WORDS OF THE SPIRIT

By
William L Mathews

Copyrights © 2024

All Rights Reserved

All rights reserved. No part of this publication may be reproduced, distributed, or transmitted in any form or by any means, including photocopying, recording, or other electronic or mechanical methods, without the author's prior written permission, except in the case of brief quotations embodied in critical reviews and certain other non-commercial uses permitted by copyright law. For permission requests, please get in touch with the author.

Email: wordsofthespiritwm@gmail.com

Contents

Dedication i
Acknowledgments ii
About the Author iii
Foreword 1
Chapter 1: January 3
Chapter 2: February 34
Chapter 3: March 63
Chapter 4: April 94
Chapter 5: May 124
Chapter 6: June 155
Chapter 7: July 185
Chapter 8: August 216
Chapter 9: September 248
Chapter 10: October 280
Chapter 11: November 311
Chapter 12: December 341

Dedication

This is dedicated to the Lord, our God, without which none of this could be possible. To Him be all the glory.

Acknowledgments

I could not have done this without the devoted support of my precious bride, Cate. We spent many hours together bouncing ideas off one another and proofing, proofing, proofing. A dear friend of ours, Betty, has been of great help, particularly in interpretation. Cat, another friend, has been of great help and has provided valuable ideas and inspiration. I must acknowledge all the wonderful pastors through my walk with the Lord who have mentored and taught me so much.

About the Author

William grew up in Western Washington very near to the Cascade Mountains. He now resides near the Catalina Mountains in Arizona with his wife Cate and their little Shih Tzu, Olive. He is a layperson that has devoted the past 50 plus years to teaching God's Word in several formats. He has a deep love for the Lord and all that's been given him through Jesus Christ. This is his testimony.

My Story:

This is how I came to the Lord. It was a winding trail of ups and downs probably not so different than what others go through.

I grew up in a small town. My mother would teach me things from the Bible, and she had a deep reverence for God. I attended Sunday School at first alone. When my oldest sister was about five and I was eight we would walk a mile each way to a church on the other side of town for Sunday School.

One day we were asked if we'd like to stay over for the church service. We did and there was an alter call. My sister and I went forward to accept the Lord. I remember a man praying over us and then saying, "Go and sin no more." There was no follow up with us. I remember feeling clean and light, but a few weeks later I realized I was back in sin and felt lost. I had so many questions and no answers. As I look back, my confession was from my heart. I believe the Lord never left me but was patient with me until the time was right for my full commitment.

I tried several different churches in my younger years and found myself confused. I ended up rejecting Jesus Christ as God. How could a loving God allow all misery, sickness, and death to continue? How could He allow wars to be more and more destructive, and not only that, but to allow them to be fought in His name? How could He be anything more than a colossal fraud? That's pretty much how the next twelve years of my life went. I was an anti-Christ and loved challenging Christians on their faith.

At about age 30, my life began to spiral downward. Nothing was working for me anymore. I had already become an anti-Christ and continued to blame all the ills of the earth on Him; all the time, giving Him a place in history, but certainly not deity. Oh, perhaps God was okay. Something had to kick start what I considered all this mess, but then what did He do? Did He just walk away and let it work itself out?

My dark thoughts had increased. My speech was pretty much like a sewer. I had an excellent technical understanding of my job, and I had surrounded myself with computers for years. People could turn on you, but certainly not the machines that surrounded my life. Then with everything else going up in flames, my job started to go the same way. Programs that I had written, which were solid proven performers, suddenly began to fail. There was no reason for it, they simply wouldn't work. It was like two and two not being four anymore. I don't mean everything was going wrong, but it was certainly so in the most critical, most visible parts of my job. I was beginning to question my sanity.

During this same period, a friend decided she wanted to go back to Church. The result of her decision was to ask me to go with her. I did not want to go but I did it for her. We went to a church a few blocks away that I didn't even know was there. I had seen a sign to it, but even going down that road had never found it. Suddenly, there it was, and so we went. It was Sierra Heights Baptist Church, a North American Baptist affiliate.

I was critical of everything that happened that day; the pastor, the congregation, the building, even the time of day. I was miserable. On the following Tuesday the pastor appeared at my home. I wasn't happy. I told him I wasn't interested in anything he had to say, I wanted no part of him or his religion. I was VERY clear about where I stood. This only seemed to embolden him. Finally, he trapped me, or that's my perception, into reading a book. It's called <u>Mere Christianity</u> by C.S. Lewis. My response was that "Certainly I'd read it. I wasn't afraid of any damn book." (Those were my exact words.)

The following day, the book appeared almost out of thin air. I knew it was from the people across the cul-de-sac. Of course, I knew they were weird too. In any event, I began to read the "damn" book. It took me a month or so to go through it. The first part was okay, since it dealt with God, not Christ. After that, I had some real problems with it. There were times where I would read only a few pages and toss it across the room only to pick it up again a few days later. I finally finished the book, and some doubts began creeping into my thinking. Could I be wrong?

During this time, my life continued to spiral downhill at an ever-accelerating pace. I've never been a particularly sensitive individual, but I could sense a battle going on around and within me. I didn't like it, and just wanted to get back to my secure little world where things worked the way they were supposed to; back to my world where two and two still equaled four. I could even sense "those people" across the cul-de-sac praying for me. It was an awful experience. I just wanted to be left alone.

To top it all off, the church pastor had asked if I would like to attend a special class on Sunday afternoons. Off I went, still against my better judgement. There were twelve of us plus the pastor. The pastor went around the room asking individuals to introduce themselves and tell where they were in their walk with the Lord. The responses were such as, "I'm searching - I want to meet Jesus - I want to know Him more," etc. When the pastor asked me that question, my response was, "I've arrived, and I don't need this." I really thought I had, and certainly didn't need this. He just looked at me and smiled while the rest of the group seemed to look at me in a different light.

Sometime shortly after finishing the book, and before the six-week class was over, I went to church and there was an alter call. I had a bad cold and wasn't feeling well. While I was standing, I began to feel a strong urge to walk up front and confess my need for Christ, but I wanted it to be real. I didn't want to be duped into something that simply wasn't real, and I wanted to be sure it wasn't just because I was worn down by the cold. I was holding the top of the pew in front of me so tightly that my knuckles were white.

Rather than going directly home after church, I went for a short drive to think things over. I had come so close to taking that huge leap in walking up to the front of the church to confess Christ, but again, it had to be real. I did not want it to be because I wasn't feeling well. It had to be right in every way.

The following week I attended church again, and wouldn't you know it, there was another alter call. I was feeling fine and had no excuses. The same urge came over me. I held back for a while but then relented, walked up front where I was met by a church deacon who asked to pray with me after I told him that I wanted to accept Christ into my life, but it had to be REAL. I didn't want any mumbo jumbo. This had to be the REAL deal. I asked Christ to really show me He was real. This is what happened.

Immediately it seemed as if a heavy weight was lifted from me. My gutter mouth stopped immediately. The thoughts behind my gutter mouth stopped immediately. Where I had surrounded myself with computers and programs which couldn't hurt me, I had an immediate love for people which I definitely didn't have before. Where I had read the Bible before and it hadn't made much sense, it immediately became much clearer. I no longer picked and chose what I thought was good but accepted the whole Bible. That's not to say that I still didn't have problems, but at least I'd reversed course. Oh yes, two and two once again became four.

At my water baptism in 1972, I had an interesting experience. I'd never seen or been to a baptism before. There were twelve of us from the class to be baptized. I thought I'd just wait and see what they did and follow along. When the order of baptism was given to me, and I saw that I was being baptized first, I began to panic. The sanctuary with the baptistry had just been finished and this was the first baptism. I didn't want to do anything wrong. I remember sitting in the front pew on the far-right seat alone. I began to pray, "Lord what do I do? I don't want to dishonor You or any of these people." As I sat there for a few moments in prayer a peace descended on me like I had never experienced before. In addition, a fire lit within me that's never gone out. I still see and feel it every time I look for it. It's still burning just as brightly as the day it started. He walks with me, and He talks with me. I'm never alone. I want everyone to have this peace and certainty.

All this is not to say that I followed on with a perfect life. No, there have been lots of challenges in my life that have left scars like everyone else. Unfortunately, after many years of marriage, it ended in divorce which always leaves scars. I have made many mistakes in my life, but my focus has moved from the world to Christ above all. Many years have passed since I asked Christ into my life. I'm happily married to my precious Cate. We have a good life. We're not rich in the physical sense, but we're comfortable despite the challenges presented by old age. We have a great richness not of this world. Most importantly, that empty hole in the heart of my soul has been filled and remains so. That empty hole is a God shaped void that only He can fill through His Spirit. No matter what we do in life, we may try to fill that hole with material goods, wealth, knowledge, etc., but nothing can fill it but His Spirit.

I've had many changes in my physical and spiritual life over the years. I received the gift of tongues about a year after accepting Christ. When I told my dear Pastor Gerlitz what had happened, he cautioned me that the gift was not for today. My response was that I didn't know what to say except that I had received the gift, and it was real. The result was minimal or no use of it at all for the next 30 years I was in the Baptist Churches. That's not a condemnation. It's part of who they are. They are God's children, and it doesn't affect their salvation. It's only been in the past three years that at the urging of Cate that I'm using that gift and having visions and hearing the Voice of God. That too is very new and unexpected. The Bible tells us that our young men will see visions and our old men will dream dreams. Perhaps I'm young at heart. I can't explain it any other way. I just want to do His will now and forever.

Foreword

I want you to feast on God's Word daily. Each of these verses is from my daily Bible reading. I read through the Bible every year and have done so for quite a while. I take a verse that leaps out at me as I'm reading and meditate on it for a while. Often there are several verses that get my attention, and I will go back to them at another time. I formulate my thoughts and write them down. Then I write what I hear from the Lord as His Spirit touches my spirit. I want you, the reader, to not only read what is written, but to always come back wanting more. I want you to immerse yourself in God's Word. Feed on it. Drink from it. Be nourished by it and pass it onto others. As His Word takes deeper roots into your heart, let it refresh your soul and receive its blessings.

There is a verse or are verses for each day of the year. For February 29 I have something a little different. I have included visions I have seen where appropriate. The beatitudes are at the end of the book. They have become very special to me, and my hope is that you will see them in the same light.

You will find some similarities as you read through, but the whole Word of God builds upon itself book by book, chapter by chapter, and verse by verse. Those similar verses that you come across are part of that scheme.

I feel an urgency in writing this book. This past October on the eighth just as I began my prayer, I was startled with a Word from the Lord.

I heard a shout from the Lord. The cry of the Lord in a very loud voice was, **"Hear Me! Hear Me!"** I saw Him looking from Heaven at a world separated from Him. I saw Him looking at a city with people going hurriedly about their business with not a single thought of Him. He continued shouting, continued over and over without letting up. There was anguish in His voice. He was very persistent and determined that He must be heard amid the chaos we are making of this world. He must be heard in the streets, in the workplace, in the homes, and yes, even in the churches. Why won't people listen? I see His heart and His overwhelming love that some at least hear His voice. I have the sense that time is very short, perhaps shorter than we ever expected. He sees us destroying ourselves with our attitudes and lack of concern for one another and for Him. We must not let their blood be on our hands.

Listen to these words I heard from the Lord:

"Hear Me! Hear Me! Listen to My Word! There is life in My Word and nowhere else. Come to Me! Leave all else aside. Lean your hearts toward Me and I will fill you with My Presence now and everlasting. Look where you are going. If it is not toward Me, it is away from Me. Move ever forward as I move ever forward to you through My Spirit. Listen and receive life. There is no life except through Me. Know Me and be filled. I am coming."

May you be blessed by not only the reading of His Word, but in doing His will as His Spirit leads you through each day.

Chapter 1: January

1 – Walk, Stand, Sit

"Blessed is the man who walks not in the counsel of the wicked, nor stands in the way of sinners, nor sits in the seat of scoffers; but his delight is in the law of the Lord, and on his law he meditates day and night."

Psalm 1:1-2 ESV

My thoughts:

Progression -- Here we go into a new year. Psalm 1 is my favorite psalm, and it is my life verse. It sets the tone for the next 149 psalms. Let's just go through the first two verses, but there's so much more in this psalm.

Walk, stand, sit. That is the progression of following those who don't follow Christ. If you walk in the counsel of the wicked, you are in their company, and it begins to rub off. If you then stand in the way of sinners, you are going their way. You are fitting in. These two things are followed by sitting in the seat of scoffers, and what do you do? Yes, you scoff at the things of God. Now you're trapped with no way out except if you reach out to the Lord.

Keep your delight in His Word. Read it. Meditate on it. Love it. Live it.

What I heard from the Lord:

"I made you in My image. I made you to love Me and to be loved by Me. Follow these words, and all will go well with you. Ignore My words at your own peril. Let My blessings adorn you from head to toe and keep your focus not on this world, but on the world to come and is at hand."

2 – The Devil Made Me Do It

"The man said, "The woman whom you gave to be with me, she gave me fruit of the tree, and I ate." Then the Lord God said to the woman, "What is this that you have done?" The woman said, "The serpent deceived me, and I ate.""

Genesis 3:12-13 ESV

My thoughts:

The Devil made me do it. Yes, we have heard that before, but here's where it began. Adam and Eve were caught in a lie. Neither would take responsibility. It makes me think of a child caught in the act of doing something they were told not to do and asked if or why they did it, they say, "It wasn't me." So, Adam blamed Eve, and Eve blamed the serpent. It still happens today, and not only with children.

We all have responsibilities. If you say, you're going to do something, do it. If you're not, then don't say you will. If it's a sin, God will forgive you, but there still may be consequences. When you make a mistake, own up to it. There's a price for everything we do, either good or bad.

What I heard from the Lord:

"Lies, lies, lies, I hate lies. Satan is the father of lies, and he and all who follow him will be banished from My sight forever. When you lie, even what you call a white lie, it is a deception, and plants seeds that lead to greater sin. Live, act, and love in My Truth."

3 – Revival and Winnowing – A Vision

"His winnowing fork is in his hand, and he will clear his threshing floor and gather his wheat into the barn, but the chaff he will burn with unquenchable fire."

Matthew 3:12 ESV

My thoughts:

Pray for your church. Pray for every church that calls Jesus the Lord. Pray for those churches that have lost Jesus as their First Love. Pray for revival and winnowing that the Church, the Bride of Christ, may be ready for Her Lord. If you don't have a church, find one. You are not designed to live your faith alone.

What I heard from the Lord, a Vision

"I see the Church in need of revival but also in need of winnowing. I see the Church embedded in the governments of the world and being corrupted by the attention placed there. I see the Church caught in its own internal political intrigues without reliance on the Lord. What I see coming is the Lord with winnowing fire for those within the Church determined with their ways over His. I also see Him with a great revival on the horizon; indeed, it is now. I see the Holy Spirit as a light coming down from Heaven and resting on each church, with light spreading out to draw the lost."

4 – God's Covenants

"And when the Lord smelled the pleasing aroma, the Lord said in his heart, "I will never again curse the ground because of man, for the intention of man's heart is evil from his youth. Neither will I ever again strike down every living creature as I have done."

Genesis 8:21 ESV

My thoughts:

Noah had just made a sacrifice to the Lord. God says our hearts are evil from our youth. We have the same sin nature that has been passed down from Adam and Eve. Even Noah had that same sin nature, but God made a covenant with him that continues to us. God makes covenants with us but never breaks them. We make covenants with Him and almost always break them. We have something better.

We have the assurance through Jesus Christ that even though we have a sin nature, all we have to do is confess that/those sin(s), and they will be forgiven by His blood on the cross. Try as we might, we still sin, but His grace is always greater than our sins. Thank You, Jesus.

What I heard from the Lord:

"What you do, the sins you have and indulge in do not only affect you, but those around you. Sometimes it affects generations. Your sins infect the very ground upon which you walk and even the air itself. The water you drink, that too is polluted by your sin. Your sins are forgiven through My Son, but there is still a price you pay. Think on that."

5 – The Pure in Heart

"Blessed are the pure in heart, for they shall see God."

Matthew 5:8 ESV

My thoughts:

Perhaps like me you have heard and even memorized the beatitudes but never really took them to heart. I just really understood the Beatitudes for the first time. For me, they finally sunk in.

Frankly, I didn't want to be meek, poor in spirit, or to be mournful. So, I just passed over them.

All of them are to define us. Of the eight, I selected the verse above. If we have pure hearts, shouldn't all the others apply?

Shouldn't we be poor in spirit when we see what's happening in the world? Shouldn't we mourn our failings before God? Shouldn't we put others before ourselves? Shouldn't righteousness be our goal in this life? Let us be merciful and forgiving. If our hearts are pure, shouldn't that be reflected in the way we live? Shouldn't we always seek peace with others? Shouldn't it be an honor to be persecuted for Christ? With all this, we can rejoice. Didn't Jesus pour His heart out to us in these verses?

The Holy Spirit resides in us as a down payment for what's to come. How great a comfort is that? Thank You, Lord, for opening our eyes just a bit further today.

At the end of this book, you will find my thoughts on all the beatitudes.

What I heard from the Lord:

"It all starts in the heart. Whether your hearts are full of the fruit of My Spirit, or whether you give yourselves over to Satan, the root is the cause. Let your roots be deeply entrenched in My Word that your hearts are pure and nothing but the fruit of My Spirit grows in your lives. Again, the root of My fruit which gives freedom and life, or the fruit of evil which produces slavery and death? It is your choice."

6 – Lead Me, Lord

"Lead me, O Lord, in your righteousness because of my enemies; make your way straight before me."

Psalm 5:8 ESV

My thoughts:

In my opening prayers each day, I ask the Lord to search my heart and take out the sins lying there and to cast them as far as the East is from the West. I ask Him to keep His Holy Spirit firmly on the throne of my heart, directing my ways and keeping me on the path He has set for me. I ask for His protection and guidance. Praise You, Lord.

Yes, lead us, Lord. Make Your way straight before us.

What I heard from the Lord:

"I have led you all your lives. Too many times, you have strayed from My path. You have paid for your waywardness, yet I have used what you and others meant for evil and changed it for your good. Now, you are finally beginning to get it. I will always care for you, and I shall never shy from your presence wherever you take Me but beware of the consequences of taking Me where you shouldn't, whether it be in physical places or even in your thoughts. Yes, beware."

7 – Where is Your Treasure?

"For where your treasure is, there your heart will be also."

Matthew 6:21 ESV

My thoughts:

What is our treasure? What is it in life that we most value? The treasure I value most on this earth is the love of my wife, our children, their children, and the lasting friendships we have made. But what is my greatest treasure? Christ is my greatest Treasure, for without Him, I am nothing. I'm a zero with the edges rubbed off. What we have here we can't take with us when we die, and why would we? It would spoil what is in Heaven. We must trust our Lord Jesus with the Love He has given us. That is our greatest treasure. If we think we love now, how much greater will that be when we are face to Face with Him? For us, it is His Love and His Presence that are our greatest treasures, and nothing can take that away.

What I heard from the Lord:

"My beloved children. Your treasure is safe with Me. It will not rot. It will not decay, but it will be preserved and waiting for you. You have an idea of what awaits but know this, what you will find is beyond your wildest imagination. I know what your imagination is for I created that too. Oh, how I love you. I give all I can to you on this earth, but there's so much more to come. Just wait."

8 – The Narrow Gate

"Enter by the narrow gate. For the gate is wide and the way is easy that leads to destruction, and those who enter by it are many. For the gate is narrow and the way is hard that leads to life, and those who find it are few. "Not everyone who says to me, 'Lord, Lord,' will enter the kingdom of heaven, but the one who does the will of my Father who is in heaven."

Matthew 7:13-14, 21 ESV

My thoughts:

The wide gate is easy. It is for those who put their comfort first. It is for those who have little or no time for the Lord but strive for the pleasures of this world. They set themselves up as gods and search for anything worldly. Their god is such as wealth, power, pleasure, and comfort. With their focus there, they will never even look for the narrow way. They think those who search for the narrow way are fools.

The narrow gate the Lord has set for us to go through may not be easy, but we know who God is and will not be deterred from His presence. Our works are because of our love for Him, not to find favor with Him. It's all in being humble before the Lord and putting His will before our own.

What I heard from the Lord:

"Remember the vision I gave you of the broad halls where everyone was bustling along in their own thoughts, committed to what they saw with their eyes, touched with their hands, and sensed for their pleasure? It all looked so good; then you saw the narrow way, a set of stairs leading away from those on the broad avenue. The stairs were steep and not as inviting, but you heard My call. You're still on those stairs of My narrow way but keep climbing in My strength. Not only am I waiting, but I am here with you now. You are blessed in My love and have My protection."

9 – Partnership in Prayer

"Now then, return the man's wife, for he is a prophet, so that he will pray for you, and you shall live. But if you do not return her, know that you shall surely die, you and all who are yours."

Genesis 20:7 ESV

My thoughts:

This is the first time in the Bible that God shows our partnership with Him through our prayers. In this verse, among other things, Abimelech is told that his life is in the hands of Abraham, and that his life is dependent on the prayer of Abraham. God values our prayers. Revelation states that our prayers are kept in golden bowls. (Revelation 5:8) When we pray, let's take heart that our prayers bring God near through the Holy Spirit. We should never take our prayers lightly. He listens. He wants our participation in communion with Him. Let us take time today and every day to be in communion with Him through our fervent prayer.

What I heard from the Lord:

"I have all power, yet I wait expectantly but patiently for you. I so love the time we spend together in communion. Yes, I give you My power in so many ways. I don't give it lightly, but with a purpose that tests you and provides light to the world. Your prayers are so very special. I always answer. You must know that. Sometimes it may seem I am far away, but look deep into your spirit, and there I am. Be careful what you pray for. I am no genie that grants wishes without thought, but the very God and Ruler of all, and you are My greatest love."

10 – The Faith of Abraham and Isaac

"When they came to the place of which God had told him, Abraham built the altar there and laid the wood in order and bound Isaac, his son, and laid him on the altar, on top of the wood."

Genesis 22:9 ESV

My thoughts:

This verse is taken from Genesis, where Abraham was about to sacrifice his son, Isaac. By this time, Isaac was probably about thirteen. Abraham was about 113 years old. We clearly see the faith of Abraham. He had been told by God that his descendants would be great in number, yet he was told to sacrifice his son anyway. Abraham's faith was unshakeable. Now, what about Isaac? What about his faith? Isaac could have easily gotten up off the altar and run, but he didn't. He was submissive all the way.

I don't have that kind of faith, not yet anyway. Abraham walked much closer to God than us, but we do have the Holy Spirit living in us. We do not expect God to give us a challenge like that, but if He ever does, make us ready, Lord Jesus. We can't do it alone.

What I heard from the Lord:

"Abraham had great faith and deserves your imitation. He didn't know I would provide a sacrifice, yet His faith was strong enough to know I am God. I do not have to tell you everything. What you do not know is for your good. As Abraham trusted, so you must trust Me. As I fulfilled my promises to Abraham, I fulfill my vows to you. Have faith."

11 – The Faithful Servant

"And he said, "O Lord, God of my master Abraham, please grant me success today and show steadfast love to my master Abraham.""

Genesis 24:12 ESV

My thoughts:

This unnamed servant shows more faith than Abraham or anyone before him, yet he is not even named. I like that. We need to be like this selfless unknown person who willingly puts the wishes and wellbeing of others above his own needs. Perhaps he had watched God bless Abraham over the years again and again. He saw that and the awe that Abraham had for the Lord. Like this servant, I want his confidence in the Lord and his selflessness. This was a man after God's own heart.

What I heard from the Lord:

"When you show and live your obedience to those placed above you as to Me, you will be given greater gifts. You will be given tasks that please not only Me but you as well. As you work, always let it be as if it were done just for Me. You have nothing to lose and only gain."

12 – Dust

"And if anyone will not receive you or listen to your words, shake off the dust from your feet when you leave that house or town."

Matthew 10:14 ESV

My thoughts:

Some people take this verse out of context. They take it out of context where this was specifically for the disciples being sent out two by two to surrounding towns that if they didn't receive or listen to their words, they should leave and shake off the dust from their feet. This clearly does not mean that if you give the Word of the Lord or witness to others, if they don't listen or receive your words, you are to do this with them. By no means are we to ever give up. We don't know what is in the hearts of others. I do not know how many times the word was given to me when I rejected it, but one day I heard and listened. We always need to be ready with the Gospel, the Word of life. We all know people who have rejected the Word given to them. I am certainly not giving up on them. It is God who will judge.

What I heard from the Lord:

"My Word gives life to those who hear it. They must not only hear it with their ears but also with their hearts. Blessed are those who give My Word and those who hear My Word with their spirits and guard it deeply in their souls. Freely give My Word, yet do not cast My pearls before swine. You will know when. Until you do, freely give My Word in this darkening world."

13 – Whomever Finds His Life

"Whoever finds his life will lose it, and whoever loses his life for my sake will find it."

Matthew 10:39 ESV

My thoughts:

At first glance, this appears to be an odd saying, but let's take a good look.

Before coming to Christ, we had life; a life built on this world. It is a life that can be lived without ever knowing Christ. Is a life without Christ really life? After living the new life, I realized that the highest point of my life without Him was lower than the lowest point with Him.

When we find Christ, we give our lives to Him. In effect, we lose our lives in giving them over to Him, and we find new life in Him. We find the abundant, overflowing life that He gives to His saints. It is constantly renewing, unlike our old life. This new life is dead to sin and alive to Christ. We need to beware, though, that at times we allow the old life to return and draw us away. We must be quick to call on Jesus, confess to Him, and reclaim the new life, the eternal life He has given us.

What I heard from the Lord:

"To lose your life for Me means life eternal, not only eternal, but abundantly as well. I am right there all over the world, knocking on the doors of hearts of men and women. I knock, but they must respond. Think of your life before you opened the door. Was that really life, or is life what you have now?"

14 – He Will Give Us Rest

"Come to me, all who labor and are heavy laden, and I will give you rest."

Matthew 11:28 ESV

My thoughts:

We are placed in the world but told not to be of the world. Being of the world can result in heavy burdens. It's so easy to be caught up in all the world has to offer. There are rewards, but they are temporary in view of eternity. Are we to work in order to receive wealth as the world gives, honors as the world gives, and praise as the world gives? These are not bad things, but they don't satisfy. We each have a God-shaped hole in our spiritual heart that only God can fill with the Holy Spirit.

Then there's Jesus, who promises to give us rest. He tells us in verse 30 that His yoke is easy, and His burden is light. What a difference to take His yoke. That means He's right beside us. It's an honor to work with Him. It's a blessing to bear His burden. He does not give as the world gives, but He gives life and peace. With this, I can be in the world doing the best I can where He places me.

What I heard from the Lord:

"My rest is not the rest the world gives, but rest that satisfies. When you are tired in this world, you must sleep. This is good for you need refreshment from what the world gives, whether good or bad. My rest is away from the cares of the world. Walk with Me. Hear My Voice. Learn from My Word and find rest from the world and refreshment in My peace."

15 – He Gives Us Rest

"Now Rachel had taken the household gods and put them in the camel's saddle and sat on them. Laban felt all about the tent but did not find them."

Genesis 31:34 ESV

My thoughts:

Deceit – The name Jacob means deceiver. Jacob had acted with deceit in actions with his brother Essau and with his father, Isaac. Now he had spent 20 years deceiving and being deceived by Laban, and even after God told Jacob to return to his father, he did that in deceit. In this verse, we see Rachel contaminated by the same thing.

To be a deceiver is to be a liar. Are we deceivers? Have we always acted honestly and openly? The answer is no. There were times before knowing Christ that we did not. There have been times since knowing Christ that we have sugar-coated truths or not told the whole story, but that was still lying.

Lord, let our yes be yes, and our no be no, and kick all deceit to the curb. Let all our dealings be straightforward and honest all our days. Let us always do the next right thing, always. Amen

What I heard from the Lord:

"Deceit, what a fine little word you use to say, "LIE." When you use fancy words and phrases to convey a lie, it's still a lie. Satan is the father of lies. Why do you want to mimic him? To lie is to lie. It isn't a little white lie. It isn't giving partial truths, which are still lies. Don't use words like an affair when it's fornication. Be open and honest with Me first of all, but you must be honest with yourself and those you are with."

16 – Wrestled With God

"Then he said, "Your name shall no longer be called Jacob, but Israel, for you have striven with God and with men and have prevailed."

Genesis 32:28 ESV

My thoughts:

Have you ever wrestled with God? Of course, you have. Jacob wrestled with God and won. Jacob means deceiver. Israel means "Wrestles with God." Jacob just got a major promotion. His life changed forever at that moment.

I remember wrestling with God. He won, but so did I. In going through my process of accepting Christ into my life, there was a terrible battle. I could sense it in my spirit. The battle between good and evil was going on in my heart. It lasted for weeks, but it all ended when I chose Christ. I remember just wanting the battle to be over. Since then, peace has reigned in my heart.

Praise God for our victory with, in, and through Christ. To Him be the Glory.

What I heard from the Lord:

"I have a special private and secret name for each of you. It is between only you and only Me. It is something attached to yourself through all eternity. It is something I will call you in private. This is a bond between us like no other. Accept it as a badge of My love for you, by the special place each of you have in My heart. You don't know it now, for many things have yet to pass. Be assured; it will be worth the wait."

17 – Roots

"Other seeds fell on rocky ground, where they did not have much soil, and immediately they sprang up since they had no depth of soil"

Matthew 13:5 ESV

My thoughts:

Our roots must be deep within the Word of God. That only happens by reading, memorization, and meditating with prayer. Does a tree work to yield its fruit? No, and neither do we if we are rooted in the Word of God. It just happens. Our job is to stay rooted and be there for God and others who are and who come into our lives. Poorly rooted trees produce inferior fruit. Lord, let the fruit I yield be the best it can be. Keep me from withering in the fiery blasts of Satan.

Prophecy from Jan. 17, 2022

What I heard from the Lord:

A prophecy

"The old order is passing away, not as time goes by, but in a flash. All you know and what you have lived through is being changed in a flash. Satan and all his minions have been unleashed from hell onto the earth. Nothing is as it seems. Prepare yourselves, for the end is at hand. Look around. What do you see? The world's governments are a hollow reed being filled by Satan. His time has come. Nothing will be as before. Hell is about to be raised on the earth. There is nowhere to run. He is everywhere. Look around. What do you see? Yes, you see the darkness of the coming, but take heart, for it is My coming. Be prepared. Don't let your oil run out. You know what to do. Yes, keep your faith, for I am greater than he who is in the world, and nothing can prevail against Me and for those I hold dear. Stand, yes, take your stand. The victory is already won. Watch and wait for I, too, am coming."

18 – Understanding Joseph's Brothers

"They saw him from afar, and before he came near to them, they conspired against him to kill him."

Genesis 37:18 ESV

My thoughts:

The story of Joseph begins, and he is the main character in the rest of the book of Genesis.

Now Dinah had been raped. We know what Joseph's brothers did to the rapist and all his family. We know these brothers by Genesis 34:2 worshiped foreign gods, and Jacob finally took them away. When they brutally killed the rapist and his family, they displayed what they had learned from their foreign gods.

This gives us a picture of who these men really were at that time. So, why not kill Joseph? Wasn't he just another thing in their way that needed killing? It didn't matter that he was their brother. He was a brat to be dispensed with.

Joseph's life may have been more dramatic than ours, but everything he did and everything that happened to him, both good and evil, made him into the person he became, and so it is with us. He came to embrace it, and so should we. So, we have no excuse not to forgive and to release those torments that cling to us out of unforgiveness. We need to thank God for the good and bad that's come to us and thank Him not only in both but for both as well. This is what I have learned, and I praise God for it.

What I heard from the Lord:

"Good or evil, it matters not for I am the Lord your God, and there is none like Me. It is I who gave you life. It is through My Son that you have life, eternal life. Too often, you think that when evil comes upon you that it isn't deserved. It doesn't matter whether or not it is deserved; it is necessary. Good and evil make you who you are. You are seasoned when evil comes upon you. You are given respite when good comes upon you. Thank Me in and for seasons of good and evil. The time is coming when evil will never again raise its ugly head."

19 – The Pearl of Great Price

"Again, the kingdom of heaven is like a merchant in search of fine pearls, who, on finding one pearl of great value, went and sold all that he had and bought it."

Matthew 13:45-46 ESV

My thoughts:

The term "kingdom of heaven" is also known as the kingdom of God. Each of us in Christ has found that Pearl of great price. We have confessed our sins and given our lives and all we have to the One who owns it all anyway. It is all on loan from Him. Our Jesus, our Pearl of great price, not only owns us by our confession but by His blood shed on the cross for our sins, past, present, and future. All we own is His. All we should want to be is His, for He has given His all for us. Even the crowns He gives us, we will throw at His feet in total submission and love, for that, too, is His. He loved us before we even knew Him. Thank You, Lord Jesus, for everything.

What I heard from the Lord:

"Yes, My Son is your pearl of great price, but you are my pearls of great price. My Son sacrificed His life for yours. Always give thanks for the price that was paid that I, too, may call you My pearl of great price."

20 – From Rags to Riches

"Then the chief cupbearer said to Pharaoh, "I remember my offenses today."

Genesis 41:9 ESV

"Then Pharaoh said to Joseph, "Since God has shown you all this, there is none so discerning and wise as you are."

Genesis 41:39 ESV

My thoughts:

Joseph was 17 when he was sold into slavery. God used 13 years of Joseph's life to groom him to be the ruler of Egypt. It took the chief baker two years to remember Joseph to the pharaoh. Those two years were critical for God's finishing school with Joseph. All the bad that had occurred to him, God meant for good and used it that way. God used Joseph to rescue his people, including his brothers, who had treated him so shamefully. Of all who came before him and all who came after him until Jesus, God was displayed openly in Joseph's heart. He is an example of what we should want our lives to be.

In ways, our lives parallel his. The good and the bad come into our lives. We must embrace both as from God; let Him have His way with us and be blessed.

What I heard from the Lord:

"Joseph, if you choose to be like anyone in My Word, think of Joseph. He may not have started well, but he finished beyond compare. He delivered his people when the famine came. You, too, are in a famine, but yours is a famine of souls for My kingdom. Stand and be ready to tell all I have given of the Pearl of great price."

21 – Love Lavishly

"But you say, 'If anyone tells his father or his mother, "What you would have gained from me is given to God," Matthew 15:5 ESV

My thoughts:

This saying of "corban" in Mark was not in the Bible but one of the many made-up laws of the Pharisees. Children were responsible for their parents in their old age. If the children told their parents they couldn't help them because that money had been dedicated to God, they were free from supporting their parents. It has nothing to do with tithing.

So, today what are we to do when family members are in need?

What I heard from the Lord:

"It is said to honor your father and mother, but when asked of My Son when He looked out in the crowd and said these are my mother and father. Those you know and love are your father and mother. Those in the church are your father and mother. If there is a need, physical, spiritual, or emotional, that you can fill, don't hesitate to be there for them. It's My love that I have poured into you. Use it lavishly."

22 – Judah's Love

"Now, therefore, please let your servant remain instead of the boy as a servant to my Lord, and let the boy go back with his brothers."

Genesis 44:33 ESV

My thoughts:

Judah and his brothers have come far from selling Joseph into slavery. Now Judah is willing to give himself into slavery to save his brother.

What I heard from the Lord:

"As Judah was willing to give his life for his brother, so did My Son give His life for you; not you alone, but for so very many over the years. I cannot look upon sin. My Son had to become this for your sake. That cost Me everything, but that's how much I love you. Can't you even love Me a little? Can't you spend just a little time in prayer and in My Word? It is true that I ask you for everything, but then I give you everything. Let My words stay in your hearts with My Spirit, Who will not lead you astray but into righteousness. Stay in My Word and be blessed. You have been given not only eternal life but abundant life through all eternity. I long for your presence."

23 – The Fool Says There is No God

"The fool says in his heart, "There is no God." They are corrupt; they do abominable deeds; there is none who does good."

Psalm 14:1 ESV

My thoughts:

Fools say there is no God.

They are corrupt.

There is none who does good.

After reading this, I realize all who reject Christ are fools indeed. They refuse to look at the evidence. They ignore the changed lives of those who accept Christ into their lives or just think they're weird. Their deeds are evil because even the good they do is tainted by their lack of interest in the Lord.

Not to say church attendance is a mark of Christians, but church attendance in total gets lower yearly in the percentage of the population. So, we live in a land of unbelievers, and their only hope is in Christ. So, how do they get there? We have been given the keys. First, we pray for them. For those who don't know the Lord, we can pray that the Lord keeps knocking on the doors of their hearts. We can show our faith through our deeds and our words. We can shower them with our love in spite of their lack of acceptance. The Lord holds off His coming until the very last soul who can be saved will be saved.

What I heard from the Lord:

"As I set you here in this time and this place, you are gifted specifically to meet the needs of unbelief in your world. Know I am beside you all the way. I never leave nor forsake you. You are here for a very specific purpose. That is to make certain that no one can say, "I didn't know." Let My Son be revealed in all you say and do on this and every day. I am with you."

24 – God First

"Trust in the Lord with all your heart, and do not lean on your own understanding. In all your ways, acknowledge him, and he will make straight your paths. Be not wise in your own eyes; fear the Lord and turn away from evil. It will be healing to your flesh and refreshment to your bones."

Proverbs 3:5-8 ESV

My thoughts:

Put God first in every part of your life, and all will be well. What do I mean by well? Even in the midst of chaos, He is there. He is with us in the good times and the bad, for both shape our future and make us stronger if only we put Him first in everything. Thank You, Jesus.

What I heard from the Lord:

"I am the Lord your God. As you bow to My Son, you bow to Me. As you listen to My Spirit, you listen to Me. I Am that I AM. No matter how you start, finish well. You can finish well only through My Son and His teachings. Write them on your heart. As I live in you, you live in Me. I will never leave nor forsake you but will be your strength and your Guide. Lean on Me."

25 – We Are Your Servants

"His brothers also came and fell down before him and said, "Behold, we are your servants." But Joseph said to them, "Do not fear, for am I in the place of God?"

Genesis 50:18-19 ESV

My thoughts:

"Do not fear, for am I in the place of God?" We must always give God His due. Never take credit for what He's done or doing. In his early years, Joseph wanted his brothers to bow down to him, but now he has been well seasoned by events, both good and bad. Joseph now did not want his brothers bowing down to him, for he knew we are all to bow down to God. He did God's bidding, as should we, but again as it says in Revelation, we will throw our crowns at the feet of Jesus, for He is the Lord. Our crowns come from Him and must return to Him. He bought and paid dearly for us. For me, to sit at His feet is more than enough.

What I heard from the Lord:

"Joseph was a man after My Own Heart. I loved him then, and I love him now. He learned well, as you must do. You have all you need and more. Joseph had neither Law nor your Christ, but he had and knew Me and looked forward to My Son. To have the heart of Joseph is to be humble to Me. Take note."

26 – Agreement

"Again, I say to you, if two of you agree on earth about anything they ask, it will be done for them by my Father in heaven."

Matthew 18:19 ESV

My thoughts:

"Again, I say to you," this adds emphasis to what He's saying. So, if two or more ask in prayer about anything, it will be done for them, does this mean if we ask for riches beyond compare, it will be given, or long life, or power over enemies? No, it is not that simple. In John chapter 15, we find there are conditions attached. It involves love and understanding. Jesus is the vine, and we are the branches.

As long as we are connected to Him, our prayers will reflect that love and communion. We will ask for those things that enrich the lives of others. We will ask for the Spirit to knock on the doors of hearts of those who don't know Him. We will pray for the welfare of others. There will be no selfishness in our prayers. Also, there is joy in our prayers, united with others to share in the experience with the Lord.

What I heard from the Lord:

"Ask not what others can do for you but ask what you can do for others. You are servants as My Son was a servant. He is a servant no more, yet He serves still. He serves through you. You are My friends, but you must still be servants because that is your role today. The time will come when you will lead, but even in leading, you will be servants."

27 – Little Children

"But Jesus said, "Let the little children come to me and do not hinder them, for to such belongs the kingdom of heaven."

Matthew 19:14 ESV

My thoughts:

What do we think of when we think of little children? Little children have an innocence about them. They are dependent. They are eager to learn. They are eager to love. They are ready to let you know how they feel.

We may not be innocent, but we need to be ready to forgive. We need to be dependent on our Lord. We need to be eager to learn from His Word and spend time with Him in prayer and Bible meditation. We need to be eager to love. We need to be honest with God. We need to let Him know how we feel and lay our concerns at His feet and leave them there. That is how we need to be like children. If we do this, we belong to the kingdom of heaven.

What I heard from the Lord:

"You are my children. You will always be my children, as your children will always be your children, but you grow. You grow by the moment in My love and grace, not only to Me but to others as well. As you sit at My feet expectantly learning, it is not enough to do only that but to pass on what you know to others whenever and wherever you can. You will know when and you will know how. Relax in My Love; it never fails."

28 – A Price For Everything

"When the young man heard this, he went away sorrowful, for he had great possessions."

Matthew 19:22 ESV

My thoughts:

When the young man was told he had to give everything he had and then follow Jesus, he decided the price was too high. What about the people of today? Is there any difference?

As we walk through our day, there is a price to be paid for every decision we make. We are all given time, talent, and treasure. We need to choose how we are going to spend our time. Will we spend it in earthly pleasure? Will we spend it for the Lord? There is a price either way. What about our talent? Each of us has a talent of some sort. How are we using that talent? Is it for the Lord or our pleasure? Then there's treasure. He asks for our first fruits. Will we obey or use it for something else? It's our choice. We must choose wisely.

If we choose to take time to go to church on Sunday, there's a price. If we decide to spend Sunday watching football instead, there is a price. Which will we choose?

What I heard from the Lord:

"Yes, there is a price for everything. My Son paid the highest price. He finished well that you might live. You have great treasure, for you have My Spirit living within you. That is life eternal for any who will listen. Spend this treasure extravagantly. It never runs out. The more you spend, the more you have."

29 – A New Sprout

"For there is hope of a tree, if it be cut down, that it will sprout again, and that the tender branch thereof will not cease."

Job 14:7 KJV

My thoughts:

When I read this, I thought about how wonderful it is to know Jesus. I was shown the gift of salvation: 'Old things are passed away, all things become new.' We must be born again,

When we give our lives and hearts to the Lord, it is like a new sprout is growing where the old tree was cut down. The new sprout may use the old root system for a time, but eventually, it builds its own and is completely separated from the old.

Each day a new sprout is formed in us; each new day, we learn not to be dependent on the old "me" but to trust the Lord in what He is doing in us.

What I heard from the Lord:

"Leave that which is behind, behind. You can't change the past, but you can and must provide for the future. You have life eternal within you. You have been given a new life. Beware that you do not go back to where you were, if only for a moment. Keep your eyes on Me and keep in step with My Spirit. It's only the beginning."

30 – The Face in Righteousness

"As for me, I shall behold your face in righteousness; when I awake, I shall be satisfied with your likeness."

Psalm 17:15 ESV

My thoughts:

It used to be that when I'd wake. the Lord would be bubbling out of my heart, and I'd sense His presence right away. It's different now for me. I want that to be the case as it once was, but sometimes I'm awake in the morning for up to an hour before I give Him a thought, then I feel bad because I've taken so long. I remedy some of this by a schedule to make certain we commune still in the morning, but it bothers me that I have to do that. My heart is in the right place, but my failing brain doesn't seem to be.

Our desire should be to have consciousness of Him in our hearts all the time. We know He's there. We should not want to miss out on anything with our Lord.

Help us, Lord, to always be conscious of Your Presence. Let us again be like the psalmist. Let us behold Your face in righteousness when we awake.

What I heard from the Lord:

"Do not fear, for I know your heart, and your heart is good. You give me what you can. Your life on earth is short and not always easy. All have failings of some kind but remember, My strength is strongest in your weakness. Pray to Me, see if I will not answer. Never fear, for I am with you always."

31 – My Redeemer

"For I know that my Redeemer lives, and at the last he will stand upon the earth."

Job 19:25 ESV

My thoughts:

Yes, my Redeemer lives. He has stood on the earth before and will do so again. There is a beautiful song about this verse, "Because He lives, I can face tomorrow. Because He lives, all fear is gone." There is more, of course, but what leaps out to me is that Job saw this way back then. Job is one of the oldest books in the Bible. It gives me comfort to realize Job knew this so many thousands of years ago.

What I heard from the Lord:

"I live. I have always been alive. I have no beginning nor no end. I did stand on the earth. Wherever My Son goes, I go. As He was here with you, so was I. That was for only a passing moment, but in the fullness of time, I will stand upon the earth, not for a fleeting moment but for all time, and you will be at My side for eternity."

Chapter 2: February

1 – Do Not Withhold Good

"Do not withhold good from those to whom it is due when it is in your power to do it."

Proverbs 3:27 ESV

My thoughts:

Why would we ever want to withhold good from those to whom it is due if we have the power to do so? So many times we can make someone's day or wreck it by just a word. Just a smile or a thank you to someone providing you with service can go a long way. When you begin to think you're better than another, it's time to re-evaluate your motives.

What I heard from the Lord:

"When I put someone or people in your presence who have physical needs, or spiritual needs, you must be swift to act on their part. You must be prepared to give of your talent, treasure, and time as is necessary. Don't all your resources come from Me? All you have is mine. When you are prompted by My Spirit, don't hesitate, but give what has been planted in your heart. Be blessed."

2 – The Fear of the Lord

"And he said to man, 'Behold, the fear of the Lord, that is wisdom, and to turn away from evil is understanding."

Job 28:28 ESV

My thoughts, my prayer:

Wisdom and understanding go together. Wisdom is what we do with understanding. Sometimes our wisdom is sound, but if it is not built on the Solid Rock, it won't stand. Our deep and full respect for the Lord is the beginning of knowing and accepting His wisdom.

My prayer:

Lord, as we walk through this day, give us Your understanding that we may make decisions and carry them out as You would. Lord, help us keep our eyes upon You so that we may not stumble as we walk on the path You have set before us. Dear Holy Spirit, take our hand as we walk together in unison. In the name of Jesus, Amen.

What I heard from the Lord:

"When you turn from evil, you can only come to Me. It's one or the other. There is no neutral ground. When you called upon My Son, that was the turning point in your lives. You allowed the work of my Son to free you from the slavery of sin. I am all wisdom. You find wisdom only in Me, for I am true wisdom, not the wisdom of man, which changes with the seasons. Count on my Truth and My Wisdom. It's already within you."

3 – Angels

"For in the resurrection they neither marry nor are given in marriage but are like angels in heaven."

Matthew 22:30 ESV

My thoughts:

We read much about angels in the Bible. We know they are messengers and guardians. We also know they are warriors.

What I heard from the Lord:

"I said you will be like angels in that way, not other ways. My angels are dear to Me. You, too, are dear to Me, but in a different way. I sent My Son for your salvation, not for the salvation of angels. I brought you up out of the miry clay and set your feet on high. I have wonders waiting for you that have never yet been seen by men or angels. No, you won't marry in heaven. You will have my eternal unblemished love flowing through you for all eternity. You will know Me like never before. You will know those in heaven like never before, and your love will flow to and through each other like never before. What I have for you is so much better than marriage on your earth. You will be married to My Son. He is your betrothed."

4 – The Law of Christ

"But woe to you, scribes and Pharisees, hypocrites! For you shut the kingdom of heaven in people's faces. For you neither enter yourselves nor allow those, who would enter to go in."

Matthew 23:13 ESV

My thoughts, my prayer:

The law of Christ is simple. Love God with all your soul and all your might. Love your neighbor as yourself, plus a new command that is to love one another as Christ loves you. That fulfills all the other laws set before Him. (John 15:12) Do this, and we will do far more than the law was ever made for. With God's love poured upon and through us, everyone should become our friend. We want the best for all and will be ready to do whatever is necessary for our brothers and sisters. To do as the Pharisees is to oppose the love of God. To oppose the love of God is to hate Him, for God is love.

My prayer:

Dear Lord, never let it be so with me. Help me, Father, to keep my eyes always on You. Keep Your Spirit firmly on the throne of my heart. In the name of Jesus, Amen.

What I heard from the Lord:

"As My kingdom is alive, so too are you. You have the keys to the kingdom. Let those you meet see it in your face and in your actions. Finally, let it be seen by your words as well. In just a little while, this will be all over, and many will never know My kingdom. Go forth in My love, and strength, and let your deeds show who I am. There is not a single soul I want to lose."

5 – Endure to the End

"But the one who endures to the end will be saved."

Matthew 24:13 ESV

My thoughts:

Once we find the Pearl of great price and give all for Him, we must become His followers. We read, memorize, and meditate upon His Word. We give Him the first fruits of our labor. We give Him our love and devotion. We love our neighbors as ourselves and more. We give Him our prayers and our fellowship. We do this because of our love for Him. We endure to the end and do not slack. This is His wish. This is our desire. Thanks be to God. These are done in His strength and not our own.

What I heard from the Lord:

"Your beginnings are one thing, and your endings are completely another thing. You entered this world in sin, but you enter My kingdom full of My glory and grace. You are no longer a slave of sin, but you are My friend. You fight the good fight and endure until the end."

6 – Be Ready

"Therefore, you also must be ready, for the Son of Man is coming at an hour you do not expect."

Matthew 24:44 ESV

My thoughts:

We don't know the hour that He will appear. Personally, I feel that we are in the season of His coming, but every generation since Jesus has felt that way. In the year 1000 AD people were waiting on mountain tops. They were so certain of His return. World War II had all the trappings of His return with an Anti-Christ ruling Europe, killing Jews at every opportunity and sending Christians to the death camps as well.

So, why do I think this is the season? Look around and see the foundations set up by God are being besieged on every front all over the world. Evil mankind is on the brink of scientific discoveries that will unleash hell on Earth. If Christ doesn't come soon, that may well happen. The Word has been preached to all nations. Yet as I see all that, I don't want Him to come until all who can be saved are; that none be lost who can be saved.

What I heard from the Lord:

"Do not be troubled, for I surely know the steps of men and women who have set foot on this earth from the very beginning out into the future. It is not in My nature that any will be lost that can be saved. That is why My delay in coming has been so long, for I know the future. Past, present, and future are all the same to Me, and the time is near for My Son's return. Keep watch!"

7 – Job's Daughters

"He had also seven sons and three daughters. And he called the name of the first daughter Jemimah, and the name of the second Keziah, and the name of the third Keren-happuch."

Job 42:13-14 ESV

My thoughts:

Here's something you don't often read in the Bible. Job's daughters are named, and his sons are not. I think to be named in the Bible is a special honor in most cases. Most people in the Old Testament lived and died without their names ever being recorded. In Genesis, it names Seth being a son of Adam and Eve, and then it goes on to say they had other sons and daughters. Biblical genealogy only lists the most prominent people in the line. I think Job's daughters must have been very special.

"Now, therefore, take seven bulls and seven rams and go to my servant Job and offer up a burnt offering for yourselves. And my servant Job shall pray for you, for I will accept his prayer not to deal with you according to your folly. For you have not spoken of me what is right, as my servant Job has." (Job 42:8) So Eliphaz the Temanite and Bildad the Shuhite and Zophar the Naamathite went and did what the Lord had told them, and the Lord accepted Job's prayer."

What I heard from the Lord:

"I covet your prayers. I covet our times of communion. Job was a man of prayer. You need only read the book. Job's daughters were also women of prayer as he was. You see this in our partnership. More times than you know, I have held back until I receive your prayers. That's how much I love and honor our relationship. Rest in My arms through the work of My Son."

8 – Betrayal

"Then one of the Twelve—the one called Judas Iscariot—went to the chief priests and asked, "What are you willing to give me if I deliver him over to you?" So they counted out for him thirty pieces of silver. From then on, Judas watched for an opportunity to hand him over."

Matthew 25:14-15 ESV

My thoughts:

As we are fitted to live in this time and place, so was Judas. Judas had all the tools to do the job he was designed for. That doesn't mean that Judas doesn't have any responsibility for his actions. He bears full responsibility. He knew Jesus. Jesus trusted him as He did the others. Remember, Jesus had hundreds if not thousands of disciples, but only these twelve were the inner circle.

The price for a common slave at that time was thirty shekels of silver. It gives the impression the temple leaders regarded the life of Jesus as no more than that of a slave. Yes, Jesus, King of the universe was so lowly regarded. I am sure they got quite a surprise when they died and saw Him for who He is. So, Judas betrayed Him.

Peter, as you will see, also betrayed Him. So, what's the difference between the two? Judas never repented. Judas hung himself after realizing what he had done. Peter, on the other hand, was repentant, and Jesus forgave him. We are able to see differences between the two men throughout the book of Matthew. I choose to be like Peter.

What I heard from the Lord:

"Here you see the beginning of liberation from sin for those who choose My Son. It had to be this way and should not be a surprise. Over and over, the Scriptures foretell what was to happen, and there was no other way. Sin can blind people, but My Word enlightens the spirit. Hold close to My Spirit and be blessed."

9 – Pharaoh

"But Pharaoh said, "Who is the Lord, that I should obey him and let Israel go? I do not know the Lord, and I will not let Israel go."

Exodus 5:2 ESV

My Thoughts:

Pharaoh asked a logical question. (I try to put myself in his place.) He'd been told all his life that he was a god. He knew nothing of the Hebrew God. He was familiar with all the gods of Egypt and was equally familiar with their power, the dark power of Satan. This was way out of left field for him. He never saw it coming. He saw Aaron and Moses as upstarts and wanted to put them down and have the Israelites blame Moses and Aaron. They did just as Pharaoh planned. Pharaoh did exactly as God planned when Pharaoh hardened his heart.

Later, God hardened Pharaoh's heart confirming Pharaoh's desires, and Pharaoh was lost from the Kingdom of God for all eternity. Our positions in this world don't matter in the Face of God. What matters is hearing His Word and keeping our hearts pliable toward His Spirit.

What I heard from the Lord:

"Pharaoh didn't know Me then, but he knows Me now. He's in a very dark place. He was always in a very dark place and elected to remain so. There are so many there with him with the same attitude, but you; you know Me and obey My commands, for I am right alongside with My Spirit that you not be fooled by what the world has to offer. Remain in Me as I remain in you."

10 – Pray – God Loves Our Prayers

"Let the words of my mouth and the meditation of my heart be acceptable in your sight, O Lord, my rock and my redeemer." Psalm 19:14 ESV

My thoughts, my prayer:

I think when you sort it out and think about our place with the Lord that this sums it up. It makes me smile when I read this. I smile with my face, but more so with my heart. He is our Rock, our foundation, our source. He is our Redeemer. He paid the price for our redemption from sin. We could not do it.

Now it gets personal:

I was moved to tell the Lord why I love Him so much:

You chose me. You not only chose me, You died for me. What more could one ask? You spent great effort in creation. All creation was for the purpose of allowing me to be born, to live, and to grow in the space where You've set me. To grow in your grace and to finally realize I love you more than life itself. I would be willing to give my life for You in a heartbeat. You've given Your life for me. Let me live my life for You. In Jesus' Name, Amen.

What I heard from the Lord:

"You have great love, not only for Me but for those you pray for daily. I love your prayers. I look forward to them. They give Me such great joy; you will never know until you reach Heaven. Keep that love, not only for yourself but willingly spread it wherever I show you. You are my beloved son. Rest in My love."

11 – Pride and Unbelief

"Then Pharaoh's servants said to him, "How long shall this man be a snare to us? Let the men go, that they may serve the Lord their God. Do you not yet understand that Egypt is ruined?"

Exodus 10:7 ESV

My thoughts:

The Pharaoh's counselors in the 8th plague said Egypt was ruined, yet two more plagues were coming. By this time, Pharaoh's heart had been hardened by the Lord, so Pharaoh couldn't repent. More ruin was yet to come, including the destruction of their army. Notice that Egypt wasn't spoken of for a very long time after God's people left. Egypt was truly ruined, and God's people were safe. Oh, what damage pride and unbelief can do.

Soften our hearts Dear Lord and chase pride from our presence. In the name of Jesus, Amen.

What I heard from the Lord:

"Oh, the travesty that could be averted if people would just listen. The Word is there for all. Just read and let your hearts decide. Read with an open mind, not jaded by the things of the world, but read in the spirit with which it was written. This is My Word. Read and gain wisdom that you evade the traps set all around you. Too many fall into their own traps. You, come to My Word and be saved."

12 – Barabbas

"Then he released for them Barabbas, and having scourged Jesus, delivered him to be crucified."

Matthew 27:26 ESV

My thoughts, my prayer:

Who is Barabbas? Barabbas was a very bad person. As good as Jesus is, Barabbas was bad. I am Barabbas. You are Barabbas. We are Barabbas. When we look at Jesus, when we really look, we see how far we fall short in our own strength. The most righteous person who has ever lived in comparison to Jesus is still Barabbas. We can never make ourselves clean, but it is by the blood of Jesus that we are made clean. It's His love, His work, His power that saves us. All we need to do is return His love by loving Him and others He brings into our presence.

My prayer:

Lord, help us to love whomever You place in our presence today with the Love You have given us, and help us to keep our focus on You throughout this day. Thank You, Lord, for accepting our confessions. Let us not be like Barabbas. In the name of Jesus, Amen.

What I heard from the Lord:

"Good and evil, My Son, the only good, and Barabbas representing the worst of the worst, yet was he worse than you? No, My children. There is no real difference between you except through My Son. Come to Me, you who are heavy laden, and I will give you rest. I will give you victory. I will give you eternal and abundant life with Me. Just ask."

13 – A Pure Heart

"Keep your heart with all vigilance, for from it flow the springs of life."

Proverbs 4:23 ESV

My thoughts:

What comes from our hearts becomes who we are. Whatever it is, it can be positive things that allow us to grow and be a blessing to others, or it can be negative and be a blight on ourselves and others. As for me, I must ask the Holy Spirit to take His rightful place on the throne of my heart. If I stay on the throne of my heart, my actions will be misguided at best and hurtful at worst. I don't want that at all. I want my witness to be as pure as possible, depending on the guidance of the Holy Spirit, not lagging nor trying to pull Him along, but walking side by side.

What I heard from the Lord:

"I sent My Spirit to keep your hearts with all vigilance. You know when you begin to stray. It starts in your heart, and if you don't listen to My Spirit, the flame is fanned until you take the next steps. Listen, listen to My Spirit. He is there for a reason beyond your comfort, to keep you from the dark one and lead you into all purity."

14 – Grumbling

"And the whole congregation of the people of Israel grumbled against Moses and Aaron in the wilderness."

Exodus 16:2 ESV

My thoughts:

I cannot imagine the people grumbling after all the wonders they had seen. It has happened repeatedly ever since Moses entered their midst before he spoke with Pharaoh. Do we grumble like this today against the Lord?

What I heard from the Lord:

"Yes, you grumble before Me whenever you stray from My Presence. When you read My Word and do the opposite, that is grumbling against Me. When you fail to love those whom I have sent in your midst, you are grumbling against Me. When you speak out against a brother or sister, that is grumbling against Me. It is your sin that is grumbling to Me. Just rest in My Love. Take My yoke. It is easy. I am right beside you in whatever I've set in your path to overcome. I will never leave nor forsake you. Rest in My Love and cease your struggle against Me."

15 – Jethro Rejoiced

"And Jethro rejoiced for all the good that the Lord had done to Israel, in that he had delivered them out of the hand of the Egyptians."

Exodus 18:9 ESV

My thoughts:

Take time to rejoice.

Jethro rejoiced in all the good God had done for Israel.

Rejoice in the Lord, and again I say rejoice is a command found in Philippians 4:4.

What I heard from the Lord:

"Rejoice in the good times and the bad times. Am I not with you in both times? Rejoice in what you see Me doing for others; for the churches; for healing, and for each breath you take. Am I not a God of Love? Do I not want the best for you, always? Have I not shown you My love at all times? I revel in your rejoicing. I want to pour out blessings from heaven, the likes you have never seen. Yes, I want to do more, and you shall see blessings beyond compare. Rejoice always and come unto Me. Let Me gather you. Come into my embrace and let your joy flow freely in all things."

16 – Faith

"And when Jesus saw their faith, he said to the paralytic, "Son, your sins are forgiven.""

Mark 2:5 ESV

My thoughts:

Where was the faith of the paralytic? We clearly see the faith of his friends, but again, what about the paralytic? Where is our faith in time of healing? Are we surprised when it happens, or fervently thanking and praising the Lord? Let us be ever thankful for His provisions.

What I heard from the Lord:

"Oh, the faith of those who carried the paralytic. It was their faith that stirred them to action. What is faith without action? Action without faith is chaotic at best. Faith guides action. Oh, those men of faith who loved their friend, knowing in their hearts what I would do. Their faith was driven by love for their fellow man. Yes, I knew of the paralytic's faith, but he was unable to act on his own, so these great friends did what he could not. They displayed his faith in themselves. It is the same with you. You are surrounded by those with faith that is misplaced or insufficient, but you of faith; pray for those with little faith. Pray for their wellness of spirit and wellness of the body. You, be their intercessor. You, be their guide. You, be their faith. In that, your love will shine."

17 – Blasphemy

"But whoever blasphemes against the Holy Spirit never has forgiveness, but is guilty of an eternal sin—"

Mark 3:29 ESV

My thoughts:

The deadly sin. The sin that brings death to the frivolous. We must pray for our friends who don't know the Lord that they do not blaspheme and sin unto death. There are those who sin unto death and those who sin unto the second death. If we know God, if we truly know Him and our sins continue, He may bring us home before our chosen time as He did to Ananias and Sapphira. Those who sin against the Holy Spirit have hardened their hearts. These are not just the hardened who commit terrible sins against God and humanity but those who go along their merry way, never thinking of God. They do not give Him a second thought even though He loves them dearly. They who love the world, and all its treasures cannot love Him. Woe to them. We must pray for those we know, friends whose lives shut Him out. Pray that He continues to knock on the doors of their hearts.

What I heard from the Lord:

"Remember Pharaoh. I offered him life until he hardened his heart. I knew him. His heart was unchangeable. It was then that I confirmed what he had already done. Have you committed the unpardonable sin? You would not be reading this if you had. When you go there, there is no turning back. You are lost and refuse to listen, and there is no further hope. I offer life for the taking. I hold my arms out to all who have not yet committed the unpardonable sin."

18 – What Will Be Measured to You?

"And he said to them, "Pay attention to what you hear: with the measure you use, it will be measured to you, and still more will be added to you."

Mark 4:24 ESV

My thoughts:

We must all be ready to hear God's Word, to let it come alive in ourselves, but also, we must be ready to present it to others in our midst. Be ready.

Lord, help us to understand.

What I heard from the Lord:

"When you read My Word; when you hear My Word, what will you do with it? Will you keep it to yourself, or will you pass it on to others? Your measure: how you measure; it is clear that what you read and hold in your heart is good, but not meant only for you but for your neighbors, friends, relatives, anyone that I put in your presence who has need of My Word. Do not hesitate to give that what I have given you. Do not hold it only for yourself, but give freely, and I will give you more. There is no end to My Word. It is fresh and new every morning; every time you read it; every time you hear it, and every time you give it away."

19 – I Shall Not Want

"The Lord is my shepherd; I shall not want."

Psalm 23:1 ESV

My thoughts:

What sweet words to open this psalm with. There are only nine words, but with such love and power.

What I heard from the Lord:

"I am your Shepherd. As you live, I provide for all your needs, physical, emotional, and spiritual. I took your hand when you called Me into your heart. I'm right there beside you at every moment, guarding you from all enemies and nourishing you with My Spirit that you shall not want. I know your needs before you are ever aware of them. Walk with Me. Talk with Me. Read My Word, even more; meditate on My Word and keep It in your heart. You are My beloved. I have loved you before you were even a substance in your mother's womb. Stay close and feel My Presence. You are never alone, for I am your Shepherd, and I will never abandon you.

Continue to let me lead you. I will never lead you astray. Do not wander off the path I have set for you. You have wandered off before, and where did it get you? I had to give my Son because of your wanderings from your path. Tell Me. What do you want that I haven't provided? I supply your wants without your even asking. I love you more than even Heaven itself. What greater sacrifice could I make? Be blessed in My presence. Just love."

20 – Clean Hands and Pure Hearts

"Who shall ascend the hill of the Lord? And who shall stand in his holy place? He who has clean hands and a pure heart, who does not lift up his soul to what is false and does not swear deceitfully."

Psalm 24:3-4 ESV

My thoughts:

Lord, we want clean hands and pure hearts without deceit. We want to be your children in every way. We have seen in recent revivals people thronging toward You in their desire to have clean hands and pure hearts, to be born again. So many of us pray for revival in this dark world. Could this be the beginning of not only a national revival so desperately needed but a world revival that many may be saved before the great and terrible tribulation to come? It is my prayer that it be so, and that this revival be allowed to continue unabated by those who think they know how it should be conducted when they, in fact, know nothing, for they have never seen one before. Lord, let your will be fulfilled.

What I heard from the Lord:

"I sent My Son. You have given your hearts to Him. He stands in His Holy Place. He has clean hands and a pure heart. There are no lies or deceit in Him. You, My children, brothers with Him, you are covered by His mantle. When I look at you, I see you without sin, for He has paid the price for you. He died in your place. You ascend the hill with Him. You stand with Him in His Holy Place. You have clean hands and pure hearts because His Spirit lives within you, and there is no deceit in you. Breathe out your sins and breathe in My Spirit that you remain clean and covered by My Son."

The Lord used the term brothers. We are all seen by God as firstborn sons with Christ, whether we are men or women.

21 – King Herod

"For Herod feared John, knowing that he was a righteous and holy man, and he kept him safe. When he heard him, he was greatly perplexed, and yet he heard him gladly."

Mark 6:20 ESV

My thoughts:

Herod was a king. Herod was a man who made mistakes, yet he loved hearing the messages of John. King Herod appeared not to be the finest specimen of the human race, yet he kept his word in the face of those around him. (In this case, not the best choice.) John was under his protection, as we are protected by our leadership. In John's case, the king failed to protect him, as will our leaders from time to time, but God is our Highest Leader and Protector. Why didn't God protect John? Hadn't John done the job he was intended to do? We are not designed to live our lives here forever. When our tasks are done, we, too, will be called to our eternal home. John was protected by God until he completed his task. We can count on Him protecting us in the same way. When our work is done here, it is just the beginning.

What I heard from the Lord:

"John, the greatest of the prophets, yet what he accomplished is dwarfed by the work of My Son. It is even dwarfed by My church. John was one man on the earth given a very difficult task, yet he was perfectly fitted out for its completion, as are you in your time. My saints are always properly fitted for their tasks on earth. You are My children, My greatest treasure."

22 – Lift Up My Soul

"To you, O Lord, I lift up my soul."

Psalm 25:1 ESV

My thoughts:

To You, Lord I lift up my soul and my spirit to intertwine with Your Spirit. I lift it up to commune with Your Spirit that I may know my identity within You. Lift up my soul and keep me steadfastly on the path you have set before me. Let us model His love wherever and whenever we can.

What I heard from the Lord:

"You are body, soul, and spirit. Your spirit is in constant contact with My Spirit. Your body, though chained to the Earth, is the tent for your soul. Your soul, how beautiful. Your essence. The real you made in My image. Yes. Come and commune with Me. Rest in my arms. Let Me speak to you about things you would otherwise never know. Rest in my love. Let your joy be full to overflowing, for we are one in the Spirit."

23 – Do the Next Right Thing

"He leads the humble in what is right and teaches the humble his way."

Psalm 25:9 ESV

My thoughts:

We attended a church that sets a theme for the year. This church is the Church of Living Water in Olympia, Washington. Several years ago, the theme was "**Do the next right thing**." That has remained with me for the past many years. I have taken it to heart and try to live my life with that in mind.

What I heard from the Lord:

"When you are led by My Spirit; when you take My Word to heart; when you are in agreement with My Word, listen to My Spirit. Not only listen, but by taking it to heart, you will do the next right thing. Revel in My Word. Keep it in the forefront of your mind. Keep in communion with Me, and I will direct you on the path I have set before you. Focus on Me, and do not stray no matter what you see the world doing. You are not part of this world, but you are of My kingdom. Rest in My love."

24 – Affliction and Trouble

"Consider my affliction and my trouble, and forgive all my sins."

Psalm 25:18 ESV

My thoughts:

"Consider my affliction, my trouble. Forgive all my sins." These words were written so long ago yet are just as alive today as when they were written.

What are our afflictions and troubles? They are the same, and they are all different for each of us. The one clear thing is that the Lord is with us in these, whether they affect us physically, emotionally, or spiritually. With His Spirit in our hearts, He knows us more deeply than we know ourselves in every way. One thing we know, though, is to come to the Lord with our afflictions and our troubles. We need to ask for His intervention first. We need to give Him first chance to deal with whatever problem we might have. King Asa in 2 Kings went to the doctors before seeking God's help. God told Asa that because he did not trust in Him first that he would die, and that's exactly what happened. Let us always bring our afflictions, troubles, and sins to God first.

What I heard from the Lord:

"I know you. I know everything about you. I know your deepest thoughts, your hopes, and your dreams. I know your deepest hurts and your greatest triumphs. I know how every part of you fits together and their inner workings, for I designed you from My innermost thoughts that you be in companionship with Me. I am the Great Physician. I am your great physician. Who could ever know you better than I? Come to me and be healed."

25 – The Eyes of Our Hearts

"Then Jesus laid his hands on his eyes again, and he opened his eyes, his sight was restored, and he saw everything clearly."

Mark 8:25 ESV

My thoughts:

Jesus laid His hands on the man's eyes twice, and his sight was restored.

Sight, what a beautiful thing, but there is more isn't there. Why was it done twice in this instance?

What I heard from the Lord:

"You have eyes to see, but more; you have the eyes of your heart to depend on as well. When Peter was walking on the water, he started with the eyes of his heart on My Son, but when he focused his physical eyes on the storm, he became afraid. Your spiritual eyes include your faith, your trust in Me, and your spiritual perception. You can only see me with the eyes of your heart. Let Me sharpen that sight. You need to see what I see. Stay close. Listen to My Word. Depend on the eyes of My Spirit. Remember, when Peter said, "You are the Christ," he saw that with the eyes of his heart."

26 – Constant Communion

"And He said to them, "This kind cannot be driven out by anything but prayer."

Mark 9:29 ESV

My thoughts:

Lord, I do not understand what this means. You commanded the spirit to come out of the boy. I did not see any prayer there. Before that, you said, "All things are possible for one who believes." Again, I do not see where You prayed. What am I missing?

What I heard from the Lord Jesus:

"What you did not see and is not in the writing is that I am and was always in prayer to My Father. There was and is always a constant communion between Us. At that time, My disciples didn't understand that. Bathe everything in prayer every day. Keep in communion with Me constantly. I reside in your heart. I know your every thought and intent. Rest in My love."

27 – Whom Shall I Fear?

"The Lord is my light and my salvation. Whom shall I fear? He is my fortress."

Psalm. 27:1 ESV

My thoughts:

The Lord lights our paths through His Holy Spirit living within us. He is our salvation, for without Him, we are eternally doomed. He is our fortress, a place where we can seek refuge from all the unholy around us. He is our protector, and without Him, we are like pillars of salt standing in the rain, being worn down and destroyed moment by moment until nothing is left.

What I heard from the Lord:

"There is no fear in you as long as your focus remains on Me. As your focus remains on Me, I light your path. Yes, I am your salvation. I am your Fortress. You know that very well. Just let my Spirit rest on you. You trust. You obey. You have My joy. You are a joy. My peace rests upon you. Rest in My peace."

28 – Wait

"Wait for the Lord; be strong, and let your heart take courage; wait for the Lord!"

Psalm 27:14 ESV

My thoughts, my prayer:

Waiting is not fun whether you're waiting for something good or something bad. The Lord waits on us more than we wait on Him, but He does wait for us. If we pray, "Lord come quickly, to bring us home," we must add, "Yet let none be lost who can be saved." Otherwise, it's a selfish prayer. The Lord does everything in the fullness of time. It is His time, not our time, but is it? Since He has called us, and we have accepted His call, we are His. We must wait on Him, but not idly. There's much to do before the time He comes to take us away or for us to pass away through death. Either way, let's keep the eyes of our hearts focused on the Lord and what He wants of us. Only then will we be fulfilled.

My prayer:

Thank You Lord, for loving us enough to wait on us as we wait on You. What would You have us do this day? In the name of Jesus, Amen.

What I heard from the Lord:

"Wait is not a bad word. It is a necessary word. My waiting for you is way beyond your current comprehension. Not only do you wait for the good things. You also wait for those people and things that can cause harm but are still necessary for your growth in My Son. Think of the times you have waited in traffic. Just think. By your waiting, you could have avoided a serious accident. There are many things happening at the same time. There is a need for coordination so that no one should be harmed or blessed unnecessarily. It is okay to wait for Me. It is okay for Me to wait for you."

29 – Vision of the Holy Spirit

My thoughts, My vision:

I saw water coming down through the rocks. The water wasn't coming straight down, but there were curves in the stream bed, and the bottom of the stream bed was smooth. The water was clear and rushing. I did not see where it was coming from or where it was going. The rocks were rough. They were in shades of brown and black.

What I heard from the Lord:

"The water is My Holy Spirit. It has no beginning and no end. The rough rocks are the unrepentant spirits of Man. Where the Spirit has flowed, there are no rough edges underneath. The bed is those who have chosen Me. The brown and black rocks My Spirit is rushing by are unrepentant humanity. They only need to come and drink of the Spirit. The rushing of the Spirit represents the speed at which time is passing. There is so little time for the unrepentant. Revival must come as a rush of water. My Spirit."

Chapter 3: March

1 – Recover My Sight

"And Jesus said to him, "What do you want me to do for you?" And the blind man said to him, "Rabbi, let me recover my sight."

Mark 10:51 ESV

My thoughts:

As I began to pray this morning, I said, "Open the eyes of my heart, Lord, that I may truly see." Then I opened a devotion I follow daily, and it was entitled "My Eyes Were Opened." Coincidence? I don't think so. What is it that we want the Lord to do for us today? What are we doing about it?

What I heard from the Lord:

"You will see shadows of who you were. You will see where you are now. That will give you enough sight to take the next step toward Me. Always walk toward Me, for I am your light. You live in a dark, sightless world, but you have no excuse for you can see. Don't close the eyes of your heart. Keep them wide open, for they are intended to see things as they truly are. I am Lord of all. I am your Lord. Walk with Me. Listen to Me. Eat from the Word I have provided. It will nourish you and keep you in My Presence. All I want is to love you. I must have your undivided love for Me. Be blessed in My Presence."

2 – My Strength and My Shield

"The Lord is my strength and my shield; in him my heart trusts, and I am helped; my heart exults, and with my song, I give thanks to him."

Psalm 28:7 ESV

My thoughts:

My Strength; my Shield; Keeper of my heart; my Helper, and so much more.

Without our Lord, we are nothing. We are lost sheep without a shepherd, but He is truly our strength, and we can be confident of His help in every need. We are clueless about all the things He shields us from, but He is always at our side, shielding us from attacks everywhere. We can come to Him in prayer, and He also becomes our Helper in every kind of need. It's so beautiful when His heart touches our hearts. Each of us has a different song in which to thank Him, whether it be with our voices, our acts of kindness, or the works that He has set aside for us to do. There's no end to the different songs we have with which to thank Him. Let's remember to do that today.

What I heard from the Lord:

"Sing to Me. Sing to Me from your hearts. I care not what you sound like to others. Did I not create your voices also when you were created? Sing with your voices. Sing with your hearts. Sing with your hands and your labor. Sing with your love. Sing when you are apart and when you are together. Sing when you are on the mountaintops. Sing when you are in the valleys. Sing unto Me and give Me My due, for you are Mine. In all you think, and you do, do it unto Me."

3 – The Splendor of Holiness

"Ascribe to the Lord the glory due his name; worship the Lord in the splendor of holiness."

Psalm 29:2 ESV

My thoughts, my prayer:

Your due is our worship. We worship You in the splendor of holiness, in Your magnificent grandeur. This can be hard to grasp.

My prayer:

Oh, Lord. You are magnificent beyond anything we have ever known. We get glimpses in looking at the stars, beautiful sunsets, the roaring ocean, and many more things we see on this earth, but we know all these beautiful things pale in comparison to your splendor and holiness. We know we cannot absorb it all in this life. Let us bow down to You, for You are God, and there is none like You. Thank You Lord, even for the glimpses we get from time to time. Let the eyes of our hearts remain focused on You. Help us in this life to continue to prepare for the life to come by honoring Your commands and loving our neighbors. Thank You, in Jesus' name, Amen.

What I heard from the Lord:

"My Holiness, My Name, what are these by themselves? There must be something to compare. I am the Creator of all. Before My creation, there was nothing; then I began the universe you inhabit. Is it not magnificent? Is it not beautiful, yet it too is set apart? Thus, you will understand, but for now, know that I am set apart. I am holy. You by My Son and My Spirit in your hearts give you My holiness, but there is more to come. This is only partial. The fullness comes soon to you."

4 – God of the Living

"He is not God of the dead, but of the living. You are quite wrong."

Mark 12:27 ESV

My thoughts:

This tells me that when we take our last breath on this earth, it will be immediately followed by our next breath in heaven. We hear it again and again. Remember the thief on the cross. What did Jesus say to him? "Truly I say to you, today you will be with me in paradise." We have it here, right out of the mouth of Jesus.

(Luke 23:43)

What I heard from the Lord:

"What purpose would I have if I were God of the dead? I promise, as you are alive on this day, you will be alive forevermore. Oh, My people. I have wonders and treasures waiting here just for you. I have prepared a place just for you. Never fear. I am with you now. I will be with you forever. Be satisfied where you are now and with what you have, but the bounty awaiting is beyond your present imagination. Live your life in My Love. It never runs out; neither does my care for you. You are my beloved children."

5 – Don't Miss the Mark

"And when Jesus saw that he answered wisely, he said to him, "You are not far from the kingdom of God." And after that, no one dared to ask him any more questions.""

Mark 12:34 ESV

My thoughts:

How do we answer the Lord? Are we honest or do we try to hold things back from Him? It doesn't work, for He knows all. There's no hiding from Him. He lives within us through His Spirit and is our guide if we only follow Him.

What I heard from the Lord:

"To not be far from the kingdom of God is to miss the kingdom. It resides in you and resides in everyone who calls upon MY Son to be in their hearts. You can read My Word, but you need to feast on it; to make it a part of your daily life. To only taste but not swallow misses the mark. If you miss the mark, you will miss My kingdom."

6 – You Will Be Hated

"And you will be hated by all for my name's sake. But the one who endures to the end will be saved."

Mark 13:13 ESV

My thoughts:

This passage is where Jesus is telling of what's to come. It doesn't look very good for the world, but it looks great for us. All we have to do is endure to the end. This sounds simple if you read it fast, but if you slow down and think about it, "enduring to the end" can be and most often is very difficult. Always remember, Jesus is with us through His Spirit, no matter where we are or what we're doing.

What I heard from the Lord:

"The end is coming. You can see the season. You only need to endure to the end, whether you come to me through your death, or I come to you in the clouds. Endure to the end. I do not love you more, nor do I love you less in what you do but know this. I am with you at this moment, and I will be with you through all eternity. There is no parting of ways between us. Count on Me to provide whatever you need during the times ahead. Persevere and be blessed, for I am with you always."

7 – Stay Awake; Be Alert

"Lest he come suddenly and find you asleep. And what I say to you, I say to all: Stay awake."

Mark 13:36-37 ESV

My thoughts:

Jesus is coming soon. People have heard that for almost 2000 years. Were they awake? Were they alert? I'm sure they were, but what did that gain them? Their readiness, their zeal in part was what gained them a closer walk with Jesus, and it should us as well. We have to live His Word. It sounds simple enough, but we know that there are always those obstacles that come up at the worst moments.

What I heard from the Lord:

"To be awake and alert is to be in My Word. It is in prayer and communion with Me. It is putting others' needs, wants, and desires before your own. Are you of the generation that will meet me in the air, or am I going to meet you when you take your leave of this earth? You were handcrafted by Me for the day in which you live. Let that be enough. Remain awake; remain alert. I am coming for you."

8 – They Never Had a Chance

"And Jesus said to them, "You will all fall away, for it is written, 'I will strike the shepherd, and the sheep will be scattered.'""

Mark 14:27 ESV

My thoughts:

They never had a chance. No matter how strong their resolve was to stay with Jesus, it had already been written that they would fall away. How do these words affect us? Will we be scattered? If we cling to His Word and let His Spirit in, then we're in His hands now and forever. He is the Good Shepherd.

What I heard from the Lord:

"It is as you say. My friends were selected long before they were born to be My friends, My pupils. As it was written for them, so it is written for you. There are some things that, no matter how hard you try to change them, no matter how hard you pray for a different outcome, it has already been written. Nothing can change it, but you are safe. You have called on Me as your Savior and Lord. I have gone and prepared a place for you. You need not fear, and neither should you have remorse when you've done everything right and the outcome doesn't meet your expectations. So it was written."

9 – This Generation

"Truly, I say to you, this generation will not pass away until all these things take place."

Mark 13:30 ESV

My thoughts:

A generation can mean many things. Is it forty years? Is it seventy years or is it something else? Lord, what generation are You talking about here? The Bible gives several instances where a generation means either forty or seventy years. Is there a way to determine what that means? Many think the establishment of Israel begins that generation. Even seventy years later would been in 2018, so I think it must refer to something else.

What I heard from the Lord:

"Some things are not for you to know. If I come to this generation, that is well and good, but if I come to another generation, that also is well and good. You are able to look back through My Word to times long ago to you, but for Me, they are still today. Your generation, like every generation before, is commanded to be on the watch. You are always to be watching for My coming. I will come like a thief in the night. You will know the time at which I will come, but not the day or the hour. Look around. What do your eyes see, not your physical eyes, but your spiritual eyes? What do they see? Yes, you know. You know. Be ever watchful. Do not be deceived."

10 – Jesus is Mocked

"So also the chief priests with the scribes mocked him to one another, saying, "He saved others; he cannot save himself."

Mark 15:31 ESV

My thoughts:

What the chief priests and scribes said was true. "He saved others; he cannot save himself." He came to suffer and die for us. He had to go willingly to the cross with all its cruelty and with its indifference. Thank You, Lord, for what You went through because of Your love for each of us. You took our cup and died in our place.

What I heard from the Lord:

"So, it was written, so it had to be done. My Son, the one greatest sacrifice for all time; My Son, the perfect sacrifice; He who bore your sins that you may be free from the penalty of sin. He who loved you before you were born; He who loved you when on the cross, and He who loves you now. You shared in His death. It should have been you, but He took your place. Ever be thankful; ever be in awe of His work on that cross. You who are free from the penalty of sin and have both eternal and abundant life, be ever thankful; be ever in praise."

11 – Iniquity

"Blessed is the man against whom the Lord counts no iniquity, and in whose spirit there is no deceit."

Psalm 32:2 ESV

My thoughts, my prayer:

Do we not have iniquity or deceit in our hearts? Who is this person that meets these requirements? When we confess our sins and are honest with God, He sees no iniquity or deceit. It's just as if we've never sinned. He sees us fresh and new every day. I like to start my morning before breakfast and before my Bible reading like this:

My prayer:

Dear Lord, I am a sinner saved only by the grace of Jesus and the work He did on the cross; search my heart and see if there is any wicked way within me. Take the sins you find and cast them as far as the East is from the West. Keep your Spirit firmly in my heart so we may have communion together, directing my path today. Lord, let Your joy be my joy. Let Your thoughts be my thoughts. Give me an understanding of Your Word today and help me to apply it to my life. In the name of Jesus, Amen.

What I heard from the Lord:

"I see you through My Son. In Him, there is no iniquity; therefore, I cannot see yours. I see no deceit in your hearts. I see only My Son. It was He who paid the price for your sins. It was He Who fulfilled the law and brought you new commandments. Rejoice in those commandments. They are given out of love that you may live and be righteous in My sight. Be blessed by My Word, and know you are loved by the Lord of all."

12 – He Spoke

"For he spoke, and it came to be; he commanded, and it stood firm."

Psalm 33:9 ESV

My thoughts, my prayer:

God's Truth stands firm. Jesus is our Truth; the very Truth of the Father is given to us for our salvation, our freedom, and He's given us an inheritance stored safely in heaven. He's given us life eternal and abundant. He never wavers. He is our firm foundation, and He calls us His friends. How cool is that to be friends with the Creator of the universe?

My prayer:

Thank You, Lord, for Your everlasting power, truth, and love. Thank You for calling us to be Your own. Thank You for Your eternal blessings. In the name of Jesus, Amen.

What I heard from the Lord:

"What I say stands. What I do is with power. Through My voice came the cosmos and all within it. What I tell you, you can believe and need not second guess Me. My Son is Truth. There is no lie in Him. As you come to Him, you come to Me. I am waiting, always waiting, for your companionship in prayer and in worship. You have My Love, and it will never be withheld."

13 – Earth Like Bronze

"I will break the pride of your power, and I will make your heavens like iron and your earth like bronze."

Leviticus 26:19 ESV

My thoughts:

If the earth is like bronze, it can't grow anything. If the heavens are like iron, it can't rain, and another thing, our prayers can't get to heaven. Our pride must be broken.

What I heard from the Lord:

"This is as true today as when it was written. Lean on Me. Let go of your pride. I will hear your prayers. I will heap blessings upon you so great that you won't be able to count them. Do not hang on so tight. Relax your hands on the reins of your heart and pass them over to Me. Let Me lead and see if you are not better for it. You know where you belong and Who you belong to. Be free with your love for Me and those you know, even those you consider unlovable. Love them with My heart. Be generous with your love, and you are going to find blessings you never thought of. Stay in My Word."

14 – Servants of the Lord

"And Mary said, "Behold, I am the servant of the Lord; let it be to me according to your word." And the angel departed from her.""

Luke 1:38 ESV

My thoughts:

Gabriel had just given Mary news that she, an unmarried virgin, was about to become the mother of God. The words thrilling and terrifying don't begin to convey the enormity of what was about to happen. Yet, her response, "Let it be to me according to your word." are the bravest words that could have been uttered.

I don't think it was so much bravery as it was a complete and total dependence on God. She was the only one who could do this, and she answered the call.

What greater service to God could there be than to be the mother of His Son? Only one person in history could do this as Mary was selected to be the mother of Jesus. Each of us has been chosen and have been selected for a purpose. Mary had to be at the right time, in the right place, and in the right spirit, as we must be in our time and place, and spirit. We can't be like Mary, yet we are exactly like Mary, for the same Spirit that came on her is the same Spirit that lives in us. As we accept what God has chosen for us to do, let us respond, "I am a servant of the Lord; let it be to me according to your Word."

What I heard from the Lord:

"You are My servants if you do My will. You are blessed as you do My will. Take up the tasks I have given you. They are not given lightly but with a purpose. You are blessed by the tasks given, but others will also be called by how you follow My commands. You know My yoke is easy. I am right beside you through My Spirit residing within you. As Mary was blessed, so therefore are you."

15 – I Will Bless the Lord

"I will bless the Lord at all times; his praise shall continually be in my mouth."

Psalm 34:1 ESV

My thoughts:

We praise Him with our lips in praise. We worship Him in everything we do as if it was all for Him. Not all of us can be in the ministry full time, but we can dedicate anything and everything we do to Him no matter our profession or whatever else we do.

What I heard from the Lord:

"You bless Me with the way you live. Your whole life should be a praise to Me. What you do for Me should be a song continually in your hearts. As you love your neighbors you are blessing me. I know the love you have for Me, and I know the many distractions that come your way. Put that all aside. Give Me My due. I ask for all you have and are, but I give to you all I have.

With My Spirit in your hearts, you must listen. You know My Word, and so you know Me. I want the very best for you. You can have that only through close communion and listening to My Spirit that never leaves nor forsakes you. You are mine. A great price has been paid for you. Watch, listen, and learn, for your lives now are but a vapor, but you have all eternity with Me."

16 – Our Calling

"And you, child, will be called the prophet of the Most High; for you will go before the Lord to prepare his ways,"

Luke 1:76 ESV

My thoughts:

This is part of the speech Zechariah gave after nine months of being unable to speak. What can we learn from what he says about his son John? How can we apply it to our lives?

John prepared the way for Jesus. John knew his calling before he was born.

What I heard from the Lord:

"You have your own calling. Do not compare what I have given you as a ministry to that of John or anyone else. Be fulfilled and satisfied with the task I have at hand for you. Be content in My Spirit living inside of you. If your task has been revealed, go forth with relish, for I am with you. If you haven't, be patient. It is coming and will be more than worth the wait. Ask, and it shall be given, more than you ever expected; ask."

17 – The Lord Bless and Keep You

"The Lord bless you and keep you; the Lord make his face shine on you and be gracious to you; the Lord turn his face toward you and give you peace."

Numbers 4:24-26 ESV

My thoughts:

The Lord blesses us. The Lord makes us happy and fills us with joy regardless of our circumstances.

The Lord keeps us. May the Lord keep us in His presence; no matter where we go, He's there. We can never be lost from Him.

The Lord makes His face shine upon us. The Lord displays His pleasure with what we think, say, and do.

The Lord is gracious to us. The Lord forgets our sins as soon as we confess them; it's as if they never happened.

The Lord turns His face toward us. The Lord of the universe and much more sees us as if there were no one else. His focus is on each one of us.

The Lord gives us peace. After all His blessings, making us His own, displaying His pleasure with us, being gracious to us, and giving His full attention to us, we will certainly have the peace of God.

What I heard from the Lord:

"All I want is your hearts as I have given you Mine. Rest assured that you are loved beyond anything else you will ever experience. I am with you all day and all night. I will never leave nor forsake you. You are My own, and I know My own. Hear My voice and listen. My Word is dependable. You can count on it and know I am God. Let there be no other gods before you. I am the only True God. Take note of that and be blessed by My Spirit."

18 – Israel First

"a light for revelation to the Gentiles, and for glory to your people Israel."

Luke 2:32 ESV

Jesus said in Mark 7:27, "And he said to her, "Let the children be fed first, for it is not right to take the children's bread and throw it to the dogs."

My thoughts:

God chose Israel as the keeper of the Law and to be a conduit for the coming Messiah. Israel's time has come and passed but it will come again. The time of the gentiles is now, but when it ends, it will be the time for Israel once again. Jesus came to Israel and was of Israel. Jesus lived under the Law.

What I heard from the Lord:

"It does not say that My Son would go to the Gentiles first. It says He would be a light for them, a revelation to them. That is right and true. When My Son met the Gentile, you refer to, He was quite right. His ministry was to the Jews first. He Himself was of their line. You can see His compassion for her and His delight in healing her. It is good that you question that which you do not understand and not test Me. And so it is; first to the Jews, and then to the Gentiles."

19 – Stumbling

"But at my stumbling, they rejoiced and gathered; they gathered together against me; wretches whom I did not know tore at me without ceasing."

Psalm 35:15 ESV

My thoughts:

Words written by David so long ago still ring true today. The Bible tells us to love our neighbors as we love ourselves. To me, that means putting ourselves out there for them in time of need but not looking for favors from them in return. When we're down, we may expect nothing at all from our neighbors, but for them to rail against us seems unthinkable to me, but I believe it is coming. One thing I have seen though, is when some televangelists have fallen from grace, those in the church seem to chime in along with those who don't know Christ, against the fallen. We are all fallen. We in Christ should understand more than anyone, that we are commanded in scripture to reach out to the fallen in Christ in loving restoration. (Matthew 17:15-18) That should not be too much to ask, and it is a command.

What I heard from the Lord:

"Think of My commands. Remember that I told you to love your neighbors as yourselves. That is true, and this is meant for those outside, those who don't know Me. I commanded you to a different love for those within My Bride. I commanded you to love one another as I have loved you. Keep that in the forefront of your hearts. Let My Spirit love through you. Who are you to hold Me back from loving others through you? Think of the love I have for you, My sacrificial love. That is how you must love one another. Be blessed in My love and know I am with and within you always."

20 – Baptisms

"John answered them all, saying, "I baptize you with water, but he who is mightier than I is coming, the strap of whose sandals I am not worthy to untie. He will baptize you with the Holy Spirit and fire."

Luke 3:16 ESV

My thoughts:

John and Jesus knew one another while they were still in their mothers' wombs. John knew his unworthiness, as we should know ours as well. As John baptized with water, Jesus would baptize with the Holy Spirit and fire.

What I heard from the Lord:

"My fire is your purity. As gold is refined in fire, so your spirits must be refined in My Purity. When you are baptized in My Spirit, I come and live in your hearts. That happens once, but you are continually being baptized in My purity. Everything you do, everything that happens to you, is part of My refining fire. Don't resist but embrace the purity growing within your hearts. You have nothing to fear; simply trust and obey. Know that My love for you transcends all you know. I'm right here within you. Bask in the fire of My presence."

21 – Grumbling

"We remember the fish we ate in Egypt that cost nothing, the cucumbers, the melons, the leeks, the onions, and the garlic."

Numbers 11:5 ESV

My thoughts:

More grumbling from the people of God for what He has given them. They want what they had in Egypt. They say the fish in Egypt cost them nothing when in fact, it cost them everything. They were enslaved by the Egyptians. They had no freedom. Their own infant sons were hunted down and killed by the Egyptians.

Where are we today? Do we ever remember our days without Christ with fondness? Whenever we get even a hint of longing, we must nip it in the bud as Jesus did with Satan when He was tempted. When or if those thoughts come upon us, we must, like Jesus, face off Satan with the Word of God. We must get the eyes of our hearts back in focus on the One who made us, our Protector, our Christ. Again, I say, my worst day with Christ is better than my best day without Him.

What I heard from the Lord:

"What I give is free for you, but it cost Me everything. My Son had to die on the cross with all your sins heaped upon Him. There is a cost for everything; if not for you, then for someone else. For everything, there is a price. Respect the Provider Who freely gave you life, not just life on this earth, but life eternal."

22 – A Word from the Lord

"Only do not rebel against the Lord. And do not fear the people of the land, for they are bread for us. Their protection is removed from them, and the Lord is with us; do not fear them."

Numbers 14:9 ESV

My thoughts:

The last portion of this verse... "Their protection is removed from them, and the Lord is with us; do not fear them." This spoke to me. For whatever reason, those who had lived in the land had been protected until the arrival of Israel. Is that how it is with us?

What I heard from the Lord: – A prophecy:

"I protect those whom I am pleased to protect. You and all like you are under my protection. There are those who have been called but are not yet chosen that I protect. My hand of protection has been on this land for many years, but because of their rebellion, My Hand of Protection is passing away. I am your Light and Salvation. I will never leave you. You will always have My protection, even in the midst of what's to come. Wait, watch, and listen. Things are about to change."

23 – Commit Your Way to the Lord

"Commit your way to the Lord; trust in him, and he will act."

Psalm 37:5 ESV

My thoughts, my prayer:

Three things:

Commit your way to the Lord.

Trust in Him.

He will act.

Lord, as You search our hearts, we ask You to not only show us Your ways but to walk beside us as we take each step. Let us not even take one step if You are not with us. Let Your way be our way.

Lord, we trust You. Your way is the only way to righteousness. As Shadrack, Meshach, and Abednego said before the furnace in Daniel 4:17-18, "If God exists, He is able to deliver us, but even if He does not, let it be known, we still won't serve your gods." So let it be with us. Lord, give us Your trust that we may resist all unholiness that comes against us.

My Prayer:

Help us, Lord, to be patient and wait for Your actions on our behalf and not try to get ahead of You. Thank You, Lord, for Your protection, Your grace, and Your healing in our lives. Let us forever show our gratefulness toward You. In the name of Jesus, Amen.

What I heard from the Lord:

"Not only will I act, but I am also already in action on your behalf. All I do is for you and never against you. You are My pride and joy. As I watch you grow to not even what you are today but what you will be, I smile upon you. Daily My Spirit is within you, showing you the way one step at a time. Walk in My Spirit and focus on Me, and your lives will be full and brimming over."

24 – Those Who Are Sick

"And Jesus answered them, "Those who are well have no need of a physician, but those who are sick. I have not come to call the righteous but sinners to repentance."

Luke 5:31-32 ESV

My thoughts:

Lord, this is hard to understand. You embarrassed those who had been following the law in favor of those who had not. I know the established religion was looking for you, but in all the wrong places, where those who were not looking for you, you embraced. What does that mean to us today?

What I heard from the Lord:

"Yes, they followed the law, but then to make certain, they increased it far beyond what was intended just to make certain they followed the letter of the law. In the process, they lost the spirit of the law. They themselves did not follow their own teachings yet expected those without power to follow them and in their self-righteousness, could not hear Me. They thought they were well, but they were the sickest of all, beyond redemption. Why would I take time with those who were irredeemably lost by their own actions when others were eager for My Salvation?

Love Me beyond all else and love your neighbor as yourself. That is the spirit of the law. Rest in My love. You have my loving protection wherever you go."

25 – Knowledge/Wisdom

"Take my instruction instead of silver, and knowledge rather than choice gold, for wisdom is better than jewels, and all that you may desire cannot compare with her."

Proverbs 8:10-11 ESV

My thoughts:

Instruction - Knowledge - Wisdom

Where would any of us be today without wisdom? I remember when I was much younger than today. I had received instructions. I had knowledge, but I was very short on wisdom.

Wisdom, not just any wisdom, but the wisdom of God's Word, the wisdom of Jesus Christ. We can never get enough. The more wisdom we gain, the more we realize how unwise we still are and keep coming back to the Well. The Fountain of Jesus Himself.

As the Holy Spirit moves within us, let us crave more and more the wisdom of Christ. Let us seek Him at every opportunity. Let us open our hearts to be filled with His Wisdom and follow His desires for us moment by moment.

What I heard from the Lord:

"You hear of the wisdom of the ages. What is that? Could it not only be hearing but listening with your whole hearts to what I say in My Word, my lifeline to you? Seek first My kingdom, and all else will be added unto you. My wisdom is not of this earth but will still inspire you to do good works and be blessed even on this earth but also to my kingdom to come. Be blessed and know My Word, the Wisdom of the ages, if you will only take it into your hearts."

26 – Our Steps Are Established

"The steps of a man are established by the Lord when he delights in his way; though he falls, he shall not be cast headlong, for the Lord upholds his hand."

Psalm 37:23-24 ESV

My thoughts, my prayer:

Our steps are established when we delight in the way of the Lord.

Even if we fall, He will catch us and hold us up.

These are great words written 1000 years before Jesus was born. We just need to stay on the path He has set for us. With our delight in Him, we acknowledge the great and terrible price paid for us on Calvary. How can we not want to keep the eyes of our hearts focused on Jesus? He catches us and holds us up even when we fall.

My prayer:

Lord, be ever in our hearts. Let us be ever ready to show and tell of the great things You have done for us when we deserve nothing. In the name of Jesus, Amen.

What I heard from the Lord:

"Yes, your path is stretched out for you. Your steps have been established, yet you must fulfill them. What good is a canvas without the paint of the painter? What good are the pages of a book without writing? I know your past. I know your present, and yes, I know your future. You still must be the painter, the writer. I am with you every step of the way, in the good and in the bad, for My Spirit lives within you, waiting to be your guide. Just call. I am always there."

27 – No Good Tree Bears Bad Fruit

"For no good tree bears bad fruit, nor again does a bad tree bear good fruit,"

Luke 6:43 ESV

My thoughts:

What kind of fruit do you bear? Look to Galatians 5:22-23.

Do others see Love, or do they see hatred?

Do they see joy, or do they see sorrow?

Do they see peace, or do they see strife?

Do they see patience, or do they see impatience?

Do they see kindness, or do they see unkindness?

Do they see goodness or evil?

Do they see faithfulness, or do they see unfaithfulness?

Do they see gentleness, or do they see roughness?

Do they see self-control, or do they see self-indulgence?

Where are you today?

What I heard from the Lord:

"What do you want your fruit to look like? Do you want people to be pleased with your speech, your thoughtfulness, your politeness, your patience, and your self-control? How about your gentleness? Those who have even a glimmer of my presence about them want that kind of fruit even if they don't show it themselves. Their fruit may not be as appealing. You, you were called to bear good fruit, not that which stinks to the high heavens. No, no one wants that. Let My Spirit direct you on your path this day. Place your hand in Mine, and your fruit will be glorious."

28 – Compassion

"And when the Lord saw her, he had compassion on her and said to her, "Do not weep."

Luke 7:13 ESV

My thoughts:

Compassion - Just what does it mean?

Sympathetic concern and pity for the suffering or misfortunes of another person.

Have you ever been moved by compassion for another? How did it feel? What did you do? Was your heart bent to an overwhelming desire to help, but you didn't know what to do? Were you overcome with a driving desire to do something, anything?

Pause and reflect. Ask how you can help. Ask the Lord to intercede. Ask Him to show you what you can do physically, emotionally, and spiritually. Ask Him to show you how He wants you to pray. Be relentless in your prayers asking God to be relentless in dealing with the problem. Above all, act in the love of Christ.

What I heard from the Lord:

"What is compassion but another aspect of love? To have compassion for your neighbors is to show your love for them. Compassion is a direct result of the love you have for Me. If you have no compassion for others, My love is not within you. If My love is not within you, you do not belong to Me. If you do not belong to Me, give up the world that taints your souls and come to Me with nothing else. Let Me give you all the riches of Heaven. All I have is yours."

29 – The Fear of the Lord

"The fear of the Lord is hatred of evil. Pride and arrogance and the way of evil and perverted speech I hate."

Proverbs 8:13 ESV

My thoughts:

Have you ever had one of those nights when out of a sound sleep, you are filled with thoughts of all your sins throughout your life? Have you laid there through the night and searched your life to see if there were any changes you could have made that would have been better? Have you then realized that this is what has made you who and what you are? All the bad and the good brought you here as you are today, and what your actions are today will make you who you will be in your tomorrow.

That's how my night went. Then I read this proverb. He is still purging me of evil, pride, and arrogance. I got up with a new awareness of how desperately we need Jesus. We have freedom only through Christ and slavery through Satan. We must choose freedom in Christ.

What I heard from the Lord:

"Put away your pride. Bury your arrogance. Who do you think you are when you think better of yourselves than of others? No, look at your lives and see where you have been. When you look at My Son, see where you need to be. You were called to be in My Presence. Let go of anything holding you from Me and rest in My unfailing arms."

30 – God of All

"Let the Lord, the God of the spirits of all flesh, appoint a man over the congregation."

Numbers 27:16 ESV

My thoughts:

This was Moses talking to the Lord when he was told his time was up on this earth. We are never alone. All we are and do are seen by the Lord. Since He lives within us, He knows us better than we know ourselves. When Moses' time was up, he asked for a successor. We are successors of those who have been before us, and our time also will come to an end on this earth.

Those who come after us come away with part of us. These people include children, friends, acquaintances, and even those who are against us. We all rub off from one another. Let us be careful that what rubs off from us comes from Christ alone. We are all teachers and students at the same time throughout our lives. Let us leave a spiritual inheritance through Christ that endures.

What I heard from the Lord:

"I am your inheritance. You provide a holy inheritance to others through your presence with Me and by following My commands. Whatever you do for My sake will not hinder others from knowing Me. To do otherwise diminishes your lives in the faces of others. Stay in My Word, keep your focus on Me, and the inheritance you provide will be priceless."

31 – Guard Our Tongues

"I said, "I will guard my ways, that I may not sin with my tongue; I will guard my mouth with a muzzle, so long as the wicked are in my presence.""

Psalm 39:1 ESV

My thoughts, my prayer:

So, if I paraphrase this verse, it seems to say I will be careful with what I say in the presence of those who don't know the Lord or anyone else.

As we think, we speak. What we speak, we will do. That is unless our hearts are bridled by the Holy Spirit. We, as David, have the Holy Spirit within us, so why was he so concerned about what he might say? When the Holy Spirit controls the reigns of our hearts, we need not fear what we might say or not say, but I think of the many times I blurt out something I shouldn't. That is when I have taken the reins from the Spirit.

My prayer:

Help us, Lord to leave the reins of our hearts in Your hands and allow You to speak to and through us in all situations. In the name of Jesus, Amen.

What I heard from the Lord:

"The tongue can be wicked, but it's not the tongue; it's your heart. All good or evil must pass through your heart. Where your thoughts come from is your heart. Purify your heart through spending time in My Word, prayer and meditation, and listen for My voice. Let this control your heart, and your tongue will be uplifting."

Chapter 4: April

1 – A New Song

"He put a new song in my mouth, a song of praise to our God. Many will see and fear and put their trust in the Lord." Psalm 40:3 ESV

My thoughts:

I have been told that I couldn't carry a tune in a bucket, and it's true, but we can sing songs of praise to our Lord by the actions and deeds the Lord places in our paths. I believe that as we place our trust in the Lord, that our songs of praise will increase and multiply. The disciples said when He asked them if they would leave Him too, when so many others had left Him. They responded with, "Where will we go?" For me, there is no other place to be but with Him. I'm sure you feel that way too. Let us praise Him together in every way we can, today and every day.

What I heard from the Lord:

"I love your praise. You were created to give praise. As you should give of your treasure, talent, and time, you should give of your praise. All is now on loan to you, but the time is coming when all will be yours. Meditate on that and see where it leads. Trust Me, but fear Me. Spend your life in praise."

2 – A Double Win

"For whoever would save his life will lose it, but whoever loses his life for my sake will save it."

Luke 9:24 ESV

My thoughts:

To give up or lose our lives in Christ is a double win. He gives us abundant and eternal life. All we need to do is say yes to Him, and we become more alive than we have ever been. Our lives are turned upside down in the best possible way. Thank You, Lord, for showing us what real life is.

What I heard from the Lord:

"Your life is to do as I will, but you know My will. It is always for your good. I do nothing for you that will not bring growth. I bring you life in all it can be. You gave Me your life, and I give it back to you better and brighter than you could have ever thought. Rest in My arms where you belong. Know that I am God, and I care for My own."

3 – From the Highest to the Lowest

"Jesus answered, "O faithless and twisted generation, how long am I to be with you and bear with you? Bring your son here."

Luke 9:41 ESV

My thoughts:

From the highest to the lowest. One day they were on the mountain with Jesus, Moses, Elijah, and even God the Father. Now here they are, unable to do the healings they had been doing the previous day. They had dropped from a mountaintop experience to a deep valley experience.

What happened?

What I heard from the Lord:

"Whenever you have high experiences, you follow with low experiences. They always come one after the other. You cannot take the high experiences for granted. Do not think the high experiences come from you. It is when you do, that the lows come. Lean on Me."

4 – No Other Gods Before Me

"You shall have no other gods before me."

Deuteronomy 5:7 ESV

My thoughts:

Our Lord is the supreme and only God of the universe. When He speaks of other gods, what is He referring to? Anything that comes between God and us becomes our god. When our focus drops from Him to anything else, that becomes our god if even for a moment. We must keep on guard and confess these instances as sin and move on with our focus on Him.

There is nothing we can do that He won't forgive except, of course, committing the unforgivable sin against the Holy Spirit. That's when we totally and completely turn our hearts away from the Lord. If we are concerned about it, then we haven't committed it. If we are not, then we probably have and there's no way back. We can look around and never know if those we see committed the unforgivable, so we simply must continue to pray for others on a continuing basis. The Lord has it all figured out. We do our part, and He does His.

What I heard from the Lord:

"I am God, Lord of all. I made you to worship Me. I made you with free will so your love for Me will come from your hearts and not from any force I place on you. If you love Me with your whole heart, I will withhold nothing from you except of course, that which could harm you. I crave your love and devotion. I see how much you love Me and know in your hearts how much more I love you, for I love you with a deep passion. You are My beloved children. Come unto Me and I will give you rest."

5 – Our Homes Await in Heaven

"Nevertheless, do not rejoice in this, that the spirits are subject to you, but rejoice that your names are written in heaven."

Luke 10:20 ESV

My thoughts:

To me, it seems to be a big deal that the spirits were subject to them, but knowing our names are written in Heaven, Wow! You honor us, Lord. We want to honor You in all we do from the least to the greatest we have to offer.

What I heard from the Lord:

"Your home awaits you in heaven. I prepared it for you long ago. As you continue on your path with Me, know I've placed before you all you will ever need, for I am always with you. Stay in My Word. Serve Me by lavishing your love on the saints. Give your life completely to Me. Let Me show you what I will do with it and be amazed."

6 – Five Things to Put First

Psalm 27:4 - "To dwell in the house of the Lord all the days of my life."

Mark 10:21 - "You lack one thing, go sell all that you have and give to the poor, and you will have treasure in heaven; and come, follow me."

Luke 10:42 - "But one thing is necessary. Mary has chosen the good portion, which will not be taken away from her."

John 9:25 - ..."One thing I do know, that though I was blind, now I see."

Philippians 3:13 - ... "But one thing I do: forgetting what lies behind and straining forward to what lies ahead."

My Thoughts:

That one thing, of course, is the choosing of the good portion, which is to listen at the feet of Jesus. The second thing is to give of your first fruits, not the last. Third is to choose life through Jesus Christ. Fourth is to recognize the great gift we have been given through the sacrifice of Christ, and fifth, putting your guilt behind you and keeping your eyes looking forward always to Christ. The past is the past.

What I heard from the Lord:

"You have chosen the good portion. Listen and learn. Put these precious moments into your heart. I am always with you. Where can you go that I can't be with you? There are moments that you need to do just that; listen and learn."

7 – Focus on the Lord

"So be careful to do what the Lord your God has commanded you; do not turn aside to the right or to the left."

Deuteronomy 5:32 NIV

My thoughts:

Lord, You tell us to do what You have commanded. You tell us not to turn aside to the right or to the left. If we do not turn aside to the right or left, our focus will be always on you.

What I heard from the Lord:

"I have fulfilled the Law through My Son. Follow His law and look neither left nor right. Keep your focus on Him, no matter what comes. I have told you before. Keep your focus on Him. Weed out anything that tries to pull your focus from Him. His burden is light."

8 – Anxiety

"And which of you, by being anxious, can add a single hour to his span of life?"

Luke 12:25 ESV

My Thoughts:

A few years ago I learned that I have a medical condition called Congenital Malrotation. It is easily taken care of in infants and the newly born, but the longer time goes by, the harder it is to correct. At my age, the procedure has never been done. In my concern, I went to the Lord. His response below matches Luke 12:25. This is true for all of us.

What I heard from the Lord:

"I made you the way you are. You are unique and special. Haven't I kept you safe from this condition for many years? I will continue to make you safe. I will allow nothing to shorten your days on this earth. Just keep your trust in Me. Keep the eyes of your heart upon Me, and I will give you peace and blessings day by day. You are My beloved."

All of us should be able to take what He said and count our blessings. We are all in His hands, no matter our condition, status in the world, age, or anything else. We are in His hands.

9 – Stay in the Race

"Why are you cast down, O my soul, and why are you in turmoil within me? Hope in God; for I shall again praise him, my salvation and my God."

Psalm 43:5 ESV

My thoughts:

I identified with this verse since I recently and somewhat unwittingly took myself out of the battle for medical reasons and found myself in the hospital. I was not out long, but it got my attention how quietly and quickly we can leave the Lord's work to others and lose the blessing. I'm not saying our salvation is at stake, but we, as vibrant Christians are in trouble when we look away from Jesus.

Praise You, Lord Jesus, that it's not how hard we hold Your hand but how hard You hold ours.

What I heard from the Lord:

"With my Spirit entwined with your spirit, how can you be downcast if you just look? You will see your spirit being enriched and ever so close to Me. If you realize how close you are, how again can you be downcast? You are my beloved children. Is there anything I will not do for you? Just ask and look up. I'm always there. Sense the warmth of My Spirit within you."

10 – First and Last

"And people will come from east and west, and from north and south, and recline at table in the kingdom of God. And behold, some are last who will be first, and some are first who will be last."

Luke 13:29-30 ESV

My thoughts:

Who may we find in Heaven? There is the narrow gate. So, we do not want to follow the crowd focused on the World. There will be some who we never expect to be there. There will be some who will be first and some who will be last. So, there is a hierarchy. I think Heaven is so full of surprises. As for me, I am as grateful as I can be just to be there.

What I heard from the Lord:

"Does it really matter if you are first or last? As long as you are in My Word and in My Spirit, what do you really care? As you have been given on earth, how much more will you be given in heaven? Fret not. All stand on the level ground beneath the cross where I gave you My greatest gift."

11 – Humility

"For everyone who exalts himself will be humbled, and he who humbles himself will be exalted."

Luke 14:11 ESV

My thoughts:

I believe some of us tend toward humility, and it is part of us, while the same can be said of others who lean toward being prideful. The Lord requires humility. If we keep God first in our lives, everything falls into place, just where it is supposed to be.

What I heard from the Lord:

"Always put others before you. It is part of your heart, who you are. This is a gift I give to you but more. It is a gift that requires exercise, but not consciously. Never focus on your humility, or it will evaporate before your eyes. Do not even give it a second thought but keep your focus on Me. Lean on Me and see what happens. In this DO test Me and give Me your honest love and worship. You must become lesser, and I must be greater in you. It must be so."

12 – Excuses

"And another said, 'I have bought five yoke of oxen, and I go to examine them. Please have me excused."

Luke 14:19 ESV

My thoughts:

There was also the man who bought a field, and a man newly married. All flimsy excuses.

What excuses do we hear today when invited to the Banquet? Surely many are set in their ways and don't want even life-changing or lifesaving changes.

Those dear friends of ours outside of Christ too often don't even want to know there is a banquet, but for us to ignore their ignorant desires leaves their blood on our hands.

What I heard from the Lord Jesus:

"Excuses, excuses, I have heard them all. What if I had an excuse for not laying My life down for you that you may have the eternal and abundant life? It was not what I wanted, but what out of love I had to do for you. Even though there are excuses, you must take the higher road and rather than make excuses, do the right thing. That which you know may cost you something but know this; there is a price for everything you do. Count the costs before making excuses."

13 – Ten Silver Coins

"Or suppose a woman has ten silver coins and loses one. Doesn't she light a lamp, sweep the house and search carefully until she finds it?"

Luke 15:8 NIV

My thoughts:

Something you may not know.

In Jesus's day, part of a bride's ornaments at her wedding was a headdress of coins and other valuables. It would be very important that she lose not even one coin from her wedding headdress, making it incomplete. In effect, she would view this as a crushing loss. It might be compared to the loss of a wedding ring. Other women of the day would have great compassion for her loss and would celebrate with her upon her finding the lost coin.

This gives us just a glimpse of how God feels when just one person asks Him into their heart.

What I heard from the Lord:

"It gives Me great joy whenever one of the lost comes into My light and receives the eternal, complete life that has eluded them throughout their lives. To see the radiant joy on their faces makes My heart glad too. Whenever one gives themselves to Me and My care, I and those with Me express their great joy throughout heaven and earth. Come and partake with Me. I am always waiting for those who haven't opened the door yet. I stand at the door and knock."

14 – No One Can Serve Two Masters

"No one can serve two masters. Either you will hate the one and love the other, or you will be devoted to the one and despise the other. You cannot serve both God and money."

Luke 16:13 ESV

My thoughts:

I remember when I was working; there were times when I had to split my time between two managers. Those times were some of the most frustrating moments I've ever worked through. The other was when I would have a manager over me, and his manager would leapfrog over my manager and add or change my workload. I don't know which was the most frustrating, but I don't recommend it.

What I heard from the Lord:

"Split loyalties spell disaster. You must choose one over another and not look back. So, do you want money to be your god or Me? What can money do for you after you are taken from this earth? What can I do for you after you leave this earth? Is that plain enough? Choose wisely."

15 – Do the Right Thing

"You shall not see your brother's ox or his sheep going astray and ignore them. You shall take them back to your brother."

Deuteronomy 22:1 ESV

My thoughts:

"And you shall love your neighbor as yourself." (Matthew 22:39) We have obligations to one another. We always need to meet those obligations. To an extent, we are responsible for one another's welfare. The concept is simple but not necessarily easy. Do the next right thing. This is taught throughout the Bible. It may not be the easiest thing to do, but we'll always feel better for doing it, and more importantly it pleases our Lord.

What I heard from the Lord:

"When I made you in My image, I made you for community, not to stand alone. I give you My companionship, but I also give you companionship in the world with others of like minds. Do not hesitate to immerse yourselves in their fellowship. Be prepared to accept help from others, and do not hesitate to help one another. There is joy in both."

16 – Unworthy Servants

"So you also, when you have done all that you were commanded, say, 'We are unworthy servants; we have only done what was our duty.'"

Luke 17:10 ESV

My thoughts:

No matter what we do for the Lord is only our duty, and we should not expect any special consideration. Just to be a servant of the Lord most high is reward enough. It's all we should ask. Thank You, Lord, for calling us to be your servants, but we are more than servants, for we are friends, close friends of Jesus.

What I heard from the Lord:

"You ask, "What is our duty that we can do more?" You have been measured and found wanting except for the fact that My Spirit lives within you. My Son did His duty and was found worthy. You are not made worthy by your works, but only by the blood freely given by My Son. It is He who receives all honor and glory. It is by that comparison you are still unworthy, but you are justified through Him."

17 – The Secret Things

"The secret things belong to the Lord our God, but the things that are revealed belong to us and our children forever, that we may do all the words of this law."

Deuteronomy 29:29 ESV

My thoughts:

As I search this out in my mind, I think there are things of God that we are not ready to hear, but the things He has shown us are for our benefit and are to be passed down to our children and others with whom we come into contact.

What I heard from the Lord:

"The time is coming and is almost here where you will know all the hidden things of My heart. Until then, it is better that you do not know them. Some things you will never grasp this side of heaven, and you would think foolish, but they are not. It is enough that the Law was given, but even more important that I gave you My Son. You follow His law, and you will never be forsaken. You will flourish. Keep your mind on that."

18 – Our Refuge/Our Strength

"God is our refuge and strength, a very present help in trouble."

Psalm 46:1 ESV

My thoughts:

Looking back on my life, I see very few bumpy areas for a long period of time. Recently all that changed. I spent almost two weeks in the hospital. The facilities and staff were unmatched.

I had an incident where I couldn't breathe for an extended time. As I looked around physically and spiritually, I couldn't find Jesus anywhere as I called on Him for help to breathe. Eventually, I was able to catch my breath now and then until all was normal. All during that time, a nurse stayed at my side, encouraging me and rubbing my back. He kept at this until I began breathing normally. It was then that I knew Jesus was at my side all the time as the nurse who never gave up on me. God placed His Spirit in this man. I shall never forget the Lord's kindness to me. As He was with me, He's with each of us in the good and bad times.

What I heard from the Lord:

"I say it again. Wherever you go, I am there. I will never leave nor forsake you. You gave your lives to Me. I don't take that lightly. You trust Me to act on your behalf, and you can count on Me, for I have loved you before time began. Remember who and where you were before you asked Me into your hearts. I hold you in the palm of my hand and will never let go."

19 – Life and Good or Death and Evil

"See, I have set before you today life and good, death and evil."

Deuteronomy 30:15 ESV

My thoughts:

Moses was near the end of his sermon, his very long sermon consisting of almost all of Deuteronomy. God has laid out His plan for the people, and yet He also has shown that the people will not follow His plan. He knows all that in advance, yet it is still our free will that determines our future, with or without Him.

Here God tells the people through Moses that He has given them instructions for life or death. He says that He has set before them life and that which is good, or death and that which is evil. It was their choice then, and now it is ours as well. We can believe and accept the teachings of Christ, which is good and brings eternal life, or we can refuse His teachings and go our own way resulting in evil and death. He shows us the way but allows us to choose which gate we will go through.

What I heard from the Lord:

"You have the freedom to choose life or death. It is of your free will that I bestow upon all people that they may know that they are truly free indeed to follow the path of their choice. It can never be said that I forced any soul to go My way. It's your choice, and none other. It is I who have given you the map of life eternal with Me, or life eternal without Me. Choose wisely, they did not."

20 – No Empty Word

"For it is no empty word for you, but your very life, and by this word you shall live long in the land that you are going over the Jordan to possess."

Deuteronomy 32:47 ESV

My thoughts:

There was a prerequisite for this verse. They had to follow the Law. They couldn't and didn't because they forgot the Spirit of the Law. God knew all this before ever giving the Law. Certainly, there were Jews who fulfilled the Spirit of the Law. David was called a man after God's own heart. We see other characters as we read through the Old Testament who shared this love for the Lord. The people would try for a while, then fall away repeatedly. The Lord was very patient, but the time came when He saw they were never going to get it and finally allowed them their own way.

What I heard from the Lord:

"And so, the same is true today. Look around. Do you see Me in gambling establishments, in prostitution, in slavery, and so many more things I could mention? No, I am with My chosen people, and I lay a hedge of protection around them. As the people have been straining to get away from My Law, I have released them to their own devices. I have lifted My hand of protection and reserved it only for My own.

You who have heard My call and answered, keep to your faith, and know I am the Lord, I Am. I have always been. I will always be, and you are with Me."

21 – Marriage in Heaven?

"but those who are considered worthy to attain to that age and to the resurrection from the dead neither marry nor are given in marriage, …"

Luke 20:35 ESV

My thoughts:

The Bible tells us there is a hierarchy in Heaven. We read of angels and archangels. It says we will be like them. There are people on earth we get along with and those we don't even in Church. We all have different personalities, most of which work together, but some grate on each other. All this goes away in heaven. Each of us will love one another as Christ loves us, but each of us still will have our own magnified personalities. I love my wife unconditionally. I believe we will have a special love for one another in Heaven through eternity. Oh, of course, there isn't any marriage in Heaven, but perhaps there is room for special bonds.

I value my marriage intensely, and now I realize this is only a foretaste of what's to come. It gives me comfort I have not had before. I hope it does for you as well.

What I heard from the Lord:

"You have eternity to make new friends. There will be no more testing your spirits with others you meet. There will simply be an instant love for one another. You will be making new friends throughout eternity, never-ending friendships. The kind of bonds in Heaven will be far superior to the bonds of marriage on Earth."

22 – Rahab

"And they went and came into the house of a prostitute whose name was Rahab and lodged there."

Joshua 2:1 ESV

My thoughts:

Joshua sent two men into the land across the Jordan to spy the area, especially Jericho. Here they found Rahab, the prostitute who is an ancestor of Jesus. It appears that Rahab didn't start very well, but she certainly finished well and is known to this day in the Bible. It shows that no matter your lineage, no matter how you start, it's how you finish. I, for one, did not have a good start, but through the grace of God, I will finish well. This is no boast in myself but a boast in Jesus, my Lord, and Savior. He paid a terrible price that each of us can walk with Him unashamed because His grace is greater than the greatest of our sins. Thank You, Lord Jesus, now and forever. You bring life, but not just life. You bring life abundantly.

What I heard from the Lord:

"I will use whatever I wish to accomplish the proper ending. If it isn't right, then it isn't finished. Do you not realize it is no mistake that you were born when you were, that you live in a special place selected just for you? It should be no mystery that the tasks given to you are given by Me, especially for you, and that you will not leave this earth until they are completed to My satisfaction. Accept your lot in life. No one can live it except you. Keep your eyes on Me, and all will be well no matter your circumstances."

23 – It Was Determined

"For the Son of Man goes as it has been determined, but woe to that man by whom he is betrayed!"

Luke 22:22 ESV

My thoughts: Continued from Yesterday

It was appointed for Jesus to be on the earth when He was. This fulfilled the prophecies perfectly. Everything had to be perfectly in place before He could come. There had to be a method of transportation fulfilled by the Roman road system. There had to be a common language to speed the gospel throughout the known world fulfilled by Latin. There had to be a people unsatisfied with the status quo yearning for change and, upon hearing the gospel spreading it far and wide.

Predestination and free will have been argued over for centuries. I believe both are in effect at the same time, though. In my opinion they go together as hand and glove. When I began writing this morning, I gave it over to the Lord, and this is how He led me. I have never had these thoughts before, but as I read and re-read them, it makes it clear to me that each of us has a role to play. I never thought of it in relation to His second coming, but I do now. For me, I only want to be in His service for whatever He wishes me to do, never letting me lead anyone astray but strengthening the faith and understanding in others to the best of my God given ability. Praise God in all His Love, Wisdom, and Grace.

What I heard from the Lord:

"I am with you unto the very end of the earth and beyond. I have so much to show you. If you love your life with Me now, just wait. I have so much to show you, and you're going to be involved in all of it, for I have called you my friends and confidants. I see your smile. Just you wait."

24 – Peter's Denial

"And he went out and wept bitterly."

Luke 22:62 ESV

My thoughts:

Peter had just denied Christ, and Christ had just looked at him. Do we ever deny Him? I think yes. I know I have. I try to not look back on those times. It fills me with guilt, and with Christ we have no guilt. I do not ever want to deny Him again.

What I heard from the Lord:

"You have denied Me, but in more subtle ways. You have denied Me when you are with friends, and everyone is having a good time. You see openings to speak of Me, but you refrain. You deny Me when you hold back from a witness when strongly prompted by My Spirit. You deny Me when you have opportunities to spread neighborhood leaflets for church events and do not show up. You deny Me when there are children to teach, and you do not take the opportunity to do so. You deny Me when there is an alter call simply for re-aligning things that are not right in your heart, and you hold fast.

Get your hearts in the game. There is so little time and so much to do. Take every opportunity, regardless of how you feel, to show My love through your witness by your words and your deeds. Always be ready. Always put the lost before yourselves that more may enter My kingdom."

25 – The Gibeonites

"For we have heard a report of him and all that he did in Egypt,"

Joshua 9:9b ESV

My thoughts:

The Gibeonites were pretty shrewd with their story of coming from a far country and fooling Joshua. It was their only hope, otherwise, they would all have been killed. Joshua did not consult the Lord even though he was suspicious. The Gibeonites knew they would be slaves, but at least they would live.

Their report of all the Lord did in Egypt is exciting. Over 40 years had passed, and still, people in the land had heard and remembered what the Lord did in Egypt, and they were still fearful of these people in the land.

Today the Lord still does awesome things in people's lives across the globe. I much prefer telling others of the Lord's infinite love for us than the terrors of the Old Testament times. Thank You, Lord, for being alive in our hearts today, leading, guiding, and protecting us on our journey through life.

What I heard from the Lord:

"Decisions, you make many decisions daily. How often do you consult Me before making those decisions? Don't you know, I want to be involved in every part of your lives? I crave our fellowship and the closeness within prayer and communion. Come to Me first and see if your decisions are not better than before. Include Me and rejoice, for I make all things new."

26 – Simon of Cyrene

"And as they led him away, they seized one Simon of Cyrene, who was coming in from the country, and laid on him the cross, to carry it behind Jesus."

Luke 23:26 ESV

My thoughts:

When Simon got up that morning, he had no inkling that he'd be carrying the cross of God that day. Simon wasn't even from Judah or Galilee but from Cyrene, a city that was in present-day Libya. There was a large Jewish settlement in Cyrene, and they also had a synagogue in Jerusalem. It appears that he just happened to be there. I do not think so. It is said that he had two sons who became Christians, but we do not know about Simon. He probably didn't feel very privileged about carrying the cross of Jesus, but there he was.

We have the honor of knowing Christ. We are told to carry our own cross, whatever that may be. We are yoked with Jesus, and He tells us His burden is light. He carries it alongside us as we go through life. What an amazing thought, doing life with Jesus.

What I heard from the Lord:

"I use what I will to accomplish My will. I involve you wherever I can, so that you may have the blessing. Simon of Cyrene was blessed even though he didn't know it at the time. There is nothing I cannot do, yet I wait for the participation of My children, so that they can be part of all that is in store not only for each of you but too for the whole universe. You think you are small in comparison, but I tell you that you are greater, for you are the crown of My creation."

27 – Create In Me a Clean Heart

"Create in me a clean heart, O God, and renew a right spirit within me. Cast me not away from your presence, and take not your Holy Spirit from me. Restore to me the joy of your salvation, and uphold me with a willing spirit."

Psalm 51:10-12 ESV

My thoughts, my prayer:

Give me a clean and right spirit

Let me stay in Your presence.

Fill me with Your Holy Spirit.

Let me be restored with the joy of Your salvation.

Let my spirit be willing to do Your Will.

My prayer:

Lord, I see with my heart what I need and desperately crave. Thank You, Lord, that when I stray, You are ever ready to welcome me, warts and all, but not only that, You restore my joy, and my faith. You bless me by Your Holy Spirit entrenched on the throne of my heart. Ever let me be a blessing to You and everyone I know and will meet. I pray this in the name of Jesus, Amen.

What I heard from the Lord:

"When you are baptized in My Spirit you have a clean heart. As you walk through life, sin will creep in. You know this, but more, know you only have to confess your sins, and I will continually wipe your slate clean. Unconfessed sin always drags you down. Your confession lifts you up by My hand. The time is coming when all will kneel in My Presence. You have nothing to fear."

28 – Spirits and Ghosts

"See my hands and my feet, that it is I myself. Touch me and see. For a spirit does not have flesh and bones as you see that I have."

Luke 24:30 ESV

My thoughts:

This should dispel the notion that there are no ghosts or spirits. Jesus was emphatic that He was not a ghost or a spirit but flesh and bone. Jesus lives in Heaven. He has the same body that He had when He left this earth. Today He is the only One in Heaven like this until the resurrection.

Christ confirms the Spirit world, as does Paul, when in Ephesians 5:6-20 we are told to put on the full armor of God because our enemies are not flesh and blood, but the princes and principalities of the spirit world. Lord, help us always to keep Your armor on and take our stand. The victory is Yours.

What I heard from the Lord:

"Yes, the victory is Mine, but the victory is also yours. It is you in My armor that stand in the gap holding your places. When you are in My armor, you are invincible. The spirits of Hell fall before you. They cannot stand in the light given you through My armor. Keep the Faith. Just a little while, and the victory that is already won will be complete."

29 – The Law

"For the law was given through Moses; grace and truth came through Jesus Christ."

John 1:17 ESV

My thoughts:

When I look at the Bible, I think of the Old Testament being in black and white compared to the New Testament being in color. I see the color of the first three gospels, but then comes John in brilliant, vibrant living color that keeps me always coming back for more. This gospel is written primarily for Christians, no matter their background. I see the black and white of the law given through Moses, but then the living color of grace and truth through Jesus Christ.

Thank You, Lord Jesus, for making it real. Thank You, Lord Jesus, for our very lives now and forever. Thank You, Lord.

What I heard from the Lord:

"Without My Son, you would still be under the law. The Jews would still be modifying it as they do today, but you would be totally lost from Me. I knew the Jews would reject Him, but their time is yet to come. Their sole purpose up until My Son arrived was to provide the framework for His arrival and then reject Him. They did so without consulting Me. History would have been so different if they had. All things work together for good for those who love Me in good times and bad. What was started with the Jews has not yet fulfilled its course."

30 – Possession

"So Joshua said to the people of Israel, "How long will you put off going in to take possession of the land which the Lord, the God of your fathers, has given you?"

Joshua 18:3 ESV

My thoughts:

What has Jesus given us that we haven't taken possession of yet?

He has given us a down payment with the Holy Spirit living in us. Have we fully accepted Him, or are we keeping Him at arm's length?

He has given us eternal life. That life began when we asked Jesus into our hearts. Have we taken possession of our eternal and abundant life, or do we sometimes shelter in place and wait for the storms to blow over?

He has placed His love into our hearts. What do others see in us? Do they see Jesus? Do they see lives on fire for Him? Do they see us loving them as we love ourselves?

Our desire should be to take possession of all He's given us. Let us look at Galatians 5:22-23. Have we taken possession of all the fruit of the Spirit? Which of the fruit do we fully possess? Lord, show us the way.

What I heard from the Lord:

"Those in Joshua's time had to be prompted to take possession of the land. Yes, it was difficult and uncomfortable for them, yet they managed to do well at the time for I was with them. Today, I ask you to take something much more important than land. I yearn for more souls to come to Me. Each of you have been given gifts to secure the present and the future so that others may come to know Me. The Jews kept what I had given them to spread to the world. Be available in the good times and the bad to spread My Word in every way you can with the gifts you have been given."

Chapter 5: May

1 – Trust

"But Jesus on his part did not entrust himself to them, because he knew all people."

John 2:24 ESV

My thoughts:

It is interesting that Jesus didn't entrust Himself to these people, but in 1 Corinthians 13:6, we are told to believe all things. So, this is what I think. The Holy Spirit lives in each of us. He guides us on our path. He protects us and points us always back to Christ. We are connected by our spirit to His Spirit. Through our spirits, we know, if we listen, what the general motives of others we meet along the way may be. Jesus knew their spirits and would not entrust Himself to them. The same is true with us when we meet others along our way. Trust the Holy Spirit to light the way. We still believe all things but also listen to the tempering of the Holy Spirit.

What I heard from the Lord:

"Know that My Spirit protects you, but don't throw yourselves into danger. As My Son refused to throw Himself from the temple, neither should you place yourselves in danger except to save another. Listen through your spirits. Mingle with My Spirit so that you may know your next step. Do not step ahead of Him, just keep in step in communion with Him, and all will be well."

2 – Get the Facts Before Acting

"Thus says the whole congregation of the Lord, 'What is this breach of faith that you have committed against the God of Israel in turning away this day from following the Lord by building yourselves an altar this day in rebellion against the Lord?'"

Joshua 22:16 ESV

My thoughts:

Early in my management career, I learned to be very careful in accusing others of misdoings. I remember a manager who had done just that by firing an employee without looking at all the evidence. That employee appealed. The manager had to hire him back. You can imagine the work environment in his area after that.

Never jump to conclusions. Gather all the facts you can. Even then, in confrontation, do not accuse. Draw the supposed offender out. I remember using words like, "It appears such and such may have happened. Could I get your take on this?" I can't tell you how much trouble this saved me over the years. Always give the other party a chance. It's the right thing to do not only in management but with all the confrontations we have in life. Israel came too close to destroying thousands of people for a simple misunderstanding.

What I heard from the Lord:

"When in doubt, come to Me. Give Me your thoughts and beseech Me for answers. Don't jump ahead. Wait for My answer. In doing so, you may gain a friend instead of an enemy. You want your voice to be heard out in any misunderstandings, provide the same courtesy to anyone you think may have offended you, and be quick to make room for amends."

3 – He Must Increase

"He must increase, but I must decrease."

John 3:30 ESV

My thoughts, my prayer:

Sometimes I think it is a never-ending battle for me to decrease and allow Christ to increase in my life. It seems as if every time I allow Him to increase that I am again taking over the reins. I pray to the Lord, asking Him to help me let go. Perhaps He is, and I am just not sensitive enough to His persuasion. It's easy enough to say, "Let go and let God," but not so easy to make it real.

I've experienced long seasons with Him increasing in my life. As I live, those long seasons increase, and the periods where I take the reins are shorter.

My prayer:

Lord, all things work for our good, even the bad. Lord, whenever we pick up the reins of our lives, make it clear to us what we're doing and push our hands away with enough force as is necessary. Help us to realize what we are doing and see things Your way. In the name of Jesus, Amen.

It's a double win when He is greater and we are lesser.

What I heard from the Lord:

"When I increase in your lives, it is always for your betterment. I only want the very best for you. That very Best is My Son. As you rest in Him and listen to the Spirit, you grow. You grow in all aspects of My Love. Your decrease then is also your increase. I am the Giver of not just life, but abundant life that Our joy may increase, for your joy is My joy as well."

4 – The Samaritan Woman – A Different View

"For you have had five husbands, and the one you now have is not your husband. What you have said is true."

John 4:18 ESV

My thoughts:

What I'm about to write is not a very accepted view but check this out. In my opinion the woman at the well has been maligned. So, she had five husbands. In those days, it was almost impossible for a woman to get a divorce, so my assumption was that with the short lifespan of men in those days, they probably died or possibly divorced her. Jesus said the man she was currently living with was not her husband. He just stated the facts. He did not condemn her.

Women in those times were almost totally dependent on men for their survival. She could have been engaged but had nowhere else to go. Note also in following verses the town's folk listened to her. First, why would they listen to her, a woman? Secondly if she were a fallen woman, she would have been shunned, and not listened to. She must have had some significance in the village.

What I heard from the Lord:

"What My Son said was true. He can only speak the truth. Most have looked at this exchange and come up with an explanation, thus putting her in a bad light. This was never a judgement on her but getting her attention onto Whom she was listening. There should not be an emphasis on her but on My Son and His ministry. Always look to Him, and all will be well."

5 – Then and Now

"And all that generation also were gathered to their fathers. And there arose another generation after them who did not know the Lord or the work that he had done for Israel."

Judges 2:10 ESV

My thoughts:

So, what happened? Moses was their leader, and they passed on the Word of God to their children. Then Joshua became their leader. The people took many lands through the protection of the Lord, but it doesn't look like they passed on the Word of God onto their children, and they, for the most part, went the way of those living in the land before them.

Growing up in the 1940s and 1950s it appeared to me that an awful lot of people were in church every Sunday, but it seemed to trickle away into the early 1960s. Even the movies had positive references to God. After almost 250 years in this land of God's Word being passed down generation to generation, has slowed down to a trickle. There has been some revival, but it seems to me we are much like those mentioned in the verse above.

Lord, light us on fire for You. Let there be a revival in the land.

What I heard from the Lord:

"Revival is coming and is at hand. Too many churches have lost their First Love. I am that First Love. Revival will come, but there will be a great winnowing with it. Some will barely feel it; for others, it will make all the difference in their lives. Whole churches and denominations will be turned on their heels, and My light will shine. Many who have never known will see the light of My Son as His Spirit moves across the land. Be patient, but also be ready. No one who can be saved shall be lost."

6 – Refuge in the Lord

"Be merciful to me, O God, be merciful to me, for in you my soul takes refuge; in the shadow of your wings I will take refuge till the storms of destruction pass by."

Psalm 57:1 ESV

My thoughts, my prayer:

I have had some health issues. It's been a difficult time. The one thing that bothers me the most is my inability to concentrate on the Lord and His Word. I've been very fortunate to have that concentration until recently, but to be unable to give my full attention to the Lord is so frustrating. This is very personal to me, and I think should be for others.

My prayer:

Lord, my soul must take refuge in the shadow of Your wings. Be merciful to me. Meet me, Lord where I can best see You and give You my full devotion. The pain and other physical difficulties I can deal with in Your strength, but not being able to meditate fully on Your Word, and Your Presence are so hard to deal with. Lord, I pray You return my ability to hear Your Word and meditate on it as before. Thank You, Lord, for listening and hearing my prayer. In the Name of Jesus I pray, Amen.

What I heard from the Lord:

"I am your Refuge. I know you. I know your needs, wants, and desires. Afterall, you were made by My hands. When your spirits are up, I am with you. When your spirits are down, am I not with you still? I have promised never to leave nor forsake you. Even when your thoughts are cloudy, know I surround you, and My Spirit indwells you. Be patient and know I am Lord. All is for your good."

7 – Faithfulness

"For your steadfast love is great to the heavens, your faithfulness to the clouds."

Psalm 57:10 ESV

My thoughts:

God's love for each of us is steadfast. It doesn't change. He can't love us anymore or any less for what we do or don't do, either good or evil. As His love is great to the heavens, it surrounds us on every side and rests within our hearts. Not only is His love so great and steadfast, but He is also faithful to us. We might break our covenant with Him, but He doesn't break His covenant with us. It's not how hard we hang on to His hand, but how hard He holds on to our hands.

What I heard from the Lord:

"This day is yours when you are finished with it; know I was there with you every moment. As you begin a new day, know that I have prepared it just for you. Whatever happens to you has been pre-ordained. All things work together for your good. Remember that, even if, at times, it seems I am far from you. Relax and know that I am God, but also, I am your Friend, for you have given your life to Me."

8 – A Different Look at Faith

"And he divided the 300 men into three companies and put trumpets into the hands of all of them and empty jars, with torches inside the jars."

Judges 7:16 ESV

My thoughts:

In reading this, I remember when I was in the military. I thought of being one of Gideon's warriors with an empty jar in one hand and a torch in the other. I wouldn't like the idea of having my hands full and unable to reach my weapon if the need arose. I thought of the faith these 300 had in Gideon and, ultimately, the Lord. They knew Gideon had been anointed. On the other hand, they also knew there were very few of them in comparison to the enemy.

Praise God for using the simple to confound the wise. Praise Him for knowing the outcome of our lives when we were not yet born. Praise Him most of all for bringing Jesus not only into the world but also within our hearts. Oh, what a great advantage we have over those warriors of Gideon. They knew of Gideon and the way the Lord was using him, but they didn't know our Lord Jesus. Praise You, Lord.

What I heard from the Lord:

"As Gideon was not trained for warfare, neither are you, but you are trained for spiritual warfare. It is there that you have been trained by Me from My Word. This war is a spiritual war, not fought with the weapons of physical war, but weapons of the heart, weapons that won't rust or decay. These weapons are My armor that I bestow on you that you are prepared far better than was Gideon, who I certainly prepared for physical warfare, but you, you stay in My armor and listen for My voice. Victory is at hand."

9 – What Can We Give

"There's a young boy here with five barley loaves and two fish. But what good is that with this huge crowd?"

John 6:9 NLT

My thoughts:

The hero outside of Jesus was the young boy. He gave all he had. That's all we know about him. As Jesus used all that the boy had, He uses all we have when we willingly give it to Him.

What an example that boy is to us. What might we willingly give Him today that He may use it for His glory?

What I heard from the Lord:

"All I want is you. All I want is all you have. All I give is all I have for you. How's that for an exchange? I love you. I will never leave you, and I will never stop giving to you through all eternity. Relax in My arms and know I am the Lord of all, beginning with you with no end ever."

10 – Too High of a Price

"then whatever or whoever comes out from the doors of my house to meet me when I return in peace from the Ammonites"

Judges 11:31 ESV

My thoughts:

What did Jephthah expect to come out of his house when he returned? It could only be his wife or daughter, perhaps a servant. This man had studied the scriptures, as shown earlier in the chapter where he told the history in Judges 11:14-37, but this man made a horrible, stupid decision that cost the life of his daughter. We can't possibly know the culture of the day without being there and don't know what kinds of pressures were on the people. So, my judgement of him is improper.

These people paid the price for the way they ran their lives, as we do for the way we run ours. The Lord never demands human sacrifice, and he doesn't condone murder, as it is here that Jephthah effectively murdered his daughter. (Once again, my judgement.)

Simply, the Lord demands no vows. If we make vows, be very certain and clear about what we are doing. He tells us, let your yes be yes and your no be no. (Matthew 5:27)

What I heard from the Lord:

"As you are instruments in your time, so was Jephthah an instrument in his time. No judgement of him is valid from you. I didn't see you there. You do not know the peer and other pressure on him. He did his best with what he had, as I expect you to do your best where you are. Remember, you will be spending all eternity with Jephthah and others throughout history who love Me just as much as you do but come from different times and places."

11 – Where Can We Go?

"Simon Peter answered him, "Lord, to whom shall we go? You have the words of eternal life,"

John 6:68 ESV

My thoughts:

The Lord had just given a hard teaching to the disciples, and many had walked away. He had just asked the twelve if they would do the same.

Jesus's disciples had Him. We have the Holy Spirit. Sometimes Jesus would display some impatience with them. The Holy Spirit is always here patiently with us.

It was that Spirit that gave these great words to Peter. What is He telling us today? Yes, Jesus has the same words of eternal life today as he had for the disciples then.

Let us stay the course with the only Giver of eternal life.

What I heard from the Lord:

"Look, look at the world today. This is where you live, but not where you belong. You have been bought for a great price, the life of My Son. With My Spirit living in your hearts, know that this is only a down payment of what's to come. You belong to Me. So, where can you go but to My loving arms that keep you now and will keep you forever? You were designed for My Love. You were designed to live it and to pass it on to your children, friends, and all within your reach by your words and your deeds. I am yours, but you also are Mine now and forever."

12 – Judging

"Do not judge by appearances, but judge with right judgment."

John 7:24 ESV

My thoughts:

In the Bible, we are told not to judge lest we be judged. Here we are told to judge with the right judgment and not by appearances. In truth, we judge all the time.

We are told to judge within the church, which is well documented in Matthew 18:15-17. But we are told to judge always toward reconciliation. We are told not to judge outside of the church, but that too is directed toward drawing the lost to redemption.

In this passage, they were judging Jesus by appearances. Many judged Him by appearances, but some judged Him with the right judgment and were saved.

When we judge, and we do, let us judge with the right motives. Let us judge to build up and not tear down. Let us examine the plank in our own eye before trying to take the splinter out of the eye of another. Let us be slow to judge but quick to forgive. Let the love of Christ flow freely through our spirits.

What I heard from the Lord:

"The final judgement must be Mine. I judge the heart. Listen to your spirit as it mingles with My Spirit. When you listen to your spirit mingled with Mine, you will know the hearts of others. To judge by appearances, that which you see with your eyes, it isn't fair, and it isn't right. You cannot know what is in the hearts of others without the discernment of your spirit. How do you judge Me? Yes, by your spirit mingled with Mine. Listen and know I am Lord."

13 – Sampson's Vengeance

"Then Samson called to the Lord and said, "O Lord God, please remember me and please strengthen me only this once, O God, that I may be avenged on the Philistines for my two eyes."

Judges 16:28 ESV

My thoughts:

Samson was a rough and tumble guy and one of the people I have judged to be unfit for the Kingdom of Heaven. (My error.) He did everything his own way with little regard for the consequences, whether from God or people, but here we see him at the very end.

"Sampson called to the Lord." He didn't do this lightly, but sincerely. With all he'd done and gone through, now he still remembers the Lord. He acknowledges where his strength has come from, and his last act is against those who would and have subverted the people of God. He is acknowledged in the book of Hebrews 11:32-40 as a hero, a man of faith.

Like the thief on the cross, Samson knew his errors and called out to the Lord. Let us not judge but give the Lord His due.

What I heard from the Lord:

"It is important to start well, but more important to finish well. Sampson is one of those. Many have starts and stops of sorts until faith finally kicks in, and they see the road not traveled by many also meant for them. Take the high and narrow road to Me and be saved. It is harder, but the rewards are greater. To do otherwise leads to slavery and eventual eternity without Me and My own."

14 – He is From Above

"He said to them, "You are from below; I am from above. You are of this world; I am not of this world."

John 8:23 ESV

My thoughts:

Jesus is from above. He came to lift us up to Him through His sacrificial life. His sacrifice did not happen only on the cross but began when He set aside His glory in Heaven to be born as a baby among us. He taught us and lives by His own teaching. When we live His teaching, we become His testimony. We become living sacrifices. That is our role by His Spirit living in us, teaching us, and growing us more in His likeness day by day.

Lord, let Your Likeness shine in us today. Show us to be Your Likeness in honor of You. Let us be living sacrifices for You with every beat of our hearts. In the name of Jesus, Amen.

What I heard from the Lord:

"It is true My Son is not of the world. He created the world. For a time, He had to live in the world for your sakes. Had He never left heaven and come to the world, you would be completely and totally lost with not even a glimmer of hope. Your whole lives would be meaningless, for without My Son, there is no meaning. First, last, and always look to Him."

15 – Abide in My Word

"So Jesus said to the Jews who had believed him, "If you abide in my word, you are truly my disciples, and you will know the truth, and the truth will set you free."

John 8:31-31 ESV

My thoughts:

Now those who believed Him had just recently come to believe. There had been no time to test their faith. What Jesus continued to say ran against the grain of their lifelong beliefs and training. So, as Jesus continued, they reacted to what their lives had been. They rebelled against what they had just accepted. In effect, they had tasted but had not yet swallowed Jesus' Word. They were the rocky soil upon which the Holy Spirit was sewn. They had no roots and no faith.

What I heard from the Lord:

"My Word is pure. My Word will set you free when you call on Him to come into your hearts. Your agreement with My Word, your faith in My Word moves you from the darkness into the Light. My Son is the Light of the world, and there is no darkness in Him. The more you lean into My Spirit, the more your understanding will grow as you dig deeper into My Word. It is a life-changing treasure trove just waiting for you."

16 – The Man Born Blind

"He answered, "Whether he is a sinner, I do not know. One thing I do know, that though I was blind, now I see."

John 9:25 ESV

My thoughts:

Let's look at the man who had been blind:

Here is a man who has been blind all his life.

Jesus healed him.

He knew it was a man named Jesus who had healed him.

He was brought before the Pharisees and questioned.

He answered truthfully.

The Pharisees brought in his parents, who threw him to the wolves.

The Pharisees called him a second time. He became exasperated with them.

The Pharisees threw him out.

Jesus found him. The man worshipped Jesus and became a disciple.

That is an incredible story. Each of us has a story. Each of us was blind to Jesus until we found Him, and He gave us spiritual sight. Now we have no excuse other than to live under His gentle rule. How is our sight today? (Galatians 5:22-23, Romans 13.)

What I heard from the Lord:

"My Son is the Pearl of Great Price. This blind man was put in His path for a purpose. You, too, have been put in His path for a purpose. As this blind man and his story are in My Word for eternity, so too are you. You, too, were put in His path for a purpose and are in My Book for eternity. Let your spirit be free to mingle with My Spirit. You will see the unimaginable."

17 – We Know His Voice

"When he has brought out all his own, he goes before them, and the sheep follow him, for they know his voice."

John 10:4 ESV

My thoughts:

During an illness I found my meditations wanting, and though I craved His voice, I couldn't get to the stillness through all the noise rushing through my mind. I went through several weeks until I again was able to immerse myself in His Word and hear His voice. This was the best start to my day I've had for a long time. I pray for you to have a great day and bathe in the Spirit of God throughout this day. Bless you.

To know His voice is to hear His voice. We hear His voice by reading, memorizing, and meditating on His Word. We hear His voice by listening to those who teach and preach. How else can we know Your voice, Lord?

What I heard from the Lord:

"My voice comes to you in the stillness of the day. When you set aside all those obstructions that come between you and Me, you hear My voice when you wait for Me in the stillness. Then I will come and commune with you, and you with Me. Never fear, I am not only a prayer away, but I dwell within you. Clear your mind and let My Word settle in and cover all the rough places of your heart. Because you know My voice, you will follow Me. Taste and see if I do not show you wonders you've never dreamed of. Rest in My love and listen for My voice."

18 – Gods

"And you know that the Scriptures cannot be altered. So if those people who received God's message were called 'gods, why do you call it blasphemy when I say, 'I am the Son of God'? After all, the Father set me apart and sent me into the world."

John 10:35-36 NLT

My thoughts:

This is not the first place in the Bible where some people are called gods. Sometimes those in authority are called gods, such as judges. They are not God but those in authority over others.

They are not immortal but are born and will die.

What I heard from the Lord:

"You have been given great authority, for you are My ambassadors. You have been entrusted with My Word. You have been given the very Word of life. You stand before Me in My Righteousness. You go with My blessing and with My Truth. My Word is true and must be kept with the utmost care. As such, you are blessed of all mankind. My Word must be spread throughout the world. Rejoice as keepers of the faith."

19 – Why Jesus Wept

"Jesus wept."

John 11:35 ESV

My thoughts:

Here we have the shortest verse in the Bible. There have been many comments and ideas about why Jesus wept. There was the sorrow of Mary and Martha with their loss of Lazarus, but He knew what He was about to do. He saw the grief of His disciples, for they too knew Lazarus. The road ahead of Him to the cross was right around the corner. These are all worthy reasons for Him to weep, but He had to call Lazarus from Paradise back to Earth to yet die again. He wept because of all these things, but the biggest reason was that He had to bring Lazarus back to life again on this earth.

We don't know how many people came to Christ because of this act, and we don't know how they lived the rest of their lives. I like to believe it is because of their great testimony that many more who might have been lost were found and are experiencing eternal life. God doesn't waste anything but uses all things for our good.

What I heard from the Lord:

"My son wept. As We are One, so too I wept. There was a good man who had given his heart to My Son. He knew not his purpose when he was born was to die twice. He knew the joys of Paradise yet had to come back in order to accomplish the rest of his mission. You, too, will not be called to heaven until your mission is complete."

20 – Kill Lazarus?

"So the chief priests made plans to put Lazarus to death as well,"

John 12:10 ESV

My thoughts:

The raising of Lazarus is the only account of Jesus raising someone from the dead who had been dead for such a long time. Also, this was done just outside of Jerusalem. They wanted Jesus dead, but there was an additional complication when Lazarus was raised from the dead with all the commotion, and Lazarus was drawing people to Jesus as well. What better than to take Jesus out of the picture, but Lazarus with Him. He could not be left with such a strong testimony to the power of Jesus. The entire issue of Jesus had to be dealt with and soon.

It's so sad that they were so blind. It's so sad that so many have been lost because of the deceit of these leaders caught in Satan's lair. It is so joyful that so many have been saved in spite of all the lies and misconceptions propagated through the centuries.

What I heard from the Lord, Jesus:

"I wept. I wept for Lazarus. I wept for Mary. I wept for Martha. I wept for the unbelief around Me. Lazarus was gone. Lazarus was very happy. Lazarus had given his all, but there was more for him to do. I had to call him back. I had to call him from Paradise. He heard My voice and accepted My command, and yes, to die yet again. But oh, what a work he did before returning not to Paradise where he was, but to Heaven itself."

21 – Whoever Loves His Life Loses It

"Whoever loves his life loses it, and whoever hates his life in this world will keep it for eternal life."

John 12:25 ESV

My thoughts:

If we follow Christ, where is our citizenship? Are we here for our comfort in this world? Are we here to embrace what we see and revel in it? The world has been the same for a very long time. Jesus lived in a world under Roman tyranny. It was a world where anything could be had for a price. And so it appears to be much the same today.

If we are happy with our lives here and want to join in with the festivities of the world, then we are lost from Christ for all eternity. Christ must always be first in our lives.

So, what does it mean to hate our lives in this world? It's a comparative thing. If we really and truly love the Lord, all else in comparison is hatred. The world is an evil place, and it's getting more so at an ever-increasing pace. Our comfort level in the world should be decreasing by the day, and we should have a greater longing for Christ's presence as the days go by.

What I heard from the Lord:

"If you feel comfort in the world, you are on thin ice, and the sun is about to come out. To find comfort in the world is to see hardships in My kingdom. It is true that there are hardships in My kingdom, but anything worthwhile has its hardships. Look to me, not for an easy life in My kingdom. To say otherwise is a lie, but My benefits far exceed any benefits you see in the world. Come to Me all who are heavy laden, and I will give you rest."

22 – Heavy Words

"The one who rejects me and does not receive my words has a judge; the word that I have spoken will judge him on the last day."

John 12:48 ESV

My thoughts:

These are very heavy words. It is God's Word, Jesus Himself Who judges. The very words of Christ judge us by our choices. What will we do with His Word this day?

What I heard from the Lord:

"I act by My Word. My Words are life. When you offer My Word to others, you are offering them life. Should you withhold My Word from others, you are withholding life from them. Use care, utmost care with My Word. It is My Word that judges. Read and know who I am. Put to memory My Word and meditate on My Word. Then you will know; for my very Word judges you."

23 – God Hears Our Prayers

"If I had cherished iniquity in my heart, the Lord would not have listened. But truly God has listened; he has attended to the voice of my prayer."

Psalm 66:18-19 ESV

My thoughts:

Lord, let us keep our focus on You and keep our hearts softened toward You. Let us not betray your Word. We know you listen, for the Word says so, and there is no lie in it.

What I heard from the Lord:

"I do not hear the prayers of the proud and unrepentant. I do not hear the prayers of the selfish. I do not hear the prayers of the double minded. These prayers will not be honored.

I hear the prayers of the repentant. I hear the prayers of intercession. I hear the prayers of the soul searchers. I hear the prayers of honesty and integrity. From those who don't know Me, I answer one prayer only. All these prayers I keep in a special place near My heart, and I attend to their voices."

24 – Satan Has No Claim on Christ

"I will no longer talk much with you, for the ruler of this world is coming. He has no claim on me,"

John 14:30 ESV

My thoughts:

This is an interesting verse. The time of Jesus on the earth was almost over. Satan was coming to gloat over his victory, but Christ just said that Satan has no claim on Him. In Genesis 3:15 it says that the Lord will crush the head of Satan and that Satan would bruise His heel. A bruised heel doesn't sound like much of a victory to me. The victory belongs to the Lord.

What I heard from the Lord Jesus:

"Satan has no claim on Me, but I have many claims on him. He thought he had won a great victory, but no, yet another defeat, and there are yet more surprises in store for him. My heel was bruised but no more than that. The final victory feast is coming very soon. It is almost here. As time goes by, events will flow faster and faster until the end. Rejoice. Satan has no power over you. You are my beloved children. Stand fast and know that I am your God."

25 – Choosing

"You did not choose me, but I chose you and appointed you that you should go and bear fruit and that your fruit should abide, so that whatever you ask the Father in my name, he may give it to you."

John 15:16 ESV

My thoughts:

John 15 is beautiful from beginning to end. There are so many beautiful verses to choose from for meditation. This chapter appears to be written to the disciples, the chosen 12. The writing is close and personal. As John wrote it, though, it also applies to us.

The disciples didn't choose Him; Jesus did choose them. Jesus chose us by calling to us from His Word. As we are the branches, we must bear fruit. Fruit doesn't grow on a grapevine, but on the branches. Those branches must remain attached to the vine as we must remain attached to the Lord that we should bear fruit. Understanding all this, our prayers will never be selfish but always in line with the Mind of Christ, as it is in His name that we pray. Our prayers then, are as of Christ to the Father.

What I heard from the Lord:

"I chose you. You had to respond one way or another. You are part of the choosing through your responses. Many are called. Few are chosen. I alone am in the Calling. As you grow, your prayers will identify more and more in line with wise requests that are selfless and pure. You pray now as My Son prayed. The time is near when we will be face-to-Face with no need for requests. Rejoice, for that day is very near."

26 – The Spirit of Truth

"When the Spirit of truth comes, he will guide you into all the truth, for he will not speak on his own authority, but whatever he hears, he will speak, and he will declare to you the things that are to come."

John 16:13 ESV

My thoughts, my prayer:

The Holy Spirit, the Spirit of Truth, guides us into all truth. He speaks to us on the authority of the Lord.

Lord, we can never thank You enough for Your Spirit residing in us, leading us into all Truth. As Pilate stood there speaking with Jesus, speaking to the Truth Himself, he asked, "What is truth?" Truth was right there in front of him, and he could not see it.

How many times have we been in the same place as Pilate having the Word right in front of us, and in some fashion asking the same thing?

My prayer:

Thank You, Lord, for being patient with us. Thank You, Lord, for sending Your Spirit that He may lead us into all Truth. We are blessed of all people in all the centuries before us because You first called us, and Your Spirit lives within. In the name of Jesus, Amen.

What I heard from the Lord:

"I, My Son, and My Spirit are Truth. We are One. The Spirit resides in your hearts. Seek Truth through Him as you further seek Truth in My Word. My Spirit will guide you in all Truth through the Scriptures, My Holy Word. My Spirit is there to help you. Stand aside and be one with Him as you grow in grace and maturity. Sense the glow of My Presence."

27 – My Spirit Resides In You

"I made known to them your name, and I will continue to make it known, that the love with which you have loved me may be in them, and I in them."

John 17:26 ESV

My thoughts:

Jesus was telling the disciples that He made the name of God known to them and will continue to do so. This is done by the Holy Spirit. Christ lives in us through His Spirit.

What I heard from the Lord:

"I had longed for the day when My Spirit would reside in you. Everything had to happen at its appointed time. That includes the sacrifice of My Son. It applies to you today. Everything is happening to and for you in its appointed time. You cannot rush it, nor can you delay it. It has to be when it has to be. Let the joy I feel through My Spirit dwelling in you reign supreme and be overflowing in your lives today. Let those around you sense and know My great love for you."

28 – What is Our Cup?

"So Jesus said to Peter, "Put your sword into its sheath; shall I not drink the cup that the Father has given me?"

John 18:11 ESV

My thoughts:

Jesus had been drinking the cup the Father had given Him for about three years. Now He will finish drinking the cup on Calvary. What might your cup be?

What I heard from the Lord:

"You indeed have a cup to drink. You drink of it daily by following the Words given to you by My Son. As He drank from the cup I had given Him so you do by every action you take in the name of My Son. I see and know all. Nothing is hidden from Me. As you drink, you are resolved to complete the tasks given to you until that final day. Draw from my strength through the Spirit living in you. Draw from My strength by your communion with me in My Word and your prayers. I'm always with you, now and forevermore."

29 – If He Were not Guilty, We Wouldn't Have Arrested Him

"They answered him, "If this man were not doing evil, we would not have delivered him over to you."

John 18:30 ESV

My thoughts:

Is this perverted justice from centuries ago? I remember when I was much younger and much more innocent that if you were arrested, you must be guilty. I had the highest esteem for police officers. I still have a high regard for them, but they are not always right, nor at times are they allowed to do their jobs because of perverted requirements from politicians that may not have the purest motives.

Here we see the same thing with, "We wouldn't have arrested him if he wasn't guilty." Here we have God being put on trial. Is He on trial today? I think more than ever, and He is being convicted by those who have never read even a sentence in the Bible. He is being convicted without a shred of evidence, and His followers, along with Him.

We must remember that this isn't the first time of persecution. Hopefully, it will be the last. Come, Lord Jesus, come.

What I heard from the Lord:

"If My Son were guilty, He would be guilty of love. First and foremost. He would be guilty of being the Truth. His guilt would be in perfection. He would be guilty of patience. He came in peace and would be guilty of that. Of all the things He would be guilty of are nothing of what He was accused of. Read My Word from beginning to end and see all He is guilty of."

30 – The Procession of God

"Your procession is seen, O God, the procession of my God, my King, into the sanctuary—"

Psalm 68:24 ESV

My thoughts:

As I read this Psalm today and the magnificence of His entry into the sanctuary, I thought of this vision and how much greater we will praise Him for each saint that enters into His presence.

My vision from the Lord:

I found myself on the outside of a huge wall. As I stood in front of a giant set of double doors, they opened outward toward me to enter. Each half of the double doors came to a peak at the top. As I walked in, I saw my guardian angel on the inside to my right. The doors then closed behind me. There was another set of double doors in front of me, identical to the pair I had just passed through. It was light inside but much dimmer than when I was outside the doors. I seemed to be in an outer room. It was very long but narrow.

Now the doors opened inward away from me, and I stepped into the light. It was very bright, and there were thousands of people shouting and praising God. It was really hard for me to see, but I know I came into the presence of my God. My guardian angel was no longer with me. Did this mean my life on earth was over, and I was in Heaven? I had no fear. I had a feeling of well-being. I was then caught up with shouting out His name and praising Him. I knew I was home, but it seemed so much different than what I expected. I'm looking forward to what's coming next.

Then there was great praise for the Lord with the entrance of each saint into Heaven. How much greater is the praise for the Lord upon His entrance and His gathering?

31 – He Gives Power and Strength

"Awesome is God from his sanctuary; the God of Israel—he is the one who gives power and strength to his people. Blessed be God!"

Psalm 68:35 ESV

My thoughts:

I remember when I was young and much stronger than today. As I have aged, my physical strength seems to be spent, and the only strength I can count on is the strength of the Lord that must be renewed daily. Each day I wake, and as I wonder what the day will bring, I rise and feel the weakness of muscle and bone, the weakness of my once nimble mind. It's a fact of life and happens to all of us.

So, where does that leave us?

What I heard from the Lord:

"I am your strength and salvation. You must depend on Me and My strength as never before. What was your strength anyway except a vapor that is here today and gone tomorrow? Let Me sustain you with My never-ending strength and power. It is for such a time as this that you can recognize and depend on Me as never before. Drink from My never-ending spring of life and be renewed. Depend on Me. I will not fail."

Chapter 6: June

1 – My Lord and My God

"Thomas answered him, "My Lord and my God!"

John 20:28 ESV

My thoughts:

Thomas is my favorite disciple. He simply says it the way he sees it. There's no filter on his mouth, yet his spirit is straight and true. I remember inviting the Lord into my heart. My prayer was, "Lord Jesus, if You're real; if you're really real, come into my heart, but Lord, I don't want to be duped. This had better be true." Yes, that was my prayer. I still remember it all these years later. It was and is still all real. He came into my life and turned it upside down and made me whole. I say with Thomas, "My Lord and my God!"

What I heard from the Lord:

"Yes, you know it's all real, and where you are today is the shadow land. Things appear to be solid, but all is transitory. Nothing will last, for sin destroys all that it touches except for My intervention. You will survive, yet your very form will be lost. As you cleave to My Word, you cleave to Me, and I hold you in My righteous right hand that you come through the fire unscathed. Come into My rest."

2 – Let Us Not Lead Anyone Astray

"Let not those who hope in you be put to shame through me, O Lord God of hosts; let not those who seek you be brought to dishonor through me, O God of Israel."

Psalm 69:6 ESV

My thoughts, my prayer:

Our past actions don't necessarily display who we are today. For all who are called by the Lord, He uses our past actions and the actions of others, either good or bad, all for good to those who belong to Him. It is good to pray for those who may have been led astray by our past actions; better, if possible, to show them who we are today, what we've become by our closer walk with Christ, and how they can be embraced by the Lord as we have been and continue to be.

My prayer:

Lord, forgive us for any dishonor through us that has led anyone astray. Lord, let our lives in You be a testimony of Your Love, Your Work, and Your Priorities in the lives of those who have accepted Your call and are blessed and protected by the love and power of our Lord Jesus and in His name we pray, Amen.

What I heard from the Lord:

"Hope, you have hope in Me, and it is well placed, for it is I who stands alone in the midst of tribulation. It is I Who holds back the flood of evil, yet the time is coming and is at the gates. Your hope, your strength is in Me. Ever let it be and you will always be safe in My arms."

3 – Come Lord Jesus, come!

"And said, "Men of Galilee, why do you stand looking into heaven? This Jesus, who was taken up from you into heaven, will come in the same way as you saw him go into heaven."

Acts 1:11 ESV

My thoughts:

They saw Him in His physical body rise up into heaven. We will either see Him in His physical body when He returns, or we will return with Him. That is true whether or not you believe in a Rapture. His return means His physical return to this earth. It is true because the apostles saw it for themselves. This was written so that we, too, may know and anticipate His return.

I sense a great deal of activity in Heaven and on the earth. We would have to be spiritually blind not to know that He will come soon. I've seen a lot of change in the past many years, but nothing like what we are living through now. Something must give. I believe it is His imminent return. I, for one, welcome Him with all my heart. Join me in that welcome. Come, Lord Jesus, come!

What I heard from the Lord:

"As it was foretold, so it is coming into being. The shadows of the past are being overcome by My Light into a new and glorious day. I have yearned for this day, yet a little while, and completion comes. I have two words for you, "Be ready.""

4 – A Dim View of Sin

"And the anger of the Lord was kindled against Uzzah, and God struck him down there because of his error, and he died there beside the ark of God."

2 Samuel 6:7 ESV

My thoughts:

Why would the Lord strike Uzzah down when he was trying to protect the ark? The bigger question is why did Ahio and Uzzah not follow God's command on how the ark should be moved? God gave Moses precise instructions on how the ark should be moved, and it was not on an ox cart. (Exodus 25:14-16, Numbers 7:6-9)

God has a very dim view of sin in any form or by any degree. There is always a price for our sins. Jesus paid a heavy price that we are saved even in our sins, but there are also consequences for our actions, as we see here with Uzzah. Some of those consequences can be hard to bear, but they, too, should always point us back to Christ.

What I heard from the Lord:

"My Word is not to be trifled with. It is there for a reason. That reason is to show My Love for you. Sometimes it appears harsh, but rest assured, I am always looking out for your welfare. There is a price for the welfare of the whole that My Son had to pay. Know though that always My actions are for your welfare even when you don't understand."

5 – Only You Can Be You

"Then King David went in and sat before the Lord and said, "Who am I, O Lord God, and what is my house, that you have brought me thus far?"

2 Samuel 7:18 ESV

My thoughts:

Ask this – Who am I, Lord, that You have brought me this far? What have I done to deserve it? In answering my own questions, I am nothing. I am nothing but a zero with the edges rubbed off. What have I done to deserve it? Again nothing. It's only by God's grace that we are where we are today. For better or for worse, He is always with us.

What I heard from the Lord:

"It is not what you have done, but the work of My Son. Only you can be you. It's your job and yours alone. Stay humble and know I am Lord. All you are and have comes from Me. Use it well. It is not for safekeeping but for you to use in My kingdom, for My kingdom is coming, and it will be on earth as it is in heaven. Use all you have for My purposes and see if I won't open the doors of My storehouse for you. Watch as I lavish My love upon you."

6 – In the Name of Jesus

"But Peter said, "I have no silver and gold, but what I do have, I give to you. In the name of Jesus Christ of Nazareth, rise up and walk!"

Acts 3:6 ESV

My thoughts:

This is the first recorded healing after the ascension of Christ. When Jesus would heal, he didn't call on anyone else's name, for He is God. When Peter heals, he does so in the name of Jesus that all the credit goes to Him.

Even our prayers to God should end in Jesus' name. Because of our sins, the Father can't look at us, but He hears our prayers through the mantle of Jesus. Peter, like each of us, is a tool for Christ. Whatever we do today, let it be blessed by the Lord, and may He receive all the glory.

What I heard from the Lord:

"Miracles, yes, the first miracle after the ascension was done through Peter, not by Peter. As you are instruments for My Will, so was Peter and all those called apostles, even to Judas. It is today as it was then. Miracles did not stop with the apostles, but continue through this day, and will continue until all My own are safely gathered into My arms. Every time one accepts My Son into their heart, that is the greatest of miracles and all Heaven rejoices."

7 – Salvation In No One Else

"And there is salvation in no one else, for there is no other name under heaven given among men by which we must be saved."

Acts 4:12 ESV

My thoughts:

What a statement. What power resides with these words? Our only salvation comes from Christ for He is God. He must be or become the master of our lives through His Spirit that lives within us.

What I heard from the Lord:

"Salvation, you are saved only by the name of My Son. In Him is the means of salvation, and in no other. He died so you might live. Has there ever been anyone else like Him? There have come many pretenders. Some of them came with pure motives. Others had evil in their hearts. The decision is so simple. Come to Me through My Son. If not, the gates of Heaven are shut up against you. You will have no part of me ever. Choose wisely whom you will serve."

8 – Proclaim the Lord to the Next Generation

"So even to old age and gray hairs, O God, do not forsake me until I proclaim your might to another generation, your power to all those to come."

Psalm 71:18 ESV

My thoughts:

One of our goals might be to live long unless the Lord comes first. It's not enough to have a long life, though, but to make the life we have count for something. My goal is to live my life so there's nothing left when the Lord takes me. I have had too many squandered years, and even though I've lived these past many years for the Lord, there will never be enough to cover those I squandered. Thank God for His interventions in our lives. Let us pass the torch on to the next generation. It's the least we can do. Praise God that He takes us and makes us His own. We need to have every moment count for Him. Let each of us consecrate our hearts to Him, pledging all we have and all we are to Him. Let Him have His way in us.

Lord, fill our hearts with Your love and Your controlled strength that the world may see Christ in us. Amen

What I heard from the Lord:

"Oh, the generations that have passed, always failing, but always succeeding. The failure comes by them not fully realizing who I am. Success comes in passing My story, My Word, and My love onto the next generation. This will continue until the very last generation. Always continue as if you are the last generation, but it is not for you to know lest you falter."

9 – Obey the Lord First

"But Peter and the apostles answered, "We must obey God rather than men."

Acts 5:29 ESV

My thoughts:

And Jesus said to render unto Caesar what belongs to Caesar and render unto God what belongs to God. (Luke 20:25) What I hear is that we should obey our governmental laws unless they contradict what the Lord says. We must be loyal first to the Lord and, following that, our national and local officials.

What I heard from the Lord:

"I must have your loyalty and obedience. My laws are not burdensome, nor are they unreasonable. They are there for your good so that you may prosper in this world and in the next. Be humble in the face of opposition, but do not yield any space to those laws contrary to Mine. Don't set yourselves as holier than others, but remain humble and firmly follow My Word without unnecessarily antagonizing those who don't belong to Me. Let your word be your bond and stand your ground. I am with you."

10 – Slavery or Freedom

"For we have heard him say that this Jesus of Nazareth will destroy this place and will change the customs that Moses delivered to us."

Acts 6:14 ESV

My thoughts:

Those who brought charges against Stephen were partly right. They didn't hear him say that Jesus would destroy the place, but they were right that the customs that Moses had delivered would be changed. The law had been fulfilled with the death of Jesus. There was no further need for sacrifices nor for the other laws with their penalties. Jesus brought freedom for all who would come and drink from Him. Apparently, they wanted to stay in bondage so that the sacrifice of Jesus would be meaningless.

Lord, why are so many so blind and deaf that they can't hear Your voice or see what You have done so that we all may be free and partake in Your great love? Why do they feel they have to work for their salvation? Why can't they see You simply love them and accept them as they are?

What I heard from the Lord:

"All are free to choose. Some choose life, but many choose death, for to be apart from Me is not to have life. There is no way to force love for Me. All have freedom of choice. You are here on this earth to point the way. You cannot make them drink, and neither do I. To remove that choice is to remove freedom. I want friends, not slaves. You are my friends when you follow My voice."

11 – The Pride of Wisdom

"When Ahithophel saw that his counsel was not followed, he saddled his donkey and went off home to his own city. He set his house in order and hanged himself, and he died and was buried in the tomb of his father."

My thoughts:

Ever-present pride. It is a sin almost if not all of us have. I have heard and believe that all sins are a result of pride. It comes from the attitude that I am better (stronger, smarter, wiser, wealthier, more beautiful, etc.) than you. If you really think about it, I think you will find that's true.

2 Samuel 17:23 ESV

What I heard from the Lord:

"Ahithophel was wise in his own eyes. He had a lifetime of wisdom through his own experience, but he was not wise in Me. He forsook My Word. He saw an opportunity to elevate himself in his wisdom which ended in folly. My Son came to confound the wise in their own eyes. My Word contains wisdom that gives life. The world gives wisdom that takes life. Be firmly planted in My Word and not end like Ahithophel but be elevated into My kingdom."

12 – Two Sides of Paul

"Then they cast him out of the city and stoned him. And the witnesses laid down their garments at the feet of a young man named Saul."

Acts 7:58 ESV

My thoughts:

Here we meet Saul for the first time, later renamed Paul. This man always gave all he could, whether right or wrong. At this time, he certainly thought he was doing the right thing, and he did it to the best of his ability. After he met Jesus on the way to Damascus, he gave his all in the cause of Christ just as he had done earlier against Christ, but the difference is now he had Jesus in his heart.

What I heard from the Lord:

"My son, Paul, had to grow through the worst before he could work through the best. Saul, never satisfied until the last of My own, would be imprisoned. My son Paul, enlightened by My Spirit, letting nothing stand in his way to bring the gentiles into My pasture. Paul, My servant then. Paul, My friend now as you too are My friend. Do all you can while you still can."

13 – Exalt Righteousness in the Land

"Righteousness exalts a nation, but sin is a reproach to any people."

Proverbs 14:34 ESV

My thoughts:

Look at our nation. It has been exalted for over two hundred years, but sin has come into the nation and is a reproach to our nation. Open your eyes, and it's so very clear. What was right is now wrong. What was wrong is now right in the World. Lord, speak to us from Your heart that we may understand.

What I heard from the Lord:

"Over and over again, nation after nation that has called Me Lord then fallen into sin has perished in that their former glory has been removed. What nation today can call itself righteous in My eyes? Not one, for all have failed. Some have come closer than others. Your country started with such promise and was protected and rescued time after time, only to increase its pursuit of sin. Soon it will be no more except for being but a shadow of its former glory. Rise and let your voice be known that time is short. The end is at hand. Rejoice, for your Savior comes."

14 – Oh, To Be Like Ananias, Or Paul, Or Anyone Else?

"But the Lord said to him, "Go, for he is a chosen instrument of mine to carry my name before the Gentiles and kings and the children of Israel."

Acts 9:15 ESV

My thoughts:

Oh, to be like Ananias, to hear the Lord and respond, "Here I am, Lord." That must be our response, though. Ananias was God's chosen instrument to minister to Paul. Paul was God's chosen instrument to minister to the Gentiles, kings, and the children of Israel. Was Paul's work greater than that of Ananias? Was the work of Ananias greater than the work set before each of us?

What I heard from the Lord:

"When you begin to measure your work and your worth against others of My flock, you take your eyes from Me and look upon the world. What matters is that I have set one to do a kind of work and another to do something different. My children, you all fit together. Not one of you is greater than another. Keep your focus on Me. I have not and will not lead you astray but make you great in My kingdom as you simply do My will."

15 – Why Does God Need to Repeat Himself?

"And the voice came to him again a second time, "What God has made clean, do not call common."

Acts 10:15 ESV

My thoughts:

The Lord had to tell this to Peter 3 times. What about us? What does the Lord have to repeat in our lives before we get it? How long does He have to repeat it? If more than three times it makes Peter look pretty good.

What I heard from the Lord?

"Who has sinned in the same way only once? Who has to be directed back to My Word repeatedly? Who among you has not sinned? A price has been paid for all, yet you go back again and again to that which was dead, to that old sin nature, and bring it up over and over again. Let you not look to Peter, who had to be told only three times, but look to yourselves, who have to be shown over and over again. Cast your eyes on Me and know My rest from sin."

16 – How Long O God?

"How long, O God, is the foe to scoff? Is the enemy to revile your name forever?"

Psalm 74:10 ESV

My thoughts, a prayer:

Lord, why do You delay Your coming? As You delay, so many more are being sent to Hell by the moment. There are hundreds of millions who scoff and revile Your name, and Hell is waiting for them. Come, Lord Jesus, that no more are relegated to eternity without You. I pray this in the name of Jesus, Amen.

What I heard from the Lord:

"It is not for you to know whether I tarry or not. All must wait for the fullness of time. Let it never be said throughout eternity that I hastened, and there were unborn who could have spent eternity with Me but were cut off by hurrying events that must come in their own time. Wait with Me. It's just a little longer. It is good that you look at the times, but yet keep your focus on Me."

Thank you, Lord. We are waiting for Your appointed time.

17 – Praying Without Believing

"They said to her, "You are out of your mind." But she kept insisting that it was so, and they kept saying, "It is his angel!""

Acts 12:15 ESV

My thoughts:

They were praying without believing, yet their prayers were answered for Peter. I think I often fit into that category. I do not think I'm alone. I even put out conditions why my prayers won't be answered so I won't be disappointed if they aren't. They are always answered though, perhaps not in the ways we think they should be answered, but they are answered.

What I heard from the Lord:

"I always answer the prayers of the faithful. I treasure each prayer. You must understand that your time may not be my time, so in addition to exercises in faith, it helps you grow in My Spirit. Do not cease to pray. I covet your prayers. Come close to Me, and I will come close to you. You are My friend through all eternity."

18 – Don't Test Good Nature

"King Solomon drafted forced labor out of all Israel, and the draft numbered 30,000 men."

1 Kings 5:13 ESV

My thoughts:

Those drafted were honored to be. They appear to have been citizens, not like the other 150,000 designated as burden-bearers and stone cutters. Those drafted were required to spend only one month out of three working on the temple. It appears, though, that this continued throughout the leadership of Solomon, and after a time, the drafts were not so lenient.

The evidence of this is seen in 1 Kings 12:4, where the people complained to King Rehoboam about the harsh labor and heavy yoke King Solomon had put on them.

It's never a good thing when one takes advantage of another's good nature as if it is something owed. Those who expect that may find the price becomes impossibly high.

What I heard from the Lord:

"You too have been drafted for My service. It is not like in the days of Solomon. You are called as burden bearers just the same, but a different kind of burden. You have been burdened with and for the souls of men and women. Know though, that I am ever at your side carrying the burden with you. I'm just a prayer away."

19 – Fasting and Prayer

"Then after fasting and praying they laid their hands on them and sent them off."

Acts 13:3 ESV

My thoughts:

The Apostles show their devotion by fasting and praying before sending Paul and Barnabus out. I see this as an example for us even today before making major good decisions. I've prayed before making major decisions, but rarely with fasting. Perhaps I need to make a change.

What I heard from the Lord:

"Prayer should always go with fasting, but not necessarily fasting with prayer. There are many kinds of decisions you have to make. It's the big decisions, the life changing decisions that you need to include fasting with your prayers before acting on them. Once you have your answer, act on it, don't go your own way."

I'm still not there on this one. Something for me to work on.

20 – We Are God's Temple

"So Solomon built the house and finished it."

1 Kings 6:14 ESV

My thoughts, my prayer:

This chapter has a detailed description of part of the temple-building process and how it was held in awe by the builders. They were building a house for God to live in. They were following a plan given by God. They were very serious about doing their part.

We live in a day where we are the temple God has built and continues to build. The Holy Spirit lives within us. We don't have to go to someplace special because we are that someplace special. Wherever God is, it is a special place. It is holy ground. As such, we are holy ground and need to conduct our lives that way. We are the bride of Christ. How can we be more blessed than that?

My prayer:

Lord, reach into our hearts and draw us nearer to You in every way; in what we think; in what we see; in what we hear, and how we react to the world around us, with You directing us on our path on this day. In the name of Jesus, Amen.

What I heard from the Lord:

"So, Solomon built My house and finished it. That is true, but the house being built since My Son came to earth is of flesh and blood. You are My temple. It is in you that My Spirit resides. You are chosen, and you are blessed to be My Body and My Bride. I can bestow no greater honor upon you."

21 – The Cloud

"and when the priests came out of the Holy Place, a cloud filled the house of the Lord, so that the priests could not stand to minister because of the cloud, for the glory of the Lord filled the house of the Lord."

1 Kings 8:10-11 ESV

My thoughts:

As in the time of Solomon where God filled the temple with His Presence, so He fills us today. We are called to be His Holy Temple, His Church. Each of us are living stones fitted together to form His Church, His Body, and His Bride throughout eternity. We are indeed a blessed people.

What I heard from the Lord:

"Ask Me to fill you with My Sprit for I do not go where I am not invited among the people. Let My Spirit mingle with your spirit and be as one. Let Me open your eyes, your spiritual eyes, not your natural eyes, to wonders unknowable without My Presence. Let My Spirit bear you up through the hard times and let you soar through the good. Be where you belong."

22 – Even the Devout

"But the Jews incited the devout women of high standing and the leading men of the city, stirred up persecution against Paul and Barnabas, and drove them out of their district."

Acts 13:50 ESV

My thoughts:

So, the devout women and men were stirred up by the enemies of Christ. If we have a lasting, living relationship with Christ, I think we can be considered devout. What would it take for us to suddenly change our attitude toward Christ after knowing Him up close and personal? Could it be by outward appearances, that we're not who we appear to be?

What I heard from the Lord:

"Satan controls more of the world of today then he did then, but even then, he stirred up discord and set obstacles wherever he could. The same is today, but tenfold more. Satan's foils cannot stand, though, against persistent prayer. Many who have been deceived by his lies in the past changed and came into My kingdom. So, it is today. There are many who need to hear My call more than once before making their commitment to Me. Be persistent in prayer and in My work. You will not be disappointed."

23 – Listen to Your Heart

"He listened to Paul speaking. And Paul, looking intently at him and seeing that he had faith to be made well,"

Acts 14:9 ESV

My thoughts:

Paul looked and knew the heart of this man. He knew this man had faith to be healed. We, too, look at people and know their hearts.

When I went into the military, I did not know anyone, but my heart did. In a matter of minutes, the troublemakers would be gathered. Those of other persuasion gathered as well. Time after time, it did not fail. I have only been deceived a few times, and those times were when I did not listen to my heart.

Think about it the next time you meet someone new. What does your heart tell you about that person? There are times, too, when the spirit of another mingles with ours. Our spirit knows before our minds do that this person will be a friend for life. Our spirit can also tell us if a new person we meet is someone we need to avoid at all costs. Listen!

What I heard from the Lord:

A vision (Detailed earlier)

"I looked and saw my spirit. It looked like a long gray ribbon. As I looked further, I saw the Holy Spirit. He was portrayed as many long beautifully colored ribbons swirling above me in dazzling beauty. I saw my spirit; my ribbon being pulled upward and reach the beautiful swirling ribbons of the Spirit. Then I saw something that was awesome. The Holy Spirit and my spirit were sealed with a holy kiss for eternity and I knew I was loved by God Himself."

24 – First Love

"So Solomon did what was evil in the sight of the Lord and did not wholly follow the Lord, as David his father had done."

1 Kings 11:6 ESV

My thoughts:

Solomon had it all. He had more earthly delights than anyone before or after him. He had all this but lost his first love. He lost the Lord of life, the Lord of all. Even though he knew what he was doing, he allowed himself to be ensnared by a thousand women who had their own ideas of what was right and true, in complete opposition to the Lord. Solomon even gave himself over to the god Molech who demanded child sacrifices that would be thrown alive into the fire. That's how far Solomon fell.

What about us 3,000 years later? How many unborn babies were torn from their mothers' wombs just today? How many sex slaves are sold on the market every day and not a peep out of our governments? How many turn a blind eye and go about their business? What will it take to get this nation to face the truth of how far it has fallen from God's grace?

What I heard from the Lord:

"My son Solomon started well but finished poorly. Many start out poorly but finish well. Solomon had everything I could give him, and if more was required it would have been given as well, yet he threw it all away, and all for pride. It is pride that brought him low. Let pride not seep into your soul lest it bring you low as well. Keep your eyes upon Me for all else is fleeting."

25 – Disagreements

"And there arose a sharp disagreement so that they separated from each other. Barnabas took Mark with him and sailed away to Cyprus, but Paul chose Silas and departed, having been commended by the brothers to the grace of the Lord."

Acts 15:39-40 ESV

My thoughts:

Paul viewed Mark as unreliable since he had left them in the last missionary journey.

Barnabas viewed Mark as his beloved cousin and wanted to give him another chance.

Looking back from here, it appears as if each was right, and each was wrong. Paul wasn't ready to take another chance with Mark. Barnabas was convinced Mark had learned his lesson. According to Christ, should they have reconciled? Of course, but sometimes distance is required before we can see more clearly. What was the lesson in this?

God works out even our bad decisions. Now instead of one missionary journey, there were two journeys. There would be more people saved for the Kingdom, and Mark would gain valuable experience and go on to write the Gospel of Mark.

Later in the Epistles, Paul would ask for Mark's help. Paul and Barnabas were eventually reconciled.

(1 Corinthians 9:6)

What I heard from the Lord:

"Paul and Barnabus were the best of friends, but sometimes even friends have their differences. I have made each of you unique. Each of you needs to be that way to show your individuality, yet all are the same. Each of you has a place in your hearts meant just for Me where My Spirit resides. Take that into account whenever you find differences you think are distasteful. Be careful in your judgements lest you be judged."

26 – Don't Take the Easy Way unless it's the Right Way

"And Jeroboam said in his heart, "Now the kingdom will turn back to the house of David."

1 Kings 12:26 ESV

My thoughts:

The ten tribes having left Rehoboam made Jeroboam King. Still, the people went to Jerusalem to bring their sacrifices and worship to the Lord. Jeroboam had already been warned by the Lord to keep His statutes, but he was more fearful the people would eventually return to King Rehoboam and leave him.

Too many people, not only those in leadership, turn their eyes to the world instead of the Lord. Jeroboam even came up with his own religion and told the people to worship the two golden calves he had that he claims led the children of Israel out of Egypt, and surprise, surprise, they did it. I'm sure that was a lot easier than going to Jerusalem.

Too many take the easy way rather than the right way in whatever they do. Let's do the next right thing. It may not be easy, but that's often the case in doing what is right. It's a lot easier than what Jesus did for us.

What I heard from the Lord:

"Jeroboam defied Me. He went his own way even after I promised if he would only follow My laws all would be well. Eventually I blotted out his entire line and they are no more. In your day there are rulers, princes, and leaders who promise Me they will listen. They even tell their followers that they belong to Me, but stand and look. What do you see. Are they really after My own heart or are they chasing their own? Do not be led astray by their actions. Keep your focus on Me."

27 – Can't We Just Get Along

"Now there was war between Rehoboam and Jeroboam all the days of his life."

1 Kings 15:6 ESV

My thoughts:

There was war off and on between Judah and Israel all through Israel's existence. That had to have weakened both countries for takeover by Assyria and then Babylon. This was a huge family squabble that ended in the premature death of many and a constant distrust between them.

What about us? Is there infighting or defense of one another? Do we come to the aid of one another when difficulties come, or do we simply pray and do nothing else? Are we pleased when one of us is dealt a blow by an outsider, or do we stand up for them?

There are many families and churches in disrepair. Let us do our part. Let us pray, but then also do what the Word says. Sometimes that means our hands get dirty, but so be it when it's the right thing to do.

What I heard from the Lord:

"War is not just for countries. Look around. See the waring between men and women, boys and girls. It has been so from the very beginning, for all sin and fall short of My Glory. You are called to be peace makers and not contribute to the turmoil. Let your yes be yes and your no be no, but above all, let love rule that you not become a part of the turmoil. Follow Me. I know it isn't easy, but that is what you have been called to do."

28 – Confusion of Unbelief

"And she said to Elijah, "What have you against me, O man of God? You have come to me to bring my sin to remembrance and to cause the death of my son!"

1 Kings 17:18 ESV

My thoughts:

Elijah had come to the woman and given her a miracle during the famine which was never-ending oil and flour that never gave out. When her son died, she took it out on Elijah. Be careful with our accusations until we're sure we have all the facts and be prepared to apologize.

What I heard from the Lord:

"Confusion for unbelief reigns in the presence of holiness. The confusion comes from a lack of understanding of who I Am. As I cannot look on sin, neither can I look on the sinful, for all have sinned and fall short of what I expect. There is salvation only through My Son. As the woman's confusion was displayed when her son fell asleep, so does confusion reign when unbelievers are in the presence of the Godly when things don't go their way. They wail against Me and say I don't exist with their mouths, but in their hearts, they know I AM! The time is coming when all will kneel and know I am God."

29 – The Sound of a Low Whisper

"And after the earthquake a fire, but the Lord was not in the fire. And after the fire the sound of a low whisper."

1 Kings 19:12 ESV

My thoughts:

Elijah had a very busy time. He stood up to the prophets of Baal, brought back countless souls to the Lord, ran from Jezebel, was ministered to by an angel, spent 40 days in the wilderness, and now here he is with the Lord. He's listening for the voice of God, and God has great things to tell him.

Do we listen for that sound of a low whisper that is from God? Do we quiet our hearts and minds before Him? Are we making ourselves available to Him? Are we holding anything back? Do we give our all?

What I heard from the Lord:

"I am there for you. I always have been and always will be. I am your Savior and your Protector. In these final days, there is not much time, for I am about to appear before you. You've prayed for it, and My coming is at hand. I am preparing souls to hear My voice. You are prepared for the reaping. It is at hand."

30 – The Cloak of Elijah

"And he took up the cloak of Elijah that had fallen from him and went back and stood on the bank of the Jordan."

2 Kings 2:13 ESV

My thoughts:

Elijah went to Paradise leaving Elisha to continue the ministry. Elisha did all his master and teacher told him to do. The torch had been passed. It took the congregation some time to accept that, but they finally got it.

What I heard from the Lord:

"When I brought My prophet Elijah to fellowship with Me in Paradise, of course, his worldly clothing had to be left behind. He has much richer Heavenly clothing than anyone has ever had on Earth. He is clothed with My righteousness; My truth; My joy; My love, and so much more. The time is coming and is almost at hand. You will soon see with your own eyes and behold the riches I've stored up for you. Keep in My Word. Bathe yourself in My love."

Chapter 7: July

1 – Prepare the Saints

"And since he would not be persuaded, we ceased and said, "Let the will of the Lord be done.""

Acts 21:14 ESV

My thoughts:

Are we not all living stones that make up the Church? Are not we all then the Bride of Christ? Doesn't that mean each of us, and the Church as a whole, need to be renewed and winnowed? I'm not a very young person anymore. By far, most of my years are behind me. I say that I don't fear death, but at the same time, I'm not trying to rush toward it. In the time we have left, let us grab onto this, "Let the will of the Lord be done." And let's get on with whatever comes next. Let us not shirk our responsibilities, but as Paul says, "I press on toward the goal for the prize of the upward call of God in Christ Jesus," Philippians 3:14.

What I heard from the Lord

July 11, 2020 "Prepare the Saints throughout the Earth for what's to come."

July 13, 2020 "Prepare the Saints throughout the Earth for what's to come. LISTEN!"

Aug. 3, 2020 "There's a great winnowing that is coming – AND IT IS AT HAND!"

Twice I heard, "Prepare the Saints throughout the Earth for what's to come." To me, that means emphasis. Then a few weeks later, I heard, "There's a great winnowing that is coming – AND IT IS AT HAND.

2 – Do Not Fear

"He said, "Do not be afraid, for those who are with us are more than those who are with them.""

2 Kings 6:16 ESV

My thoughts:

Our senses are developed so we can flourish here in this universe. We are made that way. On rare occasions, some get a glimpse of something more. Elisha had a God-given ability to see there was more than most think of God's creation.

There is a spirit realm all around us. The Bible teaches this throughout, but we need not fear, for there are more with us than with the enemy. Ephesians 6:10-20, "Be prepared in the full armor of God." Praise God from Whom all blessings flow.

What I heard from the Lord:

"I am with you. You and I together are a majority. Wherever you go, I am with you. You see great power in the world, but yours is greater for it comes from My Spirit. Without Me you can do nothing. You've been there before. You do have power and can create without involving Me, but what is the result? You become tired. You become frustrated, and the result is far better with Me than without Me. Stay with Me. Let's be a team throughout eternity."

3 – Plans

"The heart of man plans his way, but the Lord establishes his steps."

Proverbs 16:9 ESV

My thoughts:

When I look back at my life, I see plans that I made. In themselves, they were good; the details were from God. Looking back, I see the trail. There is no straight line, but it's convoluted, going here and there, sometimes doubling back upon itself. I remember back when I was a fourteen-year-old child. I had plans that took me well into retirement. Those plans were never fulfilled.

My life has turned out so totally different from what that teenage boy thought. He never dreamed of the richness and fulfillment that would fill his life. He never dreamed of the richness of life that Jesus brings. Thank you, Lord Jesus, for all You have done in this simple person's life.

What I heard from the Lord:

"I establish your steps. I give you just enough light to take your next step. I am teaching you to trust me in this way. To see the whole picture that would be for your harm and not for your good. Just trust Me. I will give you all you need. Don't try to find your own way. Just walk with Me and in My Protection."

4 – Be True to Your Word

"When it was day, the Jews made a plot and bound themselves by an oath neither to eat nor drink till they had killed Paul."

Acts 23:12 ESV

My thoughts:

Be careful of what vows you make. I've said before if you say you're going to do something, then do it. You do not have to swear anything. Jesus says in Matthew 5:37, "Let what you say be simply "Yes or No," anything more than this comes from evil.""

It doesn't look like these fellows got that message. Since they didn't do what they said, they should all have died of thirst. Somehow, I don't think that happened. Let us make sure before we say we're going to do something or not that we follow through. This needs to be part of who we are. Be in Christ. Be true to Christ. Be true to yourself.

What I heard from the Lord:

"Do I ask of you any vows? Think now, do I? There are no vows that I ask of you, but I respect the vows you voluntarily give as long as they are within the framework of My Word. As I have told you, let your yes be yes and your no be no. It will save you much trouble."

5 – God Smiles on Us

"Restore us, O Lord God of hosts! Let your face shine that we may be saved!"

Psalm 80:19 ESV

My thoughts:

Just to think of God smiling on each one of us, wow, that's incredible! Just to think the God of the universe smiles on us, how fabulous. Thankfully our Father can't look at us because of our sins, so He sees us through the mantle of Christ, who gave His life for us. That means the Father doesn't see us as we are but as we will be. For me, that is a comforting thought to know I will not be as I am but made perfect in the image of Christ.

What I heard from the Lord:

"I love to smile upon you. I know your highs and your lows. I am with you in each of them. I know when you rise up and when you lie down. There is nothing I do not know about you for I formed you in your mother's womb when there was only an unformed substance. As I am yours, you are Mine, now and forevermore."

6 – Search for a Mentor – Be a Mentor

"And Jehoash did what was right in the eyes of the Lord all his days, because Jehoiada the priest instructed him."

2 Kings 12:2 ESV

My thoughts:

Jehoash did what was right because Jehoiada, the priest, instructed him. I try to do right because of God's instruction through His Word. Not long after I accepted Christ, my spiritual father, Pastor Erv Gerlitz, spent an hour or two with me each Saturday afternoon for more than a year. He taught me all the basics I needed to know in great detail. Today I am a child of God but also of Pastor Gerlitz. He never told me anything that wasn't true. He would challenge me to test anything he said against scripture. I only did once. We had a great time discussing it.

What I heard from the Lord:

"As you grow older, you gain knowledge. With experience you use that knowledge through wisdom. Some are wise and some are foolish. Seek all the knowledge you can, but not all knowledge is good. Perceive knowledge that is worth pursuing with the wisdom gained by My Word and it will be well with your heart."

7 – Right and Wrong are as Black and White

"There is a way that seems right to a man, but its end is the way to death."

Proverbs 16:25 ESV

My thoughts:

In Judges, we often see the phrase, "and every man did what was right in his own eyes." Look around. What do we see today? There is a large portion of our population doing just that. We see so many making themselves to be gods and doing what is right in their own eyes. We have heard so much in recent times of people standing up and speaking absurdities as truth, where only a very short time ago, their truth was looked upon by the majority of the population as false, and it truly is. Truth does not change because it is inconvenient. Truth does not change, nor do falsehoods.

Right and wrong are as black and white. We may sometimes see in shades of gray, but that does not change what is right or what is wrong. Let us keep our focus where it needs to be, on the Truth, the Son of God, Who is our firm Foundation.

What I heard from the Lord:

"Too many follow the wide easy road which is the World. The way seems easy. It is easy to go with the flow, but the end results in death. When I speak of death, I speak of life without Me. I give life in all its abundance. Cling to Me and listen to My Word. You are not of the World, but you are in it. Otherwise, how could you serve the lost? Listen, learn, and do My bidding."

8 – Warnings Ignored

"But my people did not listen to my voice; Israel would not submit to me. So I gave them over to their stubborn hearts, to follow their own counsels."

Psalm 81:11-12 ESV

My thoughts:

Israel did not listen, and they have gone. The Assyrians dispersed them throughout their empire, and they have never been heard from since. Judah and Benjamin also fell but are still known to this day. The Levites are also known as they, for the most part, stayed with Judah. All others were lost. So, where does that leave us today?

Does this nation listen to the Voice of God and submit to Him? Does any nation? Show me one. There are believers in every nation. There are more in some and less in others, but not in the majority anymore. So, what has God done today? There it is in Psalm 81:11, "So I gave them over to their stubborn hearts, to follow their own counsels." Does that sound familiar? Look around. That is what you will see.

"But as for me and my house, we will serve the Lord." Joshua 24:15

What I heard from the Lord:

"Like Israel, your nation once listened to My Word, but has now cast it aside. They are going after their own gods, and they are bearing the fruit of that decision. I have given them free will; therefore, they are free to come to Me or to follow Satan. There is no in between. It is One or the other."

In a devotional, Paul Tillich said, "The first duty of love is to listen." Then George Marshall said in handling people:

"Listen to the other person's story.

Listen to the other person's full story.

Listen to the other person's full story first."

I want to make that a part of how I listen.

9 – I Told You So

"Since they had been without food for a long time, Paul stood up among them and said, "Men, you should have listened to me and not have set sail from Crete and incurred this injury and loss."

Acts 27:21 ESV

My thoughts:

No one ever wants to hear the words, "I told you so." but here it is right from Paul. He could not get an audience from those who had spent most of their lives on the sea and considered him a no-nothing land lubber just before the voyage began. Yet here, as they were reminded of his words, the light began to dawn on them. He may just be correct.

So many times, I heard the gospel preached, but for whatever reason I just didn't listen. Then finally, the dawn broke, and I did not care if I heard, "I told you so." He had risen in my heart forevermore.

Hopefully, we can say to others these same words, "I told you so. Welcome to the family of God." Saying this not in an arrogant way, but one pleased that another soul has entered into the Kingdom to share in the wonders of God.

What I heard from the Lord:

"I have told you many things. I have never lied or even stretched the truth, for I am Truth. Hear My Words. What do they say? If you stop and listen, you will hear My soft quiet voice calling those from the wilderness that is this world, into the garden I have built especially for My own."

10 – Your Enemies Are My Enemies

"They lay crafty plans against your people; they consult together against your treasured ones."

Psalm 83:3 ESV

"Fill their faces with shame, that they may seek your name, O Lord."

Psalm 83:16 ESV

My thoughts:

As in ancient times, the enemies of Israel were the enemies of God, so today, our enemies are God's enemies. In the psalm, the writer identifies the enemy and calls for God's wrath to come on them, but he also calls for them to see their shame that they may find the Lord.

What I heard from the Lord:

"My enemies are your enemies. Whomever stands against Me is My enemy. When you find resistance, ask why it's there. If you find direct conflict to Me, you should not only stand but also bring them to Me in prayer. Some may be changed and saved for My kingdom. As Satan controls this world, more so, I control and live in your hearts. That is power Satan does not have. You are mine. I gave My life for you and will never allow you to be taken from Me. Rest in your salvation."

11 – Anger

"Whoever is slow to anger is better than the mighty, and he who rules his spirit than he who takes a city."

Proverbs 16:32 ESV

My thoughts:

It is not much fun to live around angry people, people who seem angry all the time. Certainly, there are times for righteous anger, but when every little thing gets our dander up, we are treading in dangerous territory. To have constant anger is to be constantly out of touch with their spirit and, of course, the Holy Spirit. Anger is a destructive emotion. Anger also eats at us physically, emotionally, and spiritually. It can take a terrible tole and shorten our years. Who in their anger can solve the reason for that anger? Who in their anger can bring peace to their hearts and the hearts of others? Who in their anger is able to build up rather than tear down?

Have righteous anger for the things of the Lord and give it over to Him. All other anger is selfish at best and destructive at worst.

What I heard from the Lord:

"Be angry if you must but count the costs. Anger is dangerous territory. I have given you My commandments which include anger. Play it safe. Be angry with what I am angry. If your anger is directed toward something unreachable for you, let it go. That is in My purview."

12 – The Righteous Live by Faith

"For in it the righteousness of God is revealed from faith for faith, as it is written, "The righteous shall live by faith."

Romans 1:17 ESV

My thoughts:

We shall live by faith. Romans is the pinnacle of the whole Bible. There is such richness in this book that books are still written on it yet found wanting. Are we righteous?

We call on Jesus, the Author and Finisher of our faith, into our hearts. We recognize the Holy Spirit, alive and living within us. We recognize the Bible, the holy written Word of God, to be infallible and unchangeable as our guide. We come together in faith to worship our Lord and Savior. We draw our very life from the Scriptures telling us how to live holy lives. We live in a world ever-changing and looking for the next bright object, yet our faith remains unchanged in the unchangeable Truth; Jesus Himself.

Yes, we are the righteous spoken of here in Romans. Just keep the faith. Stay in the Word. Hold fast in prayer and put on the full armor of God.

What I heard from the Lord:

"The righteous live by faith. To be righteous requires faith. You have faith in things, and you exercise that faith daily. The object of your faith is more important than your faith. You can have faith that a chair won't collapse if you sit in it, but to realize that faith, you must sit in the chair. Place your faith in Me. Exercise your faith by following the commands of My Son. See if it isn't true."

13 – Who or What is Your God?

"And exchanged the glory of the immortal God for images resembling mortal man and birds and animals and creeping things."

Romans 1:23 ESV

My thoughts:

We try to emulate that which we worship. If we worship the Lord, we want to be more like Him. If we worship a man or a woman, we want to be more like them. If we worship idols, we are, in effect, worshiping ourselves.

I remember my father saying he was his own god. That's all he needed. Later he was baptized, but was that just touching the bases? I'll never know this side of heaven, but I hope he's there.

There is only one God. All others are false imitations or demons with no power over us. Our focus is on Christ and on Him alone. Let us keep the eyes of our hearts razor focused on our Lord and King.

What I heard from the Lord:

"You have natural eyes, and you have eyes of the spirit. As it is important to have your natural eyes focused in a daily basis to keep you from harm, so too do you need to keep your spiritual eyes focused on Me and the things that represent Me. My representatives are My Son, My Spirit, My Word, and all that attest to These. Let your spiritual eyes be focused there and let nothing come between you and Me."

14 – No Partiality

"For God shows no partiality."

Romans 2:11 ESV

My thoughts:

Partiality – Unfair bias in favor of one thing or person compared to another.

This is only a five-word verse, but it has tremendous promise. He can't love us more, nor can He love us less, no matter what we do. We all stand beneath the cross on level ground. No one is greater than another in His eyes.

What I heard from the Lord:

"I am no respecter of a person's worldly status. I shower blessings upon those whom I wish. My judgements are true and unbiased. No one can charge me with favoritism. I love all, but I must be true to Myself. I have great rewards for those who call on My Name. For those who have no time for Me and decide to do their own thing, I have no time for them, but I will hurry to their sides if they but call on Me for their salvation. Let no one perish that can and will be saved."

15 – Teaching

"You then who teach others, do you not teach yourself? While you preach against stealing, do you steal?"

Romans 2:21 ESV

My thoughts:

There are teachers, and then there are teachers. We all teach from the time we are older brothers or sisters to being parents and grandparents. There are schoolteachers, managers, pastors, and the list goes on. In all of our roles as teachers we also learn from those being taught. To stop learning is to shrivel up and die.

When I was teaching, and even now, I try my best to show all sides of a truth, not to bend it to my own way of thinking. Teachers and even pastors who do not show every side of the truth must be taken to task. There's no room in God's kingdom for half-truths, no matter how well intended, for a half-truth is still a lie.

We must always test what we see, hear, and read by Holy Scripture.

What I heard from the Lord:

"If you teach, teach truth. Stay as close to the Source as you can, so that you spread no falsehoods. The Truth is there for the taking. My Son is Truth and there is no lie within Him. He cannot lie. Satan is the father of lies and you can count on him to stretch any truth into a lie, and make it sound true. All you need do is peel back the layers and be enlightened unto Me."

16 – We All Fall Short

"For all have sinned and fall short of the glory of God, and are justified by his grace as a gift, through the redemption that is in Christ Jesus,"

Romans 3:23-24 ESV

My thoughts:

We all know Romans 3:23, and it's true. We all fall short no matter how Godly we are. There is not that much difference between the best of us and the worst of us compared to Christ.

Look at it like this. The world's greatest high jumper and you are standing below the Space Needle. You are both told to jump over it. You both jump. Your jump is one foot. The athlete jumps six feet. That's a big difference, but in comparison to the 500-foot Space Needle there's no real difference at all. You both come up very short. We, in our unrighteousness, will never succeed.

Christ, by His sacrifice, jumps over the Space Needle with ease, so to speak, that God's grace falls on us. We owe all to Him. "All of our righteousness is as filthy rags." Isaiah 64:6

What I heard from the Lord:

"You are justified by grace through My Son. It always goes back to Him. He took your sins upon Himself that you could not bear. He made you in My eyes to look as if you have never sinned, but wait. You are covered by Him, so I only see you through Him and as you will be, but not as you are today. Remember that. I cannot look on sin, therefore I cannot look on you. But I see you just as clearly through Him. You are loved with the greatest of love."

17 – Faith Not Works

"And to the one who does not work but believes in him who justifies the ungodly, his faith is counted as righteousness,"

Romans 4:5 ESV

My thoughts:

Justification and righteousness can seem a little complicated. I learned to think of "justification" as just as if I'd never sinned. That's what the Lord did for us. No matter how hard we work, we can't make that happen. It's our faith in our Lord that makes all the difference. Righteousness is living within Christ's law. That's how we are seen covered by Christ. All thanks glory and honor go to Him.

What I heard from the Lord:

"Faith, your faith is what counts, not just faith, but I must be the object of your faith. It is I who provided for your salvation by the cross. When you come to Me in faith, I receive you as a mother receives her newborn babe. You are washed in My blood. You are a new creature in righteousness. You have a new life. You have righteousness in Me. You are just as if you had never sinned and now only need a foot washing from time to time as you fall out of fellowship with Me.

I am always here. I live in your heart and never condemn you, but My Spirit uplifts and directs you upon the path set before you. Take My yoke. I am right beside you."

18 – Teach Me Your Way

"Teach me your way, O Lord, that I may walk in your truth; unite my heart to fear your name."

Psalm 86:11 ESV

My thoughts, my prayer:

We must always want to walk in the Truth of God. Our hearts must be united with the heart of Jesus. If we are not walking in the Truth nor united with Him, we are a tool of Satan.

My prayer:

Oh Lord, we want so badly to walk in Your Truth. Jesus is the Truth. Lord, let us walk with Him. Let us walk at His side, united by Your great Love. Unite our hearts as one with Your heart, Lord. As our hearts are united with Your heart, they are also united together with all of us who call upon Your great Name. Hold us in Your great and loving hands. Nurture us by Your Holy Word. Let us be one body, not just one body, but Your bride and body dressed for the wedding, totally united forever as one. Come, Lord Jesus, come. In His Name we pray, Amen.

What I heard from the Lord:

"Come to Me in fear. Come to Me in Truth. Come to Me to learn My ways. Walk with Me and talk with Me. I will answer. I speak in many ways. I speak through My Word. I speak through teachers, friends, and yes, even babies. I speak to you through nature itself. Just keep your hearts tuned toward Me and you will hear, but be prepared to act upon what you hear."

19 – Let Grace Abound

"Now the law came in to increase the trespass, but where sin increased, grace abounded all the more,"

Romans 5:20 ESV

My thoughts:

It is so good of God to provide grace over our sins. The more we sin, the more His grace abounds. That should not make us sin more but to reflect on what it cost our Savior and sin less by keeping our eyes on Him and our hearts clean through confession. Confession is a simple foot washing to keep us clean since we have been cleansed through our repentance in asking Christ into our hearts.

Thank You, Lord, for Your great love giving us eternal life with You now and forevermore. Thank You, Lord, that there's nowhere we can go that you won't be there with us.

What I heard from the Lord:

"Do you want to sin? Do you seek My displeasure? Why, when you have seen and know the cost for your salvation would you want to do such a thing? Yes, I know you will sin. You will not reach the perfection I have for you this side of Heaven, but if you seek My guidance and My wisdom, they are here for the taking. Just open My Word and be blessed."

20 – Crucified With Christ

"We know that our old self was crucified with him in order that the body of sin might be brought to nothing, so that we would no longer be enslaved to sin."

Romans 6:6 ESV

My thoughts:

We were there. At least our sin was there weighing on Jesus. We can say we had not been born yet and so had not sinned, but God, through Jesus, bore our sins because we would sin. When Jesus came down from the cross, His Spirit continued as He was in Paradise with the thief crucified with Him that very day. We do not know all Jesus did between the time He was taken down from the cross to the time He was resurrected from the grave. We know that we, like Him, will have a resurrection. It makes sense that, like Him, until our resurrection, we, too, will be in Heaven should our bodies die before then.

Thank You, Lord, for Your plan of salvation that we may live through Your Power and the mighty work of Jesus on the cross. Thank you for Your great undeserved love that gives not only eternal but abundant life. Amen

What I heard from the Lord:

"You may have asked who killed Jesus. Was it the Romans? Was it the Jews? This is the answer you seek. You killed Him. With love so great for you, I had to come down and take your penalty and thus fulfill the law. The law had served its purpose and now let grace abound. It was your sin that I bore that you might have life in all its abundance."

21 – The Free Gift of God

"For the wages of sin is death, but the free gift of God is eternal life in Christ Jesus our Lord."

Romans 6:23 ESV

My thoughts:

Wages are something we earn through our work for another. So, what we earn for our sins is not only death but total and eternal separation from God. For some, that is what they want. They do not want to spend eternity with a Holy God. Then we see that God's gift of eternal life is free. There's no way we could earn it no matter how hard we try. Christ earned it for us. God offers it to all. That's what it means when it says, "many are called." The gift is there, but we must reach out and receive it. It is like a judge offering a pardon for a convicted offense. The convicted defendant must receive a pardon. If not, it can't go into effect. Many do refuse the pardon, in this case, eternal life with the Lord. For those who receive, though, they are the chosen. They are the few that are chosen in Matthew 22:14. Thank You, Lord, for choosing us.

What I heard from the Lord:

"There is a price for everything. What is free for one is paid for by another. I offer you the free gift of life through My Grace. It's free for you but cost Me everything. If it were not free, you might be able to say it was something you earned. It does not work that way. Your righteousness is truly filthy rags, unfit for anything but washing out scum. You the imperfect will be perfect, but not by your efforts. It is given freely only by My Son."

22 – A Hard Passage to Digest

"Thanks be to God through Jesus Christ our Lord! So then, I myself serve the law of God with my mind, but with my flesh, I serve the law of sin."

Romans 7:25 ESV

My thoughts:

I have always found this a hard passage to digest, but let's try to break it down a bit.

This verse sounds okay but not great. Serving the love of God with our minds sounds good, but serving the law of sin with our flesh doesn't sound good at all.

John Newton said. "We're not what we should be, and not what we wish to be, but at the same time, we're not what we will be, and by the grace of God, not what we once were." I like that.

We are not free to sin, but we are free to overcome sin by the Spirit that dwells within us. Jesus is ever there to provide forgiveness. Let us not look on our sin, which will only draw us closer to it, but to look upon Jesus, Who will draw us away from it.

What I heard from the Lord:

"Whatever your spiritual focus is will become your god. It can be something you are trying to flee from or be attracted to, but if you keep your focus there instead of on Me, it will replace Me in your life. I am the Great Provider. I am your Defender. Focus on Me. Flee to Me. Put your full trust in Me that I may care for you and be your Safe Harbor."

23 – Together Forever

"You, however, are not in the flesh but in the Spirit, if in fact the Spirit of God dwells in you. Anyone who does not have the Spirit of Christ does not belong to him."

Romans 8:9 ESV

My thoughts:

Here in Romans 8, we are at the apex of the Bible. We have been declared to be in the Spirit as He dwells in us. If the Spirit isn't dwelling in us, Christ is not ours. Who would be ours, then? We will always be a slave to something, so of course, we would be slaves of Satan.

What I heard from the Lord:

"You were called out of antiquity. You were called from the edges of time itself. You were a slave, but not of Me. You chose another. You saw how that worked out for you. Finally, you heard My call and finally listened. You really listened, and reality set in. Finally, you called Me, and I listened. I had been waiting for you for so very long. Now you are Mine, and I am yours. I do not call you a slave but a friend because I withhold nothing from you. Now we share eternity together."

24 – It's All About Jesus

"For those whom he foreknew, he also predestined to be conformed to the image of his Son, in order that he might be the firstborn among many brothers."

Romans 8:29 ESV

My thoughts:

Romans 8:28 is a famous verse that many Christians cling to, including me. "... All things work together for those who love the Lord...." Many forget the following verse that goes along with it. "He knew us way before we were born. He predestined us to be in the image of Christ so that we might be like firstborn sons. This includes women as well, but "firstborn sons" is a title for us. It was the firstborn sons who were heirs to their fathers' wealth. So, in that way we are all "brothers" in Christ.

What I heard from the Lord:

"Yes, you were predestined eons before you were born. I knew you then, and I know you now. I know what you will become. You are conformed through My Word, but also adversity and peace as well. All are required for you to become that which you must be. You work out your salvation as I work out your destiny. You accepted My Son as Lord and Savior. You share in His reward."

25 – Foundations

"Righteousness and justice are the foundation of your throne; steadfast love and faithfulness go before you."

Psalm 89:14 ESV

My thoughts:

If I read this correctly, the foundation of God's throne is made up of righteousness and justice. Wherever He goes, steadfast love and faithfulness go before Him. That is all well and good, but without mercy, justice and righteousness are very cold.

What I heard from the Lord:

"Righteousness and justice cannot stand alone. If they do, there is no warmth, no mercy. Mercy is found in My love. I share My faithfulness with you. Whatever I say is true. There is no lie in Me. You can count on My ever-faithful word. It will never lead you astray. I love you. The depth of my love is limitless. You are but a shadow of that love, but I give you as much as you can handle, flowing over. You are my children. You are the apple of My eye. I so look forward to your completion, not of yourselves, but through My Son."

26 – Stumbling Over the Stumbling Stone

"But that Israel who pursued a law that would lead to righteousness did not succeed in reaching that law. Why: Because they did not pursue it by faith, but as if it were based on works. They have stumbled over the stumbling stone."

Romans 9:31-32 ESV

My thoughts:

Paul clearly states here how the Jews through thousands of years missed the mark in following the Law by their lack of faith. They got caught up in the letter of the Law and left out the spirit of the Law. The Pharisees went even further in making additional commands to make certain they did not miss anything and put unreasonable requirements on the people that they themselves didn't even follow. Thanks to God for the fulfillment of the Law through Jesus.

What I heard from the Lord:

"Paul speaks the truth. I sent My Son to fulfill the Law. He did so by His death on the Earth and His resurrection to Heaven. By His act, My love has been opened for your inclusion. As you give Him honor and praise, you also give it unto Me."

27 – Confess and Be Saved

"Because, if you confess with your mouth that Jesus is Lord and believe in your heart that God raised him from the dead, you will be saved. For with the heart one believes and is justified, and with the mouth one confesses and is saved."

Romans 10:9-10 ESV

My thoughts:

Confess with your mouth and believe in your heart, then you will be justified and saved.

That sounds easy enough. Just speak out that Jesus is Lord, but you must believe it from your innermost being. It must come from there. Okay, what if you say the words and kind of believe, but not completely? What then? Let's go back to when I accepted Christ. My prayer was something like this, "Okay, Lord, I confess I'm a sinner saved only by Your Grace. I believe You are the Christ, but I don't want to be duped." I've said all this before and I don't need to go further.

Your experience may be completely different than mine. God works in different ways with each of us. We simply need to trust and obey, as the song says.

What I heard from the Lord:

"Confess and believe. Know Me. Test Me yet test Me in love and in trepidation. Do not toy with Me. Your life is of great value to Me, or you wouldn't be here, you would never have been born. Look around and see. Your world in all its fallen beauty was created fresh and new if even you were the only person to ever live in it. I love you. That's why you are here, to be loved by Me with an intensity you can only guess."

28 – God Is Not Finished with the Jews

"For the gifts and the calling of God are irrevocable."

Romans 11:29 ESV

My thoughts:

This verse is referring to the Jews being called first, then falling away so the Gentiles could be grafted into the Vine. Remember, promises were made first to the Jews and second to the Gentiles. This is all found in Romans 11:11-32

So, what does that mean, and what happens next?

What I heard from the Lord:

"The Jews were my chosen of all the people on earth. Even though I knew they were fickle people and prone to evil, I chose them. I promised them that no matter what, they would never be forgotten. They rejected My Son, but the Gentiles believed and accepted Him. Many of the Jews did as well. Much time has passed since then, and the only way for Jew or Gentile to come to Me is through My Son. My Son is coming soon since the age of the Gentiles is at an end. I will call all who have accepted My Son to Me. Not so for those Jews who have not accepted my Christ. Woe to them. They will suffer much. A remnant will come to Me, and I will gather them to My Bosom. The price they pay is so high. If only they had accepted My Son, they would miss so much suffering. In the very end, so few will finally come to me, and I will gather them to Me at last."

29 – Do Not Be Conformed to this World

"Do not be conformed to this world, but be transformed by the renewal of your mind, that by testing you may discern what is the will of God, what is good and acceptable and perfect."

Romans 12:2 ESV

My thoughts:

When we conform to the world, we are enslaved by the world. God's Word changes our minds from conformance to the world, to conformance to Christ and His Word. We should all want the will of God to be done in our lives. To do otherwise is to oppose Him.

What I heard from the Lord:

"Keep your focus on Me. I tell you this again and again. You know it's true. With your focus on Me, you will be drawn to my Word. Take time to pray My Word back to Me. Take time to digest My Word in your heart. Let it spread through your heart and be transformed. This isn't something you do once, but it's a way of life from now through eternity. Take joy in knowing My will."

30 – Put On the Lord

"The night is far gone; the day is at hand. So then let us cast off the works of darkness and put on the armor of light. But put on the Lord Jesus Christ, and make no provision for the flesh, to gratify its desires."

Romans 13:12,14 ESV

My thoughts:

When I read these verses, I saw the intertwined connection between them. Each supports the other.

Jesus has come and swept the darkness away. We must put on the armor of Light, our Lord Jesus Christ, and keep our eyes upon Him. We must do this to make no provision for the flesh to gratify its desires in us. I emphasize again the armor of God. Ephesians 6:10-20 is our guide. Put on the belt of truth; the breastplate of righteousness; shoes to spread the Gospel; the shield of faith; the helmet of salvation, and the sword of the Spirit, which is the Word of God. We need the whole armor, lest the enemy find any chink and gain access. We must take our stand and watch.

What I heard from the Lord:

"Put on your LORD, My Son. Wrap His Spirit totally around you. Be an example to your family, neighbors, coworkers, and all you encounter, directly or indirectly to demonstrate HIS love. Pray for those in authority over you including those with which you don't agree. Let love come out of you so that everyone can see it. It is all about love."

31 – Do Not Pass Judgement

"Who are you to pass judgment on the servant of another? It is before his own master that he stands or falls. And he will be upheld, for the Lord is able to make him stand."

Romans 14:4 ESV

My thoughts:

There are many differences in people of the Christian faith from all nations and all walks of life, but all share two things in common, and that is Jesus Christ is our Lord and Savior, and the Bible is the infallible Word of God. Let the differences in the way we worship enrich us, and the bond of Christ strengthen us. Try to overlook anything that doesn't affect another's salvation. Whatever is detrimental to our salvation is, of course, sin. We must not look around trying to find sin in others. We must keep our focus where it belongs.

Let God's family live in peace with one another and let the God of Righteousness be the Judge.

What I heard from the Lord:

"I have but one church, but it is all-encompassing. My children have decided to separate for reasons that are neither good nor bad but for purposes that make My Word more relevant to them, but I still have but one church. Denominations don't matter to Me. I have no issue with that as long as they believe My Son is their Savior and Lord, that He died for your sins, and that My Word is infallible. It was written by Me. If it were not true, it would not stand. All My children need to have faith in My Word and Me. It is a living thing. My Word is there to enrich your lives, not cause divisiveness. As long as you hold these tenants as true, the rest will fall in place. Never shame another brother or sister for what they believe as long as they hold these things as true."

Chapter 8: August

1 – Make Us Mighty for Christ

"Now these are the chiefs of David's mighty men, who gave him strong support in his kingdom, together with all Israel, to make him king, according to the word of the Lord concerning Israel."

1 Chronicles 11:10 ESV

My thoughts:

David had his mighty men who followed and supported him in any and every way they could. There was nothing they would not do for him. To them, He represented God. Lord, make us mighty for you. Use us for Your Kingdom.

What I heard from the Lord:

"Love, faith, and hope, but the greatest of these is love. These men of David had all those things and loved David sacrificially. You must continue being a living sacrifice for Me. Do not shirk away even in the midst of turmoil. Remember, I have won the war, but there are battles ahead. I only ask you to stand for Me. Stand in My armor. Let no one pass who isn't of My Son. He is the key to all you hope for. Rest in His love but stand fast."

2 – Our Years Are Numbered

"The years of our life are seventy, or even by reason of strength eighty; yet their span is but toil and trouble; they are soon gone, and we fly away."

Psalm 90:10 ESV

My thoughts:

As I look back at my years, almost all of them on this earth have been spent, and I'm now left with nothing but a little change. I was thirty when I accepted the Lord, and I fretted over those lost years that I had wasted, but the Lord has been generous to me and given me fifty more to be in His service.

What I heard from the Lord:

"Use each day as if it were your last, but plan as if you will be here another thousand years. You need not know the day of your new birth in Heaven. You are of My Kingdom, doing what I command. You need not count what you might have left but take your stand and do My will."

3 – Harmony with God

"Because you did not carry it the first time, the Lord our God broke out against us, because we did not seek him according to the rule."

1 Chronicles 15:13 ESV

My thoughts:

Uzzah died because the priests were careless when they tried to bring the ark of the Lord on an ox cart. His loss moved them to search the scriptures to know the correct way to move the ark of the Lord. Perhaps pride led them to this carelessness. Lord, what should this teach us?

What I heard from the Lord:

"Everything you need to live in harmony is found in My Word. Uzzah had to die, but he is with Me to this day. Stay in My Word. Search My Word. Lay it on your hearts. My Son took your burden. He fulfilled the Law. Live, work, rest, yes, and even breathe in My Spirit."

Thank You, Lord, for Your infallible Word. Thank You, Lord, for Your Spirit that lives within each of us.

4 – Good Sense

"Good sense makes one slow to anger, and it is his glory to overlook an offense."

Proverbs 19:11 ESV

My thoughts:

I've heard we should be slow to anger, slow to speak, but quick to forgive. In other words, think before we act. Try to look at matters from the offender's perception. Perhaps it wasn't intended as offensive at all. Take everything into consideration. Once you're sure you have it correct, then speak, but at the same time be ready to forgive.

What I heard from the Lord:

"These are only words until you act on them. I forgave you. When I did, it was for every offence you had ever made or will make. When you forgive, you are showing the love I place in you through My Spirit. Allow Him to direct your speech. When in doubt, simply keep quiet until you are able to hear My Word, My Spirit. Your focus is your direction."

5 – The Foolishness of God

"For the foolishness of God is wiser than men, and the weakness of God is stronger than men."

1 Corinthians 1:25 ESV

My thoughts:

Most try to mold God into who they think He should be, and so they hold onto their own strength. I've been guilty of that many times in my life. Lately, though, as my physical strength fails, along with my mental acuity, I'm reminded to rely more and more on God's strength. I have found out that it's easier on me physically, emotionally, intellectually, and spiritually. As I read this today, I pray for God's continued reminders to depend on His strength and wisdom.

What I heard from the Lord:

"Lean on Me. I will not cast you aside. I will hold you in the good times and in the bad. The good times are coming and will be so for eternity. What you see and live in this world is as a vapor and will be gone in an instant. I make all things new as you also will be fresh, whole, and new."

6 – The Mind of the Lord

"For who has understood the mind of the Lord so as to instruct him?" But we have the mind of Christ."

1 Corinthians 2:16 ESV

My thoughts:

We have the Mind of Christ. We are primarily spiritual beings in the physical world. So, it should not seem odd that we have the mind of Christ through His Spirit being in communion with our spirits.

What I heard from the Lord:

"My Spirit resides in your hearts. My Spirit mingles with your spirit. There is a spark that is impossible for those who don't know Me to understand. You feel It. You know It. You long for those times to be in communion with Me as I am with you. My greatest attribute is love. You were made to love. Just love Me with your whole heart, and I will supply the overflow back to you so you can, will, and must love your neighbors with My Love. Rest in My Love. Work in My Love. Think in My Love. Grow in My Love. Be love to someone today.

I know all your thoughts, and you know Mine if you will only be still and listen. Listen to My still, small voice out of the rush of events and activities rolling all around you. Listen when others crowd around you. Listen in spite of what you hear coming out of the airwaves. Listen, learn, and pass it onto others. It is not meant to be kept bottled up within you but to share abundantly as I have shared with you.

I am coming soon. There is so very little time for those who don't know Me and those who have rejected Me. I am the God of second chances. I stand ever ready to hear cries for help. Use what you have, and I will magnify it as I did with My Son in the feeding of the thousands. You are here in this very short time for My purpose. Don't hide your light under a bushel basket, but let it shine out to the multitudes. You have nothing to lose, for you have Me now and forevermore."

7 – My Temple

"Do you not know that you are God's temple and that God's Spirit dwells in you?"

1 Corinthians 3:16 ESV

My thoughts:

We are God's temple. We are the Church made of living stones. Jesus made this so. His Spirit meets with our spirits and mingles with them as long we allow it. He will not push Himself on us. As God's temple we need to be mindful in how we take care of that temple for it belongs to Him. Think before you act.

What I heard from the Lord:

"You are My temple. You were made that I may dwell in you; that I may direct your paths; but more than that. We commune together in the deepest of levels. Listen to My voice. Delight in My voice. Share My voice, for We are One. Let My love flow into and through you. Feel My presence and listen. My words are life."

8 – Talk

"For the kingdom of God does not consist in talk but in power."

1 Corinthians 4:20 ESV

My thoughts:

All power is in and from God. When we look around and see the power throughout the world, it is nothing. When we look at the stars and begin to comprehend their power, it is nothing. God created it all. All power is in Him.

What I heard from the Lord:

"My kingdom does consist of power. Without power, what is there? I created the universe you live in with power. But I also created it in love. What is power without love but chaos and division? There is power in your words, your talk, but without love, it is nothing more than gossip, falsehoods, and emptiness. Stay in My Word that your thoughts and your speech will be pure, loving and kind. Continue in My kingdom."

9 – Judging

"For what have I to do with judging outsiders? Is it not those inside the church whom you are to judge?"

1 Corinthians 5:12 ESV

My thoughts:

Paul makes it clear where judgement on our part is useful. Our outreach is to those outside the Church. Therefore, we are to be in the world but not of the world. It is not our place to judge the world. That belongs to the Lord. The Church is to be holy. All who have accepted Christ as Lord and Savior are holy. Being holy means being set apart for the purpose of God. Each of us has gifts given by the Holy Spirit for the Church; that it be uplifted and that it be holy. The Church, the Bride of Christ, must be set apart for the Bridegroom. We are all living stones of the Bride of Christ.

We each have a part to play, and we must each do our part to be holy through the urging of the Holy Spirit ministering to our spirits. Let us stay in His Word. Let us keep our spiritual ears and eyes open for our instruction in His kingdom.

What I heard from the Lord:

"I look for purity in My bride. She must be pure and clean. She must put away her filthy garments and let go of the world. She is rooted in the world. She knows what she must do. I wait that no one be lost who can be saved?"

A Vision I Received on the Church

I saw a woman. She had a long braid of hair. The end of the braid was caught by something on the ground. I couldn't see what it was. She was bent over with her head toward the ground. Her hair was pure black, and her face was very white. She glanced up at me once. She was beautiful. She was dressed in clothing that covered her from her neck to her feet. It seemed to be in layers. The sky behind her was cloudless and blue. She didn't look afraid, but very determined to get her hair undamaged away from whatever had caught it.

The Interpretation

"The woman is the Church. Her long braid, her adornment is caught in the world. In some ways she is bowing to the world, but not by her desire. Her desire is to be free of the ways of the world and depend totally on her Lord. Her white face is her purity. Her beauty is the Holy Spirit that the Lord has poured into her. Her clothing shows she is not ready to meet her Bridegroom. She should never fear, but always wait on her Lord. She's already been given all the tools she needs to free herself. She must free herself to be ready for her Lord."

These words came, "The Church must free herself from the call of the world."

10 – One Spirit

"But he who is joined to the Lord becomes one spirit with him."

1 Corinthians 6:17 ESV

My thoughts, a vision:

The Holy Spirit appeared as many long strands of different colored ribbons. The ribbons are long and thin. My spirit is a single strand of dull gray. It reaches up and then is pulled, intertwining with the strands of the Holy Spirit. They whirl faster and faster, growing closer together and then they kiss. I know the Spirit, but when the kiss occurs it is explosive. I know and am fully known. I am complete. It was explosive and magnetic at the same time.

What I heard from the Lord:

My Spirit lives in each of you. Wherever you go, whatever you do, I am right there beside and inside of you. Listen to my voice as I protect you, lead you and correct you. Be careful with what I have given you. It is priceless and makes you priceless in My sight."

11 – Dust to Dust

"All go to one place. All are from the dust, and to dust all return. Who knows whether the spirit of man goes upward and the spirit of the beast goes down into the earth?"

Ecclesiastes 3:20-21 ESV

My thoughts:

I find this a very sad commentary of King Solomon who had everything possible for anyone living in that time. Even though God had spoken to him in the past, he threw it all away, and what did he find? Thank You, Lord, for Your Word.

What I heard from the Lord:

"From dust you came and to dust you will go, but if you know Me, you will live in eternity with Me. How sad for those who don't know me and have nothing to look for in life except their own personal pleasure. Search as they may; there is no fulfillment in that. There is a hole in your heart that only My Son can fill through the Spirit. That is true fulfillment. Taste and see. Know that I am God and have no place for those who reject Me in My kingdom."

12 – Bloom Where You're Planted

"Only let each person lead the life that the Lord has assigned to him, and to which God has called him. This is my rule in all the churches."

1 Corinthians 7:17 ESV

My thoughts:

The term "Bloom where you're planted" comes to mind. We change jobs. We move to other places, but there must be one constant. We must serve the Lord. We must listen for His voice. Without His guidance, we should stay put but be ready for His call; be available.

Lord, what would you have us do? Should we go, or should we stay? What would You have us do?

What I heard from the Lord:

"Your days are few; remain where you are. Listen for My voice. I will show you if you need to go or stay; change what you're doing or stay with what I have proven to you is good, healthy, and right for you. Listen and know My heart. There are things you are not ready to know, but I will never withhold what you need. Lean on Me and listen to My Word."

13 – The Wisdom of Solomon

"Then I saw all the work of God, that man cannot find out the work that is done under the sun. However much man may toil in seeking, he will not find it out. Even though a wise man claims to know, he cannot find it out."

Ecclesiastes 8:17 ESV

My thoughts:

As much as Solomon knew, his knowledge was limited by the time period he was in, but not his wisdom of the knowledge he had. Through Jesus, we know all we need to know. Solomon would not fit into today any more than we would fit in his time. We too though, need to ask for wisdom.

What I heard from the Lord:

"Solomon, My son, was gifted with greater wisdom than any man or woman before or since. He started well but stopped listening to Me. What more could I do for him? You have greater knowledge than Solomon, but your wisdom is lacking. Ask Me for wisdom and see if I will withhold it from you. Ask and receive, for you have something Solomon did not have. You have My Son."

14 – A New Song

"Oh sing to the Lord a new song; sing to the Lord, all the earth!"

Psalm 96:1 ESV

My thoughts:

Personally, I have a voice that does not sing. Music means little to me, but I love poetry. I love the words, the design, the rhythm, and the creative voice of it. I know I'm in the minority, but that's the way I was made. Even though music means little to me, I much appreciate the heartfelt songs of those who can sing, and I have a great appreciation for classical music, but that's just me. There are other ways to sing, not just with our voices. We can sing and worship through everything we do.

What I heard from the Lord:

"All of you are as a new song. All you do in My name is a new song. Sing to Me with your heart in words and deeds. I care not whether your voice can sing. It's the song your heart makes that I want to hear. Sing to Me a new song."

15 – Our Duty to Worship

"Worship the Lord in the splendor of holiness; tremble before him, all the earth!"

Psalm 96:9 ESV

My thoughts:

This verse makes me warm all over. Worship the Lord in the splendor of holiness tremble before Him. As He is all powerful, all knowing, and is everywhere, we should tremble before Him. All this gives me the greatest smile for He has called us all to be a part of it.

What I heard from the Lord:

"Your duty is worship. You are holy, for you have My very Spirit living within. It is there where I speak and commune with your spirit. It is there where you learn what is written in My Word. It is there where we commune together. It is there where your soul is refreshed and sparks into new life day by day as you walk this earth. Your truth then is to worship Me. It is I who not only gave you life, but the life I give is eternal and full to overflowing. I desire your worship in all you do. It's not only for singing praises but the way you interact with others on every level. It is the way you handle your jobs. Do everything as if it is for Me, for it truly is. Don't hold back. Let it all out. Let Me hear your voice in every action you take, for I take all your actions as unto Me. Never hold back your good work and your good service. To withhold that is to rob Me."

16 – Stand, and Not Fall

"Therefore let anyone who thinks that he stands take heed lest he fall."

1 Corinthians 10:12 ESV

My thoughts:

Too many times, I have thought I was standing firm for the Lord, only to have something come along and knock the props out from under me. I keep getting up, but after a while, it happens again. I know it is when I look away and look at myself. I know it's a pride thing. Help us Lord to stand and not give the enemy even an inch.

What I heard from the Lord:

"Many stand. Few stand firm. It is pride that draws your eyes from me and unto yourselves. It just takes a small amount, but that small amount is so destructive. Many great ones have succumbed to pride and looked away from Me. Take heed. Listen to Me. You have eyes to see, but more. You have spiritual eyes that see so much more than your natural eyes. Use them. Use them to see and understand your fulfillment comes from Me. Keep those eyes on Me, and you will not fall."

17 – When Sin Begins to Creep In

"Solomon brought Pharaoh's daughter up from the city of David to the house that he had built for her, for he said, "My wife shall not live in the house of David king of Israel, for the places to which the ark of the Lord has come are holy."

2 Chronicles 8:11 ESV

My thoughts:

Because Solomon's wife from Egypt had her own gods, she had to stay away from that which was holy. Solomon had to know he was wrong in marrying her but did it anyway. Maybe for political reasons. In any event, even at this early stage in his reign, he was already pulling away from the Lord. The thing is, he knew when he was going to do something wrong and did it anyway.

This was a sin of commission. When we know something is wrong and do it anyway, God will forgive us but remember to refrain from sin for our own protection.

What I heard from the Lord:

"My son David did many things right, but at times he drifted off course. You too have drifted off course from time to time. Does that make Me to love you less? No, for I can't love you anymore than I do. David always came back to Me. In this way follow His example and all will be well with you. Solomon drifted and went his own way."

18 – The Foxes

"Catch the foxes for us, the little foxes that spoil the vineyards, for our vineyards are in blossom."

Song of Solomon 2:15 ESV

My thoughts:

What are the little foxes that try to spoil our lives, from the smallest kernel to the largest successes? How can we identify them and bring them before the Lord in confession when they come from within?

Lord, we ask you to protect our lives, our reputations, and our walk with You from anything that can spoil what You have provided from outside as well as inside. Let us not allow the small things to grow into what we can't control.

What I heard from the Lord:

"You may consider your lives with one another as your vineyards. I gave you life. I brought others into your life and you into theirs. You gave your life to Me. I will prune your vineyards. I will provide the sun and the rain. I will provide the nutrients of the soil. That is you I'm talking about. Those foxes, oh those foxes that work their way into your lives, the spawn of Satan. They work their wiles; they bring poor but attractive thoughts for you to dwell upon. Pray that through My Spirit, anything that comes between Us be stricken and cast out. Keep your focus on Me. I will tend your vineyards. All will be well, as long as your dependence is on Me."

19 – Love Defined

"Love is patient and kind; love does not envy or boast; is not arrogant or rude. It does not insist on its own way; it is not irritable or resentful; it does not rejoice at wrong doing, but rejoices with the truth. Love bears all things, believes all things, hopes all things, endures all things. Love never fails....."

1 Corinthians 13:4-8 ESV

My thoughts and what I heard from the Lord:

When I love, am I being kind,
Or simply being of another mind?
Is my love patient with you:
Loving, from God's point of view?

Do I let envy shut love out,
And let my boasting make me pout?
Do I always need my way?
I so hope not, that I pray.

Does resentment rest in me?
I hope not, that is my plea.
Have I joy when others hurt?
Am I short or am I curt?

No, my love must all things bear,
Believing the best and always care,
To be a light for all to see,
That all may know Christ in me.

20 – Our Steps Are from the Lord

"A man's steps are from the Lord; how then can man understand his way?"

Proverbs 20:24 ESV

My thoughts:

I had such thoughts of my future in my youth. In school, I envied those kids who seemed to know exactly what they were going to do. I had no clue, but the Lord has directed my steps in directions I never imagined, and I'm better for it.

What I heard from the Lord:

"Your steps are ordered by Me. You may twist and turn, but my will shall be accomplished through you. You ask, "How shall I know God's will?" Look to the scriptures. Come to Me in prayer and ask. Ask, and then listen for My voice, be it in scripture, advice from another, or My opening and closing doors to send you where you should be. If you pray and ask Me what to do and what is right, will I not direct your path so it is true and right? Believe in My Word. Believe in My Son. Believe in Me. I will not leave nor forsake you. Let everything you do be bathed in prayer."

21 – A Perverse Heart

"A perverse heart shall be far from me; I will know nothing of evil."

Psalm 101:4 ESV

My thoughts:

To be perverse is to be deliberately obstinate and unreasonable regardless of consequences. I have known too many people who are perverse, including me. I, too, was once that way, doing what I wanted and not caring what others thought or what effect my actions had on them. It is a pretty sorry way to be. The psalm says these thoughts and actions should be far from us, and we should know nothing of evil.

What I heard from the Lord:

"I have dealt with perverse people. My children in the desert were perverse beyond reason, and I had to deal with them. So, it is now with this generation. What shall I do with them? They shall be dealt with, but it's within all of you to hear My Word; to follow it, and to freely give it away even to the perverse but be careful lest you cast pearls before swine. It is not for you to judge. That is for Me. Do your duty. I will do mine."

22 – Our Faith is Not Futile

"And if Christ has not been raised, your faith is futile, and you are still in your sins."

1 Corinthians 15:17 ESV

"If in Christ we have hope in this life only, we are of all people to be pitied."

1 Corinthians 15:20

My thoughts:

For me, life has been so much better after accepting Christ into my life that even if there was nothing else after this life, it still would have been worth it. Before Christ, we were existing but not really living. We were alive to the world but dead in our spirits. I am convinced that God does not lie, and that Jesus is the only way. I do not want eternal life without Christ, but only to live it for and with our Lord.

What I heard from the Lord:

"I cannot lie. Satan is the father of lies. I am the Father of Truth. My Truth brings life. Satan's lies bring death. My Word is folly to the world but be of good cheer. You are alive unto Me through My Word, My Son, and My Spirit. Your faith is well founded. I will not let you go. It is My great desire for you to spend eternity with Me. Be at peace in My Spirit."

23 – We Will Bear the Image of Christ

"Just as we have borne the image of the man of dust, we shall also bear the image of the man of heaven."

1 Corinthians 15:49 ESV

My thoughts:

In our present form, we have the image of Adam. In the future, we will have the image of Christ. I see that we have a down payment of that future by the Holy Spirit alive within each of us who have called Jesus our Lord and Savior.

What I heard from the Lord:

"You are of dust, and to dust you will return. You are now as Adam was after the fall. They lost communion with Me, and I with them, but there was a relationship still. You have My Spirit living in you. Your hearts have been changed, but there is so much more to come. You are but a seed compared to what you will be. You love Me now, but when you are changed, oh, what a difference. You will be like My Son. Your future is so far beyond you in your present. The time is not yet but very soon."

24 – Our Labor is Not in Vain

"Therefore, my beloved brothers, be steadfast, immovable, always abounding in the work of the Lord, knowing that in the Lord your labor is not in vain."

1 Corinthians 15:58 ESV

My thoughts:

Whatever job we have, whether in paid ministry or otherwise, our job is to do the very best we can. We are all in the ministry, one way or another. That is our service unto the Lord. In doing this, "your labor is not in vain." I remember telling my children when they were young that no matter what job they had, even if it was a ditch digger, to do the best job they could. Oddly enough, my son was a ditch digger in the Army for a period and received an award for his work.

What I heard from the Lord:

"Whatever you do, do it for Me. That means everything you do should be of worship for Me. Thank Me in all your labor; that I have given you the ability and tools to accomplish your work."

25 – Our Lord, Come

"If anyone has no love for the Lord, let him be accursed. Our Lord, come!"

1 Corinthians 16:22 ESV

My thoughts:

If Christ came today, how would He see our church? Would He see love and devotion for and to Him? Would He see us as giving?

Would He see us as a light in our neighborhood? Would He see division or unity?

Would He see spiritual growth and safety for the saints and a place of love and teaching for those searching? Would He see His living stones being taught and reaching out to their neighbors?

Would He see us as a help or a hinderance to His Church? Would He need to winnow, or would there be a collection of His saints? Would He see us as living stones for Him?

Show us Lord, what can we do to further Your Kingdom?

What I heard from the Lord:

"There is not a single child that I do not love. There are many without love for Me, and that is to their detriment. I love all the same. No matter what you do or don't do, I will still love you the same. For you who show your love for Me, will I not unleash the riches of Heaven on you? Will I not show My love for you in ways unimaginable? Yet, for those who have no love for Me, it would be better if they had never been born, for their future must be without Me. They have made their own bed. That is where they must lie forever."

26 – Bless the Lord

"Bless the Lord, O my soul, and all that is within me, bless his holy name!"

Psalm 103:1 ESV

My thoughts, my prayer:

Bless the Lord with all that is within us.

Lord, You have poured Your Spirit into us. We can bless You by listening and acting upon what the Holy Spirit puts in our hearts. Can we bless You without His Spirit? No, for all our righteousness without Your Spirit are as filthy rags. It is only by Your Spirit living in us that we have any righteousness at all. Lord, fill us with Your Spirit to overflowing so that we may bless You this day and every day.

Lord, teach us through Your Spirit. You are such a blessing. We could never understand even an iota about You before You came into our hearts. We bless You today with all that is within us. In Jesus' Name, Amen.

What I heard from the Lord:

"Yes, I have poured My Spirit into you that you may know Me. That you may follow Me, and that you may model Me to the best of your ability as you grow in your faith. I do not want a part of you, I want all of you, as I give all of Me to you. Stay in My Word and listen to My Spirit."

27 – Humble Yourselves

"However, some men of Asher, of Manasseh, and of Zebulun humbled themselves and came to Jerusalem."

2 Chronicles 30:11 ESV

My thoughts:

Israel was taken captive in 722 BC by Assyria. King Hezekiah began his reign in 715 BC. Hezekiah invited all of Judea and all that was left of Israel to join in the restored Passover. As this verse states, only some humbled themselves and came to Jerusalem.

What I heard from the Lord:

"You go your own way without satisfaction. There's always something missing when you do. I am that Something that's missing. This world is not your home. Don't try to make it your home. My plans for the world are not your plans. If things do not look right today in the world, just wait until tomorrow. I am rocking the world from its foundations. Watch and see. The time is near when all things will be put right, and I will gather you in My arms as a mother hen gathers her chicks. Rest in this knowledge and know I am the Lord.

The way the world is today is because of what's in the hearts of men and women throughout the world. They must have their own way, just like my children Israel so many years ago. Human nature never changes. You are inventive and have many great inventions to help you do things easier. All that has gained you is that you become more and more lazy. Your inventions are about to cease. Your laziness will cause your death. You, who are too lazy to even call on Me. I know who you are, both you who give Me lip service yet do your own thing. Death is upon you. You who do not care and don't even pretend to acknowledge Me. You, too, can expect nothing but death and eternal damnation. Awaken, awaken. The time is now. Rouse yourselves from your slumber. Call on Me. You can call on no one else that can save you. Call on Me!"

28 – Bless the Lord

"Bless the Lord, all his hosts, his ministers, who do his will! Bless the Lord, all his works, in all places of his dominion. Bless the Lord, O my soul!"

Psalm 103:21-22 ESV

My thoughts:

This was written nearly 3000 years ago, yet it's as fresh and new today as it was when it was written. Bless the Lord O my soul and all that is within me. There is a caveat here, "who do His will." It's different now than it was then. Now we have the Holy Spirit within us. We are part of His hosts. We are ministers. He works with and through us. Praise the Lord.

What I heard from the Lord:

"You get up, and you fall. You get up, and you fall. This goes on and on, but as you earnestly reach for Me, your falls are not as far and are less often. Stay on My path and listen to My voice in My Word and by My Spirit living in you. Do not despair, for I am with you always. Rejoice in My Presence."

29 – He HEARD God's Word

"And when the king heard the words of the Law, he tore his clothes."

2 Chronicles 34:19 ESV

My thoughts:

King Josiah was the best of the best. Why? He followed the Lord the best he knew how, and then when he was confronted with the Word of God, he was devastated. He knew with his whole heart how far his people had fallen, and he knew the price to come. I repeat, Josiah was the best of the best. He followed the Lord totally without reservation. He threw himself totally on God's mercy.

What I heard from the Lord:

"I anointed this man. He served his purpose without complaint and agonized over his people. He never knew My Son, but he knew My Spirit. I anointed him with My Spirit. What he did, all he accomplished, was by My Spirit. He knew what was to come, and by his duty many were saved. He is an example for you to follow even today. He is a picture of servant leadership. He gave his all in My service. I cannot ask for more."

30 – There is Freedom Only in the Lord

"Now the Lord is the Spirit, and where the Spirit of the Lord is, there is freedom."

2 Corinthians 3:17 ESV

My thoughts:

This is a famous and beautiful, often quoted verse. (Freedom in the Lord.) Freedom can take many forms. It is freedom from or freedom to do something that could otherwise be restricted. We have many freedoms in this country. Freedom in the Lord is for the taking, but it must be accepted for it to be valid. It will not be pushed on us.

What I heard from the Lord:

"**My Spirit covers the earth. Indeed, it covers over all. Where is the freedom in My Spirit? Freedom without rules is anarchy. Freedom with rules brings order. Where there is order there is freedom. My Son brought you rules that are easy. Your very lives were created to live within the boundaries of His rules. Let My Spirit guide you into all holiness. That being the fact, you are set apart for Me and My good pleasure. That should not frighten you, for you are My great creation and my great love. Live within the bounds set before you, and you will be truly free. Do not test the limits of your freedom. Just enjoy what has been provided for your life and welfare. Know you are loved in a way you can never match or completely understand. I gave My All for you.**"

31 – Treasure in Jars of Clay

"But we have this treasure in jars of clay, to show that the surpassing power belongs to God and not to us."

2 Corinthians 4:7 ESV

My thoughts:

Are we empty jars of clay without the Holy Spirit? I don't think so. I think if we are not filled with the Holy Spirit, we will be filled with something else. I think it's like the person who was cleansed from the seven spirits. If not filled with the Holy Spirit, not only would the seven evil spirits return, but they'd bring their buddies as well.

What I heard from the Lord:

"Your hearts are shaped for My Spirit. Nothing else satisfies. Only Me. You are earthen vessels, for you come from the earth. I come from above as, of course, does My Spirit. When He enters your hearts, you are elevated so that you are no longer of the world but only in the world. To be of the world is to be subject to My wrath. You chose wisely, as did I when I chose you. You are my dear friends, for I tell you all you need to know to flourish."

Chapter 9: September

1 – We Groan

"For while we are still in this tent, we groan, being burdened—not that we would be unclothed, but that we would be further clothed so that what is mortal may be swallowed up by life."

2 Corinthians 5:4 ESV

My thoughts:

The phrase "so that what is mortal may be swallowed up by life." That's quite a statement. I think the lives we have on this Earth are poor substitutes for the life to come. We shouldn't get too attached to the here and now for it will all pass away. On the other hand, since our time is so short here, it is very precious, and we need to do all we can with the time we do have. Let us give our utmost on this earth for His Highest.

What I heard from the Lord:

"You live, yet you are not fully alive. You have My Spirit, but that is only a down payment of what is to come. You see in a glass dimly but then face to Face. Yes, that is the difference. What a time when We are face to Face with nothing between Us. I look forward to that much more than you. Yes, cling to the life you have, but know what is to come will be life in all its fullness. Now, walk with My Spirit."

2 – Do Justice, Love Kindness, Walk Humbly

"He has told you, O man, what is good; and what does the Lord require of you but to do justice, and to love kindness, and to walk humbly with your God?"

Micah 6:8 ESV

My thoughts:

Among other things the Lord requires that we:

Do justice.

Love kindness.

Walk humbly with Him.

Right out of Micah in the Old Testament. I think if we can do these three things through the love and Power of Jesus, our lives will have counted.

What I heard from the Lord:

"Justice, kindness, and humility are earmarks of My son Micah. These are not things to strive for. These come out of the natural abundance you have received through My Son. These are things that mark you as belonging to Me. Rest in Me, and let My love, joy, peace, patience, kindness, goodness, faithfulness, gentleness, and self-control mark your lives so that others may see Me in you. You are My beloved children. Let My love shine through you."

3 – The Father in the Son

"That is, in Christ God was reconciling the world to himself, not counting their trespasses against them, and entrusting to us the message of reconciliation."

2 Corinthians 5:19 ESV

My thoughts:

In Christ, God was reconciling the world to Himself. The Lord God was in His Son. Whatever the Son (Jesus) felt, so did the Father, God. They were together through the entire ministry of Jesus on the earth. The only separation was when Jesus was on the cross, and the whole sin of the world fell upon His shoulders. The Father cannot look on sin. He had to look away. Still, He knew what Jesus was going through and still shared His misery.

What I heard from the Lord:

"You could not and cannot save yourselves. Therefore, I had to send My Only Son. Yes, I was there. Yes, I knew. Yes, I had to look away. It was all agreed before there was one of you through our love for you that sending My Son was the only way to save you. That's how great Our love is for you. My Son and I are One. What He feels, I feel. What He does, I do. What He knows, I know. It was all for you. Be blessed and know you are loved by God, Father, Son, and Holy Spirit. We are One."

4 – Good and Evil

"Woe to those who call evil good and good evil, who put darkness for light and light for darkness, who put bitter for sweet and sweet for bitter!"

Isaiah 5:20 ESV

My thoughts:

As I read this verse, the leadership in our world today came to mind. I've been around for a while, and I've seen a lot of things. I remember the lies of Pravda, the Soviet Union state news, but not so much in this country until recently. The news media and our leadership would have us believe what was right is wrong, and what was wrong is now right. It's a chapter right out of Pravda, and by Isaiah's account, it's been with us since Adam. I find myself in a world that I don't know, understand, or frankly want to. It leads me to pray, "Come, Lord Jesus, come."

What I heard from the Lord:

"The world has always been so except for those who call Me Lord and walk in My ways. You have glanced away and seen what the world has to offer. In the end, it is despair, hatred, folly, and death eternal. You have glimpsed enough. Look back to Me."

5 – Be Available

"And I heard the voice of the Lord saying, "Whom shall I send, and who will go for us?" Then I said, "Here I am! Send me."

Isaiah 6:8 ESV

My thoughts:

"Here I am! Send me." What comes into my mind is, "I'm available." We all need to be available to the Lord for His good pleasure whenever and wherever He may place us. Keep our eyes on Him.

What I heard from the Lord:

"Always be available to Me. You are My chosen. You have been chosen for this time. Listen and hear Me. I have gone before you, and I go before you now. I have won the battle, yet it is still to be fought. Stand and watch the things I am doing and will do. You stand. You watch. You do not give way, but My strength will be shown not only in what you see Me do but with what I do in you, for you are Mine. The victory is Mine, and the victory is won."

6 – The Rod of God's Anger

"Woe to Assyria, the rod of my anger; the staff in their hands is my fury!"

Isaiah 10:5 ESV

My thoughts:

Now Assyria was at the gates of Jerusalem. Israel had already been conquered and never seen again. Judah was following Israel, and Isaiah was warning Judah to turn from their ways. Now this verse in its context is very interesting. Assyria conquered many nations and was pretty much THE war machine of the day. No nation had withstood them. They had no idea they were an instrument of God.

What I heard from the Lord:

"Assyria was an instrument for My purpose. I may use anything that submits to Me or holds Me in contempt for My own purposes. Assyria was a Godless nation but look around. How many Godless nations are there today arrayed against Me and My own? I will use whatever I will to complete what I have promised. Nothing is offensive to me for the purpose at hand. I use the elect and those not elected for My purpose. You must accept that I will use whatever is necessary to bring My people home and end this rebellious age."

7 – God is Our Salvation

"Behold, God is my salvation; I will trust, and will not be afraid; for the Lord God is my strength and my song, and he has become my salvation."

Isaiah 12:2 ESV

My thoughts:

Salvation, trust, strength, song, and again salvation; when you put it all together, what do you get?

Our lord has provided our salvation through the work and resurrection of Jesus. We can and must trust Him. Where else can we go? He is the Rock upon which we stand. We have human strength that gives out. His strength is shown best in our weakness and never fails. Whatever we do must be our song to Him in all circumstances. Again, our salvation is emphasized. He has given us life eternal but also abundantly. What would it be like to live forever in a miserly way? Shout for joy with the life-giving love He has given us now and forever.

What I heard from the Lord:

"I am your salvation. I am your strength. I Am that I Am. Live your lives in the security of My presence. I will not fail you in times of adversity but will always make a way for you. I am always here at your side. Never be afraid or look elsewhere for your security, for I am at hand. I am nearer than your closest friend, for I live not only beside you but inside as well through My Spirit. Depend on Me first, last, and always."

8 – Giving

"Each one must give as he has decided in his heart, not reluctantly or under compulsion, for God loves a cheerful giver."

2 Corinthians 9:7 ESV

My thoughts:

To tithe or not to tithe, or to give as you have decided in your heart. Can it be both? The Old Testament tithe was a tenth of your first fruits. Paul knew that when he wrote this. He's writing to gentiles, not Jews, though. I remember a pastor saying once upon a time, "Don't give until it hurts, give until it feels good." This is not in a prideful way, but a joyful way.

Christ gives us freedom. That means freedom in our giving as well, whether it is a tenth or whether it is more or less. God loves a cheerful giver. Remember, too, that you cannot out-give God.

What I heard from the Lord:

"You have been given much for you have My Spirit. What I give you, I give freely. What you give, you should give freely. There's no test to see who has given the most. It's just between you and Me. Give as your Spirit-filled heart tells you. The law of Moses was fulfilled by My Son. You are free indeed."

9 – True Freedom

"For such men are false apostles, deceitful workmen, disguising themselves as apostles of Christ."

2 Corinthians 11:13 ESV

My thoughts:

Here Paul is speaking about those teaching another gospel. The gospel of Christ is freedom. Other teachings are of works and result in enslavement. These were the cults in the day of Paul, and they are alive today. Any church that preaches works or faith plus works is a cult and should not be listened to. If our works gain us salvation, then Christ's death on the cross was for nothing. In plain words, cults are evil. In my younger years, I was in a cult. It seemed free at the time. I wanted to do the works they taught. It felt good to be working toward my salvation. I learned everything I could about what they taught.

Years later when I truly invited Christ into my life, I had to unlearn all I had been taught before. It was a daunting task and took a long time, but each time I exchanged a learned falsehood with the Truth, I found greater freedom.

What I heard from the Lord:

"When I walked the streets of Jerusalem, they preached a gospel of slavery. I came to free those enslaved and give the pure good news. You can't buy salvation no matter how hard you work. I gave My life for your freedom. For anyone to think they have to work for their salvation is a slap in My face and a lie. Those who preach such lies are doomed to an eternity far away from Me and My own. My gift of salvation is precious and cannot be earned, but only accepted as a free gift. Stand against those who would try to take that freedom from you and those you love. I will never lead you astray. When you came to Me, you came to the Truth. My Son is the Truth."

10 – Be Prepared

"Your dead shall live; their bodies shall rise. You who dwell in the dust, awake and sing for joy! For your dew is a dew of light, and the earth will give birth to the dead."

Isaiah 26:19 ESV

My thoughts:

This was written long before I Thessalonians chapters 4 and 5. I find it comforting to see this written in the Old Testament as well as the New. This verse is supported by this and the previous two chapters. Paul mirrors these words in 1 Thessalonians. As Jesus rose first, so will we who follow Him.

What I heard from the Lord:

"It shall be done as it has been written. All who rise will be given bodies like that of My Son. Bodies that will not grow old and die but bodies that will last forever. The current tents you have are but a patchwork. The new is without blemish and a beauty to see in every way. Be ready, for I am coming soon. This time I speak of soon not in the sense I have used it before, but soon for you. Be prepared."

11 – Power in Weakness

"But he said to me, "My grace is sufficient for you, for my power is made perfect in weakness." Therefore I will boast all the more gladly of my weaknesses, so that the power of Christ may rest upon me."

2 Corinthians 12:9 ESV

My thoughts:

I once thought of myself as strong, but that was physically. Physical strength isn't what the Lord is looking for. He gives strength in our spiritual weakness. When our spirits are connected to His Spirit, we are truly strong. When our dependence is on ourselves, we are alone and frail. Today we should be stronger than we have ever been, but that's only because of God's strength poured into us. When we acknowledge our weakness, we are ready to receive His strength and be His vessels. That is where I want to be.

What I heard from the Lord:

"All you have; all you are comes from Me. I was there when you came into this world, and I have been with you all your life. You finally listened, and I was there for you. When you fell, I lifted you up. When you were in trouble, I came to your rescue. When you were lost, I found you. Yes, I've been with you all the way in this world and will be into the next. Your success, your real success, is My success. Your failures are your own because those were the times you pushed Me away, but I was only a prayer away when you called upon Me. If you boast, let it be in Me; to boast in yourself is a lie."

12 – The Lord Waits for Us

"Therefore the Lord waits to be gracious to you, and therefore he exalts himself to show mercy to you. For the Lord is a God of justice; blessed are all those who wait for him."

Isaiah 30:18 ESV

My thoughts:

In this verse, again, we see the Lord waiting to be gracious to us. We see further that He blesses us when we wait for Him. I do not want Him to have to wait for me, yet there are times when He does. He is a God of holiness who has set us apart to be holy. If He has set us apart for Himself, a people delivered by the Living God, should we not allow His Spirit to be alive in us? Should we not listen to Him? Should we not yearn to be like Him in all His ways? Yes, Lord, again we pray, search our hearts. Cast every sin away as far as the East is from the West and direct my path this day.

What I heard from the Lord:

"Yes, I wait for you. You think you are waiting for Me, but I wait far more for you. It is you who needs to come to Me with an open and contrite heart. All you have to bring Me is yourselves. I ask for nothing else. I set your feet on solid level ground beneath the cross. All are equal in My sight, and I wait to lavish My greatest blessings upon you. Stay in My Word, Listen to My Spirit. Let Him guide you."

13 – Hear the Words of the Wise

"Incline your ear, and hear the words of the wise, and apply your heart to my knowledge, for it will be pleasant if you keep them within you, if all of them are ready on your lips."

Proverbs 22:17-18 ESV

My thoughts:

I have tried to live my life and learn through others I trust. I've always shied away from ignoring the advice of seasoned others. I've heard people say over the years something to the effect, "I'll do it my own way." Personally I do not like the "School of Hard Knocks." The few times I've tried, it didn't work out well, however, I did learn.

What I heard from the Lord:

"Apply your hearts to My knowledge. Hear from My Word. Hear from those teachers and prophets I have set in your midst. Hear of my knowledge when your hearts are quiet, and you know the quiet whisper of Me speaking in your ears. My knowledge brings wisdom. Man's knowledge brings folly. Listen to My Spirit, Who lives within you. Let Him direct you on the path set before you lest you veer to the right or to the left. Let your eyes, those spiritual eyes, discern My Word and the direction set before you."

14 – Only One Gospel

"As we have said before, so now I say again: If anyone is preaching to you a gospel contrary to the one you received, let him be accursed."

Galatians 1:9 ESV

My thoughts:

This is closely related to what we looked at on September 9, True Freedom in 2 Corinthians 11:13. Paul was speaking out against cults, that is, any church that adds works to the gospel. That doesn't mean we don't do works of the Spirit because of love for Christ, but that we don't try to get to Heaven by works or works plus Christ. If that is the case, it will give us pride to say Christ did His part, but I did my part, so what I did got me or helped me get to Heaven. Heavens, no, it is by the work of Christ that we are saved and nothing else. Ephesians 2:8-9 "For by grace you have been saved through faith. And this not of your doing, it is the gift of God not a result of works that no one may boast." Isaiah 64:6 NIV "All our righteous acts are like filthy rags......" I don't want my filthy rags. I want the righteousness of Christ.

What I heard from the Lord:

"Don't make it complicated. Just read My Word. It isn't that hard unless you make it so. Even children have faith enough to receive Me. When you receive Me, you receive the Father, and My Spirit lives in you. Let My Spirit lead you into all holiness. It is that simple."

15 – Purity of the Gospel

"To them we did not yield in submission even for a moment, so that the truth of the gospel might be preserved for you."

Galatians 2:5 ESV

My thoughts:

This verse refers to those who were trying to add to the gospel and say that circumcision was required as well as faith. Following up from yesterday, here we see how important it is that the gospel be preserved, that it not be changed or taught in any way that may allow any chink in the armor of the gospel. The Jews were so particular in their copying of the Word of God that when the Dead Sea scrolls were found in 1947 there was no difference other than syntax, to those words written more than 2000 years ago to our current Bible. This continued all the way through the Middle Ages, where each word copied by monks was verified by other proofreaders. It's a really big deal that the gospel remains pure.

What I heard from the Lord:

"You can be sure My Word is pure. As My Word is pure, so you should strive to work out your salvation. It isn't that you are not saved by faith, but that in working out your salvation, you are in My Word and practicing those things so approved by Me. You are not a slave but a friend. You must walk the path set before you. It is the only way. Trust in My Word and live in My Word."

16 – Wait

"But they who wait for the Lord shall renew their strength; they shall mount up with wings like eagles; they shall run and not be weary; they shall walk and not faint."

Isaiah 40:31 ESV

My thoughts:

Many years ago, there was a song we used to sing:

"They that upon the Lord shall renew their strength. They shall mount up with wings as an eagle.

They will run and not be weary.

They will walk and not faint.

Teach me, Lord, teach me, Lord to wait."

I still remember this song as if it were today. Our physical, emotional, and spiritual strength are like vapor before the Lord, Who's strength renews us, strengthens us, and is everlasting. We only need to ask and know that He will supply our needs beyond our understanding.

What I heard from the Lord:

"Remember when you used to get so tired, frustrated, and angry about that which you couldn't handle? After this you would finally come to Me. Do not wait. I am ever ready to supply all your needs beyond all your expectations and give you My rest, My peace, and renew you from within."

17 – No Fear

"Fear not, for I am with you; be not dismayed, for I am your God; I will strengthen you, I will help you, I will uphold you with my righteous right hand."

Isaiah 41:10 ESV

My thoughts:

Oh Lord, when I take my eyes away from you and look at what's happening in the world, I am dismayed. I see no hope for those in this world who do not call on Your name. Oh Lord, strengthen me, for I have no strength without You. I see a world in a collision with turmoil. I see no escape except in You.

What I heard from the Lord:

"Fear not, for I am with you. I called you before there was an Earth. You were called, and you were chosen. There is a breadth of brethren about you, both near and far, who are the elect, born for this time and this season to do My will. I am your righteous right hand. I will not forsake you. Why do you take your eyes from Me? Follow Peter's example. I will hold you and keep you in this dark world. The times are upon you. Rest in My Power and My Word."

18 – He Blots Out Our Transgressions

"I am he who blots out your transgressions for my own sake, and I will not remember your sins."

Isaiah 43:25 ESV

My thoughts:

Here's a verse I've read many times but somehow never saw how significant it is. Just think, here He says He blots our transgressions out for His own sake and forgets our sins. I've always gotten the part where He blots out our transgressions for our sake but never for His. That's how much He loves us. Let it be clear, if you were the only one who ever lived, He would have given His Son just for you. That is how much He loves us. If that is how much He loves us, how can we show our love for Him? I don't know about you, but when I realize His love for me. I want to cast all else aside and let Him live and love through me. Again, we must focus, love Him, and sense His love for us.

What I heard from the Lord:

"Would I have created you if I didn't love you even before your creation? Do you think I didn't know the heartache you would bring? Do you not think I could have created something else instead of you? No, it is you who, out of all My creation, I love with enduring, never-ending love. I did it all for you. I ask so little of you. Hear Me and know Me. Fellowship with Me. Is that so much to ask? You are My very image. Think on that."

19 – Cyrus Called by Name

"Thus says the Lord to his anointed, to Cyrus, whose right hand I have grasped, to subdue nations before him and to loose the belts of kings, to open doors before him that gates may not be closed:"

Isaiah 45:1 ESV

My thoughts:

Cyrus was called by name about 100 or so years before he was born. It was foretold Judah would be conquered and exiled for 70 years. At the end of that time, a king named Cyrus would free Judah and allow them to return to their homeland. At that time, it was common for conquering nations to exile the conquered nations throughout their kingdoms and move others into the area vacated by them in order to assimilate and increase their power. It all happened just as prophesied. This is the first time his name has been mentioned. The Babylonians had taken several nations captive. Cyrus not only freed Judah but several other nations as well.

God does what He says He will do. He cannot lie.

What I heard from the Lord:

"I will use that which I will use whether it be a king or a pauper. Whether it be one who knows Me or one who does not. In this regard, I am no respecter of people, but I do it all for my chosen, you whom I have called, and you who have accepted My call. It is all because of My love for you. Know this and be free of and from fear."

20 – The Fruit of the Spirit – Keep in Step

"But the fruit of the Spirit is love, joy, peace, patience, kindness, goodness, faithfulness, gentleness, self-control; against such things there is no law. If we live by the Spirit, let us also keep in step with the Spirit."

Galatians 5:22-23,25 ESV

My thoughts:

Michael Timmis wrote, "The way I define love is by using the fruit of the Spirit, which starts with love. I believe that joy is love rejoicing, peace is love at rest, patience is love waiting, kindness is love interacting, goodness is love initiating, faithfulness is love keeping its word, gentleness is love empathizing, and self-control is love resisting temptation."

I try to look at it by putting it into questions:

Ask yourself these questions.

Am I filled with love for my Lord and my neighbor?

Do I take joy in the life the Lord has given me, and does it show in how I live?

Do I have peace in my heart that cannot be disturbed because of the Spirit in me?

Is there patience in what I say, do, and in my reactions to the Lord and to others?

Do I show kindness to those I live with and to those in need?

Does my faith show by what I do and how I react to the Lord and others?

Does the goodness of God flow through me so others can know it in spite of circumstances?

Is my demeanor gentle, and do the words and deeds that come from me show it?

Do I have self-control in the face of all temptation?

What I heard from the Lord:

"Love your neighbor as yourselves. If you do this, you have fulfilled the law. By loving your neighbor and displaying the fruit of My Spirit, you are displaying to the whole world your love for Me. Show it not only by your actions and deeds but with the words that come from your mouths. I know you love me, but that is just a reflection of the love I have for you. Soon though, we will be Face to face. What a glorious day!"

21 – Share All Good Things

"Let the one who is taught the word share all good things with the one who teaches."

Galatians 6:6 ESV

My thoughts:

This verse is pointed toward support of one who teaches by those who are being taught, but as I read this, I see something else as well.

I have the spiritual gift of teaching. I didn't know that when I began teaching. I tried it like other spiritual gifts. This is the one that stuck far more than any of the other gifts. It's in teaching that I find my great joy. I love to learn from others, and I love for others to learn through what's been given to me. I pray that if you haven't searched out your Spiritual gift(s), you will, and it will give you as much joy as my gift has given me. Our greatest joy, though, must be in the Giver.

What I heard from the Lord:

"I am the One from through all knowledge and wisdom comes. I am the Fountain of Truth. Come to My Fountain and partake of it. It is always flowing. All who would learn of My Word and how to share it with others must drink of it. Be free with what you learn and know. Share it with others, but also be quick to hear what I have shown others and test it."

22 – Just One of those Days

"Even as he chose us in him before the foundation of the world, that we should be holy and blameless before him. In love he predestined us for adoption to himself as sons through Jesus Christ, according to the purpose of his will,"

Ephesians 1:4-5 ESV

My thoughts:

Sometimes things just get to us without explanation. Then I read that He chose us, that we should be holy and blameless before Him.

So, where do we go from here?

He chose us before the foundation of the world.

He made us holy and blameless before Him.

He predestined us for adoption to Himself.

Thank God that our salvation isn't dependent on our feelings; that in spite of ourselves, we are holy and blameless and are adopted sons of God Himself. We're all sons, by the way. In fact, we're all firstborn sons in the sight of God. It was the firstborn son who received the inheritance, and that's where we are.

So, when things start to get to us, what does that do for us in our present state? It does give us hope in spite of ourselves. Yes, these times will pass, and we'll get our focus back where it belongs. Our focus now should be: <u>What, God, are You teaching us through this?</u>

What I heard from the Lord:

"You are my sons and daughters. You are in Me, and I am in you. Where you go, I go. Where I go, you go. This is how it is to be. I see no blame in you, for I see you through the eyes of My Son. When you pray to Me, it is His voice that I hear. I called you from beyond eternity, and you answered. You accepted My call. Now you are forever Mine as I am yours. You will never be forsaken. As for you, My Son is the Pearl of Great Price, so you are to Me."

23 – YOU ARE MINE!

"For by grace you have been saved through faith. And this is not your own doing; it is the gift of God, not a result of works, so that no one may boast. For we are his workmanship, created in Christ Jesus for good works, which God prepared beforehand, that we should walk in them."

Ephesians 2:8-10 ESV

My thoughts:

Until recently I had looked at verses 8 and 9 and memorized them and meditated on them. What I overlooked is that verse 10 must be included as well. It adds a new element.

Verses 8 and 9 say we are saved through faith. That is true. It is not of our own doing for then we could boast. That is true. So, I still say we are saved through faith alone, but we must look at verse 10. We are saved through faith and faith alone, but we are also at the time of our salvation created in Jesus for good works.

The Lord knew us from eternity and prepared us to do these good works beforehand. Nothing else that we do will satisfy us except doing these assigned works, whatever they may be. We are all gifted differently and given the express ability for these works. As we are not able to boast about being saved by Christ through faith alone, neither are we able to boast about the good works He has assigned us. He has given us all the means to accomplish them as His Spirit lives inside us, leading and helping us along the way.

What I heard from the Lord:

"You receive pleasure and peace in doing My works, those works I have set aside for you since eternity. You are right, as you cannot boast in your salvation, neither can you boast in the works I have set before you. You have the joy of knowing you are doing My work, and I find pleasure in your pleasure. You are Mine. I will never let you go or allow the evil one to snatch you away. YOU ARE MINE!"

24 – Be Filled with the Fullness of God

"And to know the love of Christ that surpasses knowledge, that you may be filled with all the fullness of God."

Ephesians 3:19 ESV

My thoughts:

To be filled with all the fullness of God is also to be filled with the Spirit, which is of Christ. When I think of God the Father, the first thing that comes to my mind is power. When I think of the Spirit, I think of communion. When I think of Christ, I think of love. Now, that's just me, but I know all are God, and All are One. Sometimes it's hard to wrap my little mind around God, and sometimes in my feeble attempts to know Him, I compartmentalize.

I think of my grasp of God as looking at a large picture, but from my vantage point, I can only see a little bit at a time. I can never step far enough away to see it in all of His glory. As the Spirit fills my heart, and as I read His Word and meditate on it, I know I'll never grasp all of Him on this Earth, but what He's given me is enough, but still, I thirst for more.

What I heard from the Lord:

"You have answered My call. You have invited Me in as I knocked on the door of your heart. Now I live not only with you but in you as well. Let me heap riches upon you as you could never believe. I speak not of the riches of the world, but My riches that never rot nor decay. My riches sustain you and keep you close. Let us commune together now and forever. Bathe in My Love that surrounds and gives life."

25 – Humble and Gentle

"Always be humble and gentle. Be patient with each other, making allowance for each other's faults because of your love."

Ephesians 4:2 NLT

My thoughts:

Can we ALWAYS be humble and gentle? How can we be patient, always overlooking others' faults? It is because of the love God has placed in us. All of that sounds so good, but what about when it doesn't happen?

What I heard from the Lord:

"When your eyes are upon Me, the Focus of your life, you will be humble and gentle. That is My Spirit flowing through you. As for overlooking the faults in others, remember not to overlook your own faults first. Allow Me to restore you to your proper focus and place in you My abundant love. You have enough to do in your walk with Me. My Spirit is in you. My Spirit is there to bear you up when you stumble. If you simply walk alongside My Spirit, there will be a lot less stumbling and a lot more focus on Me."

26 – Light Dawns in the Darkness

"Light dawns in the darkness for the upright; he is gracious, merciful, and righteous. It is well with the man who deals generously and lends; who conducts his affairs with justice."

Psalm 112:4-5 ESV

My thoughts, my prayer:

Two short verses that hold so much. The basis in the Old Testament is to be revealed in the New Testament in Galatians 5:22-23. We were in darkness, and the Light of the Lord dawns upon us through His Spirit alive within each of our hearts.

My prayer:

Lord, help us to stay upright in Your Presence despite the pressures of this world. Let us display Your mercy in our lives. Let righteousness be seen in our hearts and in all we do. Let us be generous in our prayers and our earthly treasures. Let us not only lend but give from our hearts. Lord, let those around us see Your justice in all we do and in the way we conduct our lives. In the name of Jesus, Amen.

What I heard from the Lord:

"May your hearts glow with My love that surpasses all others. May others see Me when they look upon you. Be ready in every season to display the fruit hidden in your hearts. Be lavish with the fruit that grows in season and out. Share your abundance as I share Mine with you. Be a lamp in this ever-darkening world."

27 – Husbands, Love Your Wives; Wives, Respect Your Husbands

"Husbands, love your wives, as Christ loved the church and gave himself up for her, that he might sanctify her, having cleansed her by the washing of water with the word, so that he might present the church to himself in splendor, without spot or wrinkle or any such thing, that she might be holy and without blemish."

Ephesians 5:25-27 ESV

My thoughts:

The previous verses relate to a wife's place in marriage, but Paul had a lot to say about the husband's place as well. This tells us how much a husband must love his wife. It is not a suggestion. It is a command. Like all His commands, they are for our own good. As we are all living stones of the Church, we are all part of the bride of Christ. He gave Himself up for us, the Church.

It's a two-way street. Husbands are commanded to treat their wives with this same kind of care. How difficult can it be for a wife loved by her husband as Christ loves the Church to respond in kind; to one who puts her interests before his own?

What I heard from the Lord:

"I love you. I love you deeply and completely. My love for you brings not only words but a deep commitment. You are of My very soul. I have given so much to you. How much more can I give you than My own life? Wives, respect your husbands. Husbands love your wives as I love My bride. Love in a sacrificial manner for all eternity to see. You will be blessed beyond anything you ever expected."

28 – Withstand in the Armor of God

"Therefore take up the whole armor of God, that you may be able to withstand in the evil day, and having done all, to stand firm."

Ephesians 6:13 ESV

My thoughts - A Vision:

I saw a man armed with a bow and arrow. He was in dark armor. He was slightly crouched, with a bow getting ready to shoot me. I had no fear, for I had on the full armor of God. The surroundings were dark, but I could see him clearly. He was crouching in some kind of rubble around him. I was meditating on "Christ is in you," so, therefore, you can look forward to sharing in God's glory. It's that simple.

A dear friend helps when I cannot understand a vision which was the case with this one. Here is part of what she said, "Dark is the enemy. Crouched, ready to shoot flaming arrows, but you have on the whole armor, which startled him; he wasn't ready for that. The fact that you could see him clearly shows that God is showing you the truth for spiritual warfare."

My thoughts:

She was right on. Unfortunately, we are not always in the full armor of God, or where we need to be. Being in His armor is so important. He is always at our right hand, ready for our call when we see trouble, but also He heads off much of what we don't know. Sometimes though, we need to call before He acts. For me, my goal is to constantly be in His full armor. I know I am being a bit redundant here, but it can't be stressed enough.

What I heard from the Lord:

"I am your strength. I am your protection. When you put on My armor, you arm yourselves with My Son. He is your armor. He is your strength. He is your peace in the midst of battle, for He has overcome the world. You may rest in that armor, for you rest in Him. Think now. He is Truth. He is Salvation. He is Righteousness. He is your Faith. He is your

Sword. He is the Word. It is His strength that takes salvation to others. It's not about you and what you can do, but your faith in Him and what He can do."

29 – He Will Bring Your Good Works to Completion

"And I am sure of this, that he who began a good work in you will bring it to completion at the day of Jesus Christ."

Philippians 1:6 ESV

My thoughts, my prayer:

Oh Lord, my God, Who's promises never fail. When you sent your Holy Spirit to live in our hearts, the GOOD work began. Thank You, Father, for Your Spirit living in me. Whatever I do, wherever I go, You are with me. You will never let me go. I cannot hide from You, but why would I ever want to do that? You are my Savior and Lord. I never want anything to come between us. As for the ups and downs in my life, some were meant for evil, but You changed them for good. Yes, Lord, You licked my wounds and made me stronger than ever. Thank You, Lord, for Your promises that never fail. Thank You, Lord, for what You're making me to be now and forever. Amen

What I heard from the Lord:

"Rest assured, what I start, I finish. I have begun a good work in you. That good work continues through today. There are good works beyond what you do here. Wait and see what wonderful works I have ready for you at the proper time and place. I love My people, My Church, My Bride. Stand and let Me wash over you with My love, extravagant and pure. Rest assured; I am with you always."

30 – A Fortified City

"And I, behold, I make you this day a fortified city, an iron pillar, and bronze walls, against the whole land, against the kings of Judah, its officials, its priests, and the people of the land."

Jeremiah 1:18 ESV

My thoughts:

Jeremiah was created in his time at a place of God's choosing to bring His Word to a country run amuck. He was given strength as that of a fortified city against the whole land of Judah. He was set not only against the king and his officials, but the people themselves.

What I heard from the Lord:

"You have been fortified by My Spirit against your land. Your land began in service to Me and flourished for a time, but now that time is at an end, as was Judah. I created you for this time and in this place that you, like Jeremiah, may stand against the princes and principalities of the land. You must stand against those souls that have walked away from Me and gone their own way. Their care is only for themselves and what they can get from this world. They have lost their way. Their focus is only on their self-gratification. You, you stand in the gap. Let it be known that by your actions, I am still here, but the time is short. Stand in the gap."

Chapter 10: October

1 – Work for His Good Pleasure

"For it is God who works in you, both to will and to work for his good pleasure."

Philippians 2:13 ESV

My thoughts:

God works in us.

He gives pleasure in our hearts to do His work.

That work is for His good pleasure.

God works in each of us who know Him. It is by His will that we work for His pleasure. As we listen to His Spirit, the works we do will also be our pleasure. How is He working in you today?

What I heard from the Lord:

"Live your lives as for Me. You work when you don't even know you are working, for by My Spirit you must do the works I have ordered for you. You take pleasure in those works, but My pleasure is greater for I know where you came from, where you are now, and where you are going. Take joy in doing that what I have set before you for it was by design that the works you do can only be done best by you, but beware. If you step away, My works will yet be done, but by another. Take hold and accept My blessings."

2 – Let the Past Stay in the Past

"Brothers, I do not consider that I have made it my own. But one thing I do: forgetting what lies behind and straining forward to what lies ahead,"

Philippians 3:13 ESV

My thoughts, my prayer:

Everything we are is measured by our past. What we did, how we handled adversity, and how we dealt with praise. Looking forward, we are strengthened or weakened by our past. It's never good to dwell on the past, for it can't be changed, but our future is a different thing altogether.

My Prayer:

Oh Lord, help me keep the past in the past as far as following You. Let my focus ever be upon You. Our pasts are made up of good, bad, and neutral memories in our sight. You worked for good in all of them. Let us look forward each day to what You will do in our lives and how we may serve You. You are the Potter, and we are the clay, yet made in Your image with Your Holy Spirit living within each of us, protecting and leading us onward. Teach us, Lord, to wait as You wait on us. In the name of Jesus, Amen.

What I heard from the Lord:

"You forget, then you forget not. If you focus on your failures, you will not have your focus on Me. That is where your focus must be. Live today for Me. Let today be the foundation for tomorrow. Grow from My Word. Grow from your lives as you see My Hand in each moment. Look to Me as I care for you and nurse your self-inflicted wounds. Grow in My love and love one another as I have loved you."

3 – Anxiety or Peace

"Do not be anxious about anything, but in everything by prayer and supplication with thanksgiving let your requests be made known to God. And the peace of God, which surpasses all understanding, will guard your hearts and your minds in Christ Jesus."

Philippians 4:6-7 ESV

My thoughts:

Anxiety: intense, excessive, and persistent worry and fear about everyday situations. Why should we have it? If we believe in God, is that not enough? Even the demons know God. What are our prayers? Do we think God is our genie who should give us whatever we ask? NO, by asking with prayer and supplication WITH thanksgiving that we bring our requests and allow Him to weigh them. Let it go and let God's peace surround and envelop us. Let Him guard our hearts and minds through His Spirit dwelling in us.

What I heard from the Lord:

"My peace I give you, not as the world gives, but true peace without any anxiety. Turn your anxieties into prayer, and I will turn your prayer into peace. Let go of worry. Embrace My Spirit. Do you think you can change anything by your worry? No, of course not. Worry generates stress, and the world has stress enough. Give yourselves wholeheartedly to Me. Let me hold you, caress you, and prepare you for what's to come in My strength and love and not that of the world. The world will fail you, but I, NEVER!"

4 – All Things for and Through Him

"For by him, all things were created, in heaven and on earth, visible and invisible, whether thrones or dominions or rulers or authorities—all things were created through him and for him."

Colossians 1:16 ESV

My thoughts:

Wow! That says a lot. You and I were created by and for Him. All we can see and all we can't see or know was created by Him and for Him. Even those who rule us, whether good or bad, were created by and for Him. It should give us a small inkling about the presence and power of our Lord and Savior.

Thank You, Lord, for lifting up such a worm as I. Psalm 22:6

What I heard from the Lord:

"When you complain, I hear the murmuring of My people in the wilderness. How can you complain when I have given you everything to sustain you on this earth? No grumbling. I won't hear it. Whenever you even get a hint of grumbling in your hearts, think back on My graciousness to you. My Son had to suffer and die so that you might live an abundant, never-ending life. When you look around your world and see injustice, murder, theft, and every kind of evil, look too at all the good that still remains. That good comes from Me. You live in a time long ago prophesized. Be thankful for who you are and when you are. I am the Lord your God."

5 – Hope of Glory

"To them, God chose to make known how great among the Gentiles are the riches of the glory of this mystery, which is Christ in you, the hope of glory."

Colossians 1:27 ESV

My thoughts:

We have been given Christ. He resides in us through the Holy Spirit. He has given us the Hope of Glory. The Holy Spirit residing in us is the down payment of what is to come. In the meantime, He lives in each of our hearts preparing us for the path we must follow each and every day. He seals our hearts.

What I heard from the Lord:

"You are my chosen in all the earth. You are My beloved of all peoples. It's for you that I gave My all. Stay close in My protection. You are woven into My Son. Trust in Him as you trust in Me. Live in My love but share it whenever and wherever you can to fulfill My commission."

6 – Walk in Him

"Therefore, as you received Christ Jesus the Lord, so walk in him, rooted and built up in him and established in the faith, just as you were taught, abounding in thanksgiving."

Colossians 2:6-7 ESV

My thoughts:

We have received Christ, so we are privileged to walk with Him, not in front, not behind but beside Him. When His Word is rooted in our hearts, it builds us up, and our faith is established, yet that faith needs to be exercised to make it ever stronger. It is rooted in our hearts as we are rooted in His Word. As our faith grows so does our love for Christ with thanksgiving when it all comes together, what an incredible blessing.

What I heard from the Lord:

"As you walk in My Spirit, you become more and more rooted in My Son. As your roots grow deeper, My Spirit and My Word will nourish your spirit beyond your dreams. Eat of My Word. Walk in My Spirit. Drink of My Presence."

7 – Do Not Rejoice at the Fall of an Enemy

"Do not rejoice when your enemy falls, and let not your heart be glad when he stumbles,"

Proverbs 24:17 ESV

My thoughts:

The first question is, "Who is our enemy?" At this point in my life, I don't recognize anyone I know as my enemy. But what about those we don't know who are in power above us, and we perceive them as enemies for their evil?

These are people we know of but have no personal knowledge. I often find myself with a critical spirit towards them. When I do, I try to get my focus back on Christ. I repent and repent again but fall back into the same place. Lord, what am I to do?

What I heard from the Lord:

"Is it not I who put your leaders in power? Are they not cut from the same cloth as those around you? As the people turn further against Me, I will allow and confirm those who are in power as I did with Manasseh. People today are no different than in the time of Jeremiah; no, all have the same sinful nature. You, you who know Me. Don't fret; don't grumble. Pray to Me and let it go. Do you think I have no power over them? You, get and keep your focus on Me. If you have to do it over and over again, so be it, but keep on."

8 – How to Answer

"Let your speech always be gracious, seasoned with salt, so that you may know how you ought to answer each person."

Colossians 4:6 ESV

My thoughts and my prayer:

The previous verse tells us to walk in wisdom toward outsiders making the best use of the time.

Lord, let our speech always be gracious and seasoned with salt. Show us how we should answer each person, no matter the subject. Lord, let our dependence be upon you and not ourselves. Let us reach toward Your Word and the strength of Your Spirit in our hearts. In the name of Jesus, Amen.

What I heard from the Lord:

"How you answer others comes after you know how to answer Me. If you can't answer My Word, how can you answer anyone else, whether brothers and sisters or those outside the Church? Just stop putting your effort into it and allow Me to work through you. Let Me speak through your hearts that you may not only know but give the glory to Me. When you do that, do you not think that I won't raise you up? Let My love live in you."

9 – Keeping the Lord's Statutes

"Oh, that my ways may be steadfast in keeping your statutes! Then I shall not be put to shame, having my eyes fixed on all your commandments. I will praise you with an upright heart when I learn your righteous rules. I will keep your statutes; do not utterly forsake me!"

Psalm 119:5-8 ESV

My thoughts:

I love Psalm 119. It's all about the Lord and his statutes, precepts, and laws, but we shouldn't get caught up on these, but only on Jesus. It is His statutes, precepts, and laws we must guard in our hearts that we may not sin against Him. The Word (Bible) was given so that we might not perish. It showed the way to Jesus. I am so grateful that He took upon Himself my sins. The law led the way, but Jesus fulfilled it when not one of us could. He loves us that much and won't let us go.

What I heard from the Lord:

"My Word from old was wrapped in a Mystery. That Mystery is My Son. Listen to Him, and the Mystery is revealed. My laws are many, but they were all fulfilled in My Son. His yoke is easy. With His Word, you are free of the old law but subject to His commands. Embrace them, for they are life. Do not be discouraged. Look deep in your hearts, and there you will find Him fresh and new. His Spirit lives in you, walks with you, and calls you His own."

10 – God's Word in Our Hearts

"Thy word have I hid in mine heart, that I might not sin against thee."

Psalm 119:11 KJV

My thoughts:

Today, I call upon the King James Version because that's how I memorized this verse. This is a verse to memorize in any translation. It's very clear. It tells us what to do and why to do it. It sets the reason for memorizing scripture. It's always been hard for me to memorize scripture. When I was younger, I persevered and memorized even chapters. I did this specifically so I could bring those verses back up and meditate on them at any time. Just keep in the Word. Read it and meditate on it. You might be surprised at what may happen.

What I heard from the Lord:

"My Word, promises made, and promises kept; words that bring life if only you will listen and keep My commands. My Son is that Word. With My Spirit in your hearts and your eyes on My Word, you are safe and in My arms. I will never leave nor forsake you, for you are the living breathing stones that reign with Me forever. Stay in My Word. As I live in your hearts, so you live in Mine."

11 – The Coming of the Lord

"For the Lord himself will descend from heaven with a cry of command, with the voice of an archangel, and with the sound of the trumpet of God. And the dead in Christ will rise first. Then we who are alive, who are left, will be caught up together with them in the clouds to meet the Lord in the air, and so we will always be with the Lord."

1 Thessalonians. 4:16-17 ESV

My Thoughts:

I don't know when this will be. I sense that it is not that far off. We need to be ready. We need to continually stand in His armor. Take every opportunity to make certain all know how important this is. It is for all eternity. Let not anyone be lost that can be saved. That is what I sense, but there are many who take these verses differently. I see it as a separate event than the resurrection. They do not. Am I wrong? Are they wrong? Does it affect our salvation? I don't see how it does, but I think we just need to keep our minds on Christ. That is enough. Let His Will be done.

What I heard and saw from the Lord - A Vision:

"I see a golden eagle surrounded by clouds of gold. Those are the colors I see. Something great is happening. Jesus is coming even more majestic than we could ever understand. I see the dead rise. They have already been consummated with their eternal flesh. I see now those golden clouds were those who have passed on to be in Heaven and now return for the finale. I see more coming up; it is those who have never seen heaven. As they rise, their bodies are changed, and they are clothed with heavenly garments. I see not only joy but awe on their radiant faces. It is happening so fast, I can't keep up, but now there I am in their midst, rising with them. It is a glorious day. Thank You, Jesus."

12 – Be Sober

"But since we belong to the day, let us be sober, having put on the breastplate of faith and love, and for a helmet the hope of salvation. For God has not destined us for wrath, but to obtain salvation through our Lord Jesus Christ,"

1 Thessalonians. 5:8-9 ESV

My thoughts:

It's interesting that Paul in Ephesians 6:16 wrote, "The breastplate is of righteousness," whereas here it is of faith and love. The helmet of salvation is the same in both passages. Ephesians goes on to speak about the full armor of God. Do not faith and love follow along with righteousness?

What I heard from the Lord:

"Love, faith, and salvation; No matter what, love is the first and last. All else will fail, but love is forever. Your faith in acting out with the love I have given you demonstrates My love. Your salvation is because of My love for you and your faith in Me. These are the basic framework, but it is wise to be in My full armor. Be sober, and don't be caught off guard."

13 – Seek Him with All Your Heart

"You will seek me and find me, when you seek me with all your heart."

Jeremiah 29:13 ESV

My thoughts:

Only He can fill our hearts. That is how He has made us. For those who speak out, "There is no God," they know deep down inside that they are speaking a lie. Seek wherever they may, they cannot be satisfied in life without Him in their hearts.

What I heard from the Lord:

"You are born with a quest in your hearts. You are born with empty hearts that only My Spirit can fill. Seek Me. I am in My Word. I am in the forests and rivers. I am in the ocean. I am in the mountains and the skies but know this, I surround you on every side. Just call on Me with all your hearts, and I am there. Look inside, not on the surface, but deep inside. Can't you see Me? My Spirit is within you. I protect you. I commune with you deeper and with greater love than you can ever know elsewhere. Stay with Me. Abide with Me. Love Me, for I give you the greatest love you can ever know. Love one another with My love. I am here in your midst."

14 – Turn From Worthless Things

"Turn my eyes from looking at worthless things; and give me life in your ways."

Psalm 119:37 ESV

My thoughts:

What are the worthless things in our lives? Could it be anything that draws our focus from God? What does it mean that He gives us life in His ways? Most of us have a lot of leisure time to spend however we wish. How much of that time do we spend in God's Word, in prayer, or in His ministry? I know I can do more. All of us can always do more, at the same time it should not be drudgery for us. Look for balance.

What I heard from the Lord:

"There are many things in this world that are good for your life. There is food, sleep, and love of others, but not love of things. Whatever builds you up in this world, for Me, is good. Worthless things are those that draw your attention away from Me. You have been given an allotted number of years. Use them wisely, not fretting about the next new great thing in the world, but about who I am and My love for you. I have the greatest of love for My people, those who call on Me as Lord and Savior. In My Word, there is life. Rest in love given you moment by moment with My Spirit living in you. He guides you into that which is good, loving, and righteous. Listen and allow Him to be your guide."

15 – Do the Right Thing

"And we have confidence in the Lord about you, that you are doing and will do the things that we command."

2 Thessalonians 3:4 ESV

My thoughts:

A Church word for the year, **"Do the Next Right Thing."** hit me like a ton of bricks several years ago. I've made it a part of my life. It has become my motto. We must always strive to do the next right thing regardless of the cost. Don't look back. Keep looking forward. Keep your focus on the Lord. Let it be your goal to do what's right and be blessed as you move closer to the Lord. For those times we are wrong, we need to remedy the problem by admitting our error and doing what is right.

What I heard from the Lord:

"Follow My commands, and all will be well with you. Doing My commands is doing the right thing. Sometimes it will be easy for you, but then there will be hard times when I still ask the same from you. Even then, you must do the right thing and follow My commands. All My commands are for your good and the good of others in your lives. In doing the right thing, do not count the costs; just do the right thing."

16 – Great and Hidden Things

"Call to me and I will answer you, and will tell you great and hidden things that you have not known."

Jeremiah. 33:3 ESV

My thoughts, my prayer:

Lord, the more I know, the more I realize I know so little. You have shown me great and hidden things that, before asking You into my heart, I was clueless about. As I go through Your Word, I find nuggets of gold that I've never noticed before. That is the case with this verse. I pause, Lord, to think on these great words, this promise. What great wonder will come next? I can hardly wait. I pray in the name of Jesus, Amen.

What I heard from the Lord:

"Look at your life. What can you tell Me about what I have shown you? I lit up your life when you called Me into your heart. I opened a whole new way of looking at things; people, possessions, My handiwork, where you fit in My plan, but only partially there. There is so much yet to come. So much I want you to see and enjoy. Now you only see in shadows, but what's to come is the real thing. You, yourself, are but a shadow upon this shadow world, but you will find reality in all its fullness, in all its glory. Yes, think of this as but a poor reflection of My reality. Just wait a little while, and it will come."

17 – No One Listened – Is Anyone Listening Now?

"But neither he nor his servants nor the people of the land listened to the words of the Lord that he spoke through Jeremiah the prophet."

Jeremiah 37:2 ESV

My thoughts:

Jeremiah was working his heart out for the Lord. Barach, the servant of Jeremiah, fearlessly and tirelessly did everything Jeremiah asked, all to no avail. The hearts of the people were hard and were going about their business even as the Babylonians were at the city gates. It's kind of what was happening on the Titanic when it was sinking. The band kept playing, and those on-board thought, "Surely, we are safe."

Those who listened to Jeremiah were ignored by the mass of the population. Does anything sound familiar here? Our nation, our world seems to be assailed on every side, from pandemics to border issues and far more, but how many who are looking for real answers are ready? I sense a revival along with a winnowing in the Church at large. I also see it as our last hope. I hope I'm wrong, but I don't get that sense.

What I heard from the Lord:

"As Jeremiah was born for his time, so you have been born for your time. All I ask is that you give Me your unconditional love as I give Mine to you. You can see the season, but the time must yet be hidden. Follow My commands. Love your neighbors so much that you can't stand the thought of them perishing and not doing My will. There is still time. I will not let one perish who can be saved."

18 – Follow the Commands of Christ

"I am a companion of all who fear you, of those who keep your precepts."

Psalm 119:63 ESV

My thoughts, my prayer:

All Your People Lord; all who call You Lord and worship You; of these we are companions. We share Your love. We worship You. We give You our hearts. We give You free reign in our lives. We look forward for opportunities to share Your great love with one another and with those who don't know You. We encourage one another in every way we can and refrain from discouragement. We rejoice in one another's victories and share in the bad times. Lord, we are Your children, and our desire is to keep the commands of Jesus to the best of our ability with Your Holy Spirit guiding us moment by moment. Thank You, Lord, for not only calling us but choosing us as well. Lord, I pray you are not disappointed in us today but that You give us Your approval. In Jesus' precious name, Amen.

What I heard from the Lord:

"Fellowship, joyous fellowship is what we have when you follow the Words of My Son. Boast in Him. Share what has been given to you with your blessed companions in communion with Me. When you draw close to one another, you draw closer to Me. That gives Me great joy. You are made for community and not to stand alone. Draw from My love and share it liberally throughout your daily walk."

19 – Wait on the Lord

"Whether it is good or bad, we will obey the voice of the Lord our God to whom we are sending you, that it may be well with us when we obey the voice of the Lord our God."

Jeremiah 42:6 ESV

My thoughts:

The remnant left in Jerusalem after Babylon had victory over the people, showed themselves to have learned nothing. In this case, they had already made up their minds to leave and go to Egypt no matter what God said. They wanted God's blessing, but they would carry out their own plans no matter what God said. There is a lesson here:

Pray first for direction with thankfulness to Him.

Prepare your heart for God's answer.

Listen for His answer. It may come from another; from His Word; opened or closed doors, or from His quiet voice in your ear.

What if you cannot hear His voice? Is that telling you to go on anyway unless He stops you? Or is it telling you to wait? If you feel you cannot wait, what then? Wait some more. Jeremiah, in this case, waited ten days before receiving a response from God. Perhaps He is trying to teach us patience.

We've all been in their shoes. The next time we're in this position, give God a chance to give us His answer. These are brave words from someone who has been on both sides of this, but for my future, I pray I will wait on the Lord no matter what.

What I heard from the Lord:

"There is never any bad in what I tell you to do. You may perceive some things as bad, but I use everything for your good, no matter what your perceptions may be. When you want My direction, ask Me. Wait for Me, and follow my Word. I will not lead you astray but in fulfillment of your destiny. Call upon Me in time of decisions and wait. Is that so hard? Think about how much I wait for you."

20 – Encourage One Another

"Do not rebuke an older man but encourage him as you would a father, younger men as brothers, older women as mothers, younger women as sisters, in all purity."

1 Timothy 5:1-2 ESV

My thoughts:

This is wise advice from Paul that should ring as true today as when it was written. We should be respectful of our elders, and younger men as our brothers. In the last part of verse 2, it says, "(encourage) younger women as sisters, in all purity."

In Paul's day, young women needed an extra measure of protection, especially if they had no father or husband to protect them. The word here is not to take advantage of women in any way. In today's society, there are men who still take advantage of women. It is sad when anyone takes advantage of another for any reason. Let us have fewer rebukes with one another and more encouragement.

What I heard from the Lord:

"Today, love one another as I have loved you, taking no advantage of another but looking out for the betterment of all you encounter. Be especially nurturing to all who come to you in love and in need. Guard them up to and including your life. Let My love flow through you in ever-increasing measure."

21 – My Hands Have Fashioned You

"Your hands have made and fashioned me, give me understanding that I may learn your commandments."

Psalm 119:73 ESV

My thoughts; my prayer:

Your hands have fashioned me. Give me understanding. When, O Lord, did You decide to fashion us? When, O Lord, did You decide to give us understanding? Yes, Lord, I see You from before time; He who exists outside of time. He who has all eternity to spend with each one of us. Yes, Lord, You have made us for Your good pleasure. I pray, Lord, that our lives do and will always give You pleasure, for that is why You made us. As we were made to have a need for You, it is true that You have a need for us. You crave our worship, and that is what we were made to do. Lord, we ask that You enjoy our worship on this day as You fill the void in our hearts with Your Holy Spirit so that we may enjoy Your presence. In the name of Jesus, Amen.

What I heard from the Lord:

"Before there was time, I envisioned you in My heart. I knew you before you were born. It was Me who set you in this time and in this place that you may flourish before Me. I gave you the understanding that the only thing that can satisfy you is Me, so I have sent My Spirit to live in your hearts as you live in this world. This is but a down payment of what's to come. Take My yoke, for it is easy. These are my commandments for your good that you may not stray and suffer harm. Be blessed in what you have been given, and do not hide it from others."

22 – What I Have Entrusted to You

"Which is why I suffer as I do. But I am not ashamed, for I know whom I have believed, and I am convinced that he is able to guard until that day what has been entrusted to me."

2 Timothy 1:12 ESV

My thoughts:

There were times I should have spoken out and didn't. There were times when I should have stood up, and I didn't. There are times when I should have testified, and I didn't. We must put those things behind us, though, and look forward. We must keep on the path set before us and keep our focus on Jesus. To look back is to look at failure. To look forward is to look on Christ. He has entrusted us with His Word, our faith, and the love of God Himself. Let us never be afraid to show His love to those in need, those who are desperate to know the Creator, but also to withhold it from those who would trample it in the dust. We shall not cast His pearls to the swine but to every living person hungry for those pearls. Let us listen to the Holy Spirit and do His will.

What I heard from the Lord:

"I have entrusted to you My Word that you may pass it on to those in need and to those who hunger and thirst for it. You must humble yourselves and thirst for My Word, but let your thirst be quenched by My Spirit. Let your hunger be abated by the reading of My Word. Look around. What do you see? Look closely, and you will see a world without shame, a world in turmoil. Time is short, and I am coming. Keep the faith and pass it on whenever and wherever you can. You are in My embrace."

23 – Nor Should the Church Entangle Herself in the World

"No soldier gets entangled in civilian pursuits since his aim is to please the one who enlisted him."

2 Timothy 2:4 ESV

My thoughts:

As I read this, I was reminded of a word I received some time ago. When I entered the military. I agreed to give three years of my life to the government in the protection of our country and to use me as they saw best. I trusted the government with my life no matter what. When I accepted Christ, I agreed to give Him the rest of my life to use as He sees best. I must trust Christ with my life no matter what.

I know where my focus is today, but where is the focus of the Church? When I look into the Church, I see others just like me with their focus on Christ, yet I know some have their focus elsewhere.

I wrote about a vision of the Church earlier. This is a more recent vision where I saw her again, only much different. This time I saw her not as she is now, but what she will be.

What I heard from the Lord – A vision of the Church

"I see the Bride of Christ again. This time she is dressed in pure white, kneeling to her Master; no longer caught by the World. He turned to her, took her hands in His and lifted her up. They stood there for a moment gazing at one another then He took her into His arms, and they embraced. They were on a dance floor. As they danced, the bride kept in perfect step with her Master no matter the changes in music or tempo. She never took her eyes off Him. There were others on the floor, but my vision was filled only with Them. Revival and winnowing are on the way."

24 – God's Breath

"All Scripture is breathed out by God and profitable for teaching, for reproof, for correction, and for training in righteousness, that the man of God may be complete, equipped for every good work."

2 Timothy 3:16-17 ESV

My thoughts:

All scripture breathed out by God is profitable for our teaching, our reproof, our correction and for our training in righteousness.

This is all so we may be complete and equipped for every good work.

If scripture is breathed out by God, shouldn't it be inhaled by us? God's Word can be counted on to teach us, show us where we are wrong, and lead us to righteousness. With all this, we are ready to do whatever good work God sets before us.

A warning - if you feel like you are righteous, you are not. You have missed the mark. Ever understand that it is God's righteousness that lives within us, that we may feed from that righteousness through the Holy Spirit and give Him the glory.

What I heard from the Lord:

"As I breathed out into Adam, so he breathed in from Me. It was life to him. It is so with you today. As I breathe out My Word to you, you breathe it in. As My Word comes into you, your spirit is energized and fulfilled. It draws you toward fulfillment in Me, and it draws you to Me. Keep breathing in what I breathe into you through My Word, and it will be accounted well for you."

25 – The Time is Now

"For the time is coming when people will not endure sound teaching, but having itching ears they will accumulate for themselves teachers to suit their own passions,"

2 Timothy 4:3 ESV

My Thoughts:

When I read this, I couldn't help but wonder if Paul was referring to today's world. I remember the Billy Graham Crusades. I remember all the preparation months in advance for the churches to be ready for the coming crusade. There was training for participants of all levels; funds would be raised, and the word would go out by individuals, radio, and TV. Then the great week would begin. Thousands would be brought to Christ or rededicate their lives to Christ. The follow-up on those who had accepted Christ was another major part.

Today much of the world is a desolate land for the Lord. Where is He to be found? What about the U.S. and Canada? Millions here profess their faith in Christ, but where are they? Somewhere along the way, parents stopped teaching their children about Christ. Perhaps this is the time when people seem to put everything else between themselves and God and just give Him lip service or even less. Perhaps this is the time Paul was talking about in 2 Timothy.

What I heard from the Lord:

"Look around. What do you see? Look everywhere. The land is full of those who preach a different testament. There are mediums, worshipers of Satan, those who believe in nothing, and those who hear a gospel in their own churches that have left Me outside. Pray that awakening comes, no, a great awakening where My Word is spoken from the mountain tops, in the streets, the marketplaces, and yes, even in the churches. That time is at hand."

26 – Light My Path

"Your word is a lamp to my feet and a light to my path."

Psalm 119:105 ESV

My thoughts:

In the 1950's Jimmy Durante, a singer/actor/comedian, had a variety show on TV. At the end of each show, he would begin singing his farewell song for the week. It would be dark except for a single spotlight on him. As he sang, he would walk, one slow step at a time. A second spotlight would appear as he took his second step, then a third, and so forth. As he walked, his path behind would be lit up, but only enough light was provided for his next step.

God gives us enough light for the task at hand that He has given us. When we complete that task, He gives us enough light for the next task and so forth through our lives. We may be satisfied where we are, but as long as we breathe on this earth, God isn't finished with us, and there's always a next step. God is in control, and He gives us enough light for our needs.

What I heard from the Lord:

"You will never be left in darkness. I am Light. My Son is the Light of the World. In Him, there is no darkness. My Spirit resides in you, therefore, there is no darkness in you except for those doors that you have not yet opened to Me. Always look to the Light. Be restored in My love and My compassion. When you see the world, you see darkness, but still, you see the light of others who have My Spirit within them. They, too, are lights in a dark and darkening world. Take joy in the Light within you and cast this light wherever you go, in whatever you do."

27 – Listen for God's Voice

"I will take my stand at my watchpost and station myself on the tower and look out to see what he will say to me and what I will answer concerning my complaint. And the Lord answered me: Write the vision; make it plain on tablets, so he may run who reads it. For still the vision awaits its appointed time; it hastens to the end—it will not lie. If it seems slow, wait for it; it will surely come; it will not delay."

Habakkuk 2:1-3 ESV

My Thoughts:

Habakkuk had complaints about all the evil around him. He brought those complaints to the Lord. If we have complaints, shouldn't we be honest with the Lord and take them to Him like Thomas did in the Gospels? If our complaints are hidden, they can fester and get worse. If we put them out in the open to the Lord, He can cleanse us with His Spirit.

Habakkuk took a stand at his watch post and looked out to see what God would tell him and waited patiently for God's response. In our prayers, shouldn't we stand and wait to hear from God rather than going off on our own?

God's response is that Habakkuk should plainly write down what he heard and saw from the Lord. When we really listen, we will know the Lord's response. Consider journaling. We should write down what the Lord is telling us as plainly as we can for our reference so we can always refer to it not only for ourselves, but for others who may be included.

What I heard from the Lord:

"I wait for you. You have My Word. Read it. Believe it. Meditate on it. See if I will not come to you in a small voice and teach you meanings you may miss. Listen for My Voice. Write what I tell you. Test it against My Holy Word. Let us commune together. Let Me completely into your heart and see if I do not bless you beyond anything you have ever expected. Be blessed in My Word and in My Presence."

28 – Just Love One Another

"But avoid foolish controversies, genealogies, dissensions, and quarrels about the law, for they are unprofitable and worthless."

Titus 3:9 ESV

My thoughts:

There are many things this verse says to avoid. What stands out to me is to avoid meaningless quarrels. There are many different churches and denominations. There are only two things that we must agree on. Jesus is our Lord and Savior. The Bible is the infallible Word of God. It is these two things that unite us in faith. If there are arguments, ask, "Does this affect our salvation?" If not, let it go; if it does, perhaps it is an opportunity to share the LOVE of Christ.

What I heard from the Lord:

"My Word and My Son are One. All that came before He was born on earth pointed to Him. He gave you my Word as He walked the earth. All history is in His hands, including what has not yet occurred on the earth. As you love Him, I am loved by you. We are connected, and there is no seam between Us. Love one another as I have loved you. Let that sink in. That is how much I want you to love one another. Love without reservation or convenience. Just love!"

29 – His Mercies Renew Constantly

"The steadfast love of the Lord never ceases; his mercies never come to an end; they are new every morning; great is your faithfulness."

Lamentations 3:22-23 ESV

My thoughts:

Recently I have had several hospital stays, but I was always in God's hands, dependent on Him. Regardless of all the discomforts, it was still a good place to be. I took every advantage of showing Christ in me. I was reminded that, "The steadfast love of my Jesus never ever ceases. His mercies never end. They are new every morning. Great is His faithfulness" to us. Thank You, Lord, for Your never-ending mercies.

What I heard from the Lord:

"My mercies never end. They are constantly renewed in your lives. Think of what that means. Mercy! Mercy is for the lost; for those who have rebelled against Me. You, too, rebel against Me. It is your nature from before you receive your first gasp of air. I love you. It is that simple. I made you out of My love and desire for your companionship. Commune with Me today, in prayer, in meditation, in song, and in everything you do. Remember, I will always have mercy for you. Remember to have mercy toward all you meet."

30 – Steady Our Steps

"Keep steady my steps according to your promise, and let no iniquity get dominion over me."

Psalm 119:133 ESV

My thoughts; my prayer:

You, Lord, have made many promises. Some promises are to destruction, but more to graciousness for those who call You Lord and Savior. As we go on the journey You have planned for us, may our steps always be toward You and never away from You. "Lead us not into temptation but deliver us from evil." My prayer is that You and You alone have dominion over us. Whatever may come our way, help us to weigh it on Your scales. Let us keep short accounts with You. Let your desires be our desires as we take each step through the days you have given us on this Earth. Thank You, Lord, for Your Word and for each breath we take. May you forever be in our hearts. In the name of Jesus, Amen.

What I heard from the Lord:

"No, I will never let iniquity have dominion over you. My Spirit lives in you. You are guided by My Spirit. Yes, you sin. Yes, you stray. To have dominion over something is to dominate it and rob it of its freedom. Keep your accounts short with Me. Let yourselves allow Me to cleanse your hearts and give you restoration. Come to Me and remain in My presence."

31 – Temptation

"For because he himself has suffered when tempted, he is able to help those who are being tempted."

Hebrews 2:18 ESV

My thoughts:

To be tempted is not a sin unless you linger on it or follow through. Jesus was tempted yet did not sin. He is our Help if only we allow it.

What I heard from the Lord:

"**You can be tempted and not sin, yet you can be tempted and sin. When you let the temptation linger even for a moment, you have sinned. A fleeting thought or glance is temptation without sin, but to linger in the thought or glance is. Keep short accounts with Me. Keep in My Word. Stay in My presence. Keep your focus on Me, and all will be well with your soul.**"

Chapter 11: November

1 – Unbelief

"So we see that they were unable to enter because of unbelief."

Hebrews 3:19 ESV

My thoughts:

Israel lost everything because of unbelief. Those who started with Moses never entered the promised land, nor did Moses. They would believe for a while after seeing miracle after miracle but then slip back into their unbelief, and they lost everything. Where are we without our beliefs today? Without belief in the Lord, do we really have anything?

What I heard from the Lord:

"As I showed My people with Moses, I show you. They had miracles upon miracles yet still fell away. Look at the miracles in your own lives. Do you see them? Examine your past and your present. Is My call to you not a miracle? Think of the times you thought for certain you were going to be injured or even die. Did you see the miracles when I snatched you away so you could live for another day? You are where you are for a set time and for My purposes, yet you are here to flourish and have My Spirit in your hearts. Think about that miracle. My Spirit living in you? Why? Because of My great love for you. Enjoy My provisions and keep My Holy Word. You are loved far beyond your comprehension."

2 – Enter into God's Rest

"For whoever has entered God's rest has also rested from his works as God did from his."

Hebrews 4:10 ESV

My thoughts:

How do we enter God's rest? When God finished creation, He rested, yet He is still active. What have we finished? How have we experienced God's rest?

What I heard from the Lord:

"Think of your striving before you accepted My Son into your hearts. What were you doing if not striving, striving for the next bright object that entered your vision? Striving to get ahead in a world obsessed with power. Yet in all that, you were never satisfied until you took My Son into your heart and entered My rest. Here there is no more striving after things of the world but taking His yoke upon yourself, for His yoke is easy, and you find fulfillment only in Him. That is the rest you sought before He entered your heart. You are blessed in My Presence only through Him."

3 – Do Good People Go to Heaven?

"Salvation is far from the wicked, for they do not seek your statutes."

Psalm 119:155 ESV

My thoughts:

There are so many good people we should care for and pray for daily who do not know the Lord. We think they are lost at present, so we must continually pray for the Lord to keep knocking on the doors of their hearts. We desperately want their salvation, but they seem so distant, so disinterested in God's Word. They go on day after day, happy or sad with whatever the day brings them, never lifting their eyes to the Lord. They are sometimes polite when we bring up the Lord, just waiting for us to finish so they can go back to their lives.

Lord, what can we do for them except pray?

What I heard from the Lord:

"Live your life as a living sacrifice to Me. Keep your focus on Me but be an example of My Love so they may see My Spirit on your countenance. Let them see by your actions, including your patience. Let My patience be your patience. Let My love be your love. Let them see the joy on your face as you walk through your life on earth day by day, whether in good times or bad times. Focus, focus, focus on Me and My Word and trust My Word with all your heart. Trust in Me."

4 – Live God's Word

"And we desire each one of you to show the same earnestness to have the full assurance of hope until the end,"

Hebrews 6:11 ESV

My thoughts, a vision:

I had a vision. I couldn't see anything because of the total darkness. As I looked, I saw a light. It was moving. As I looked closer, I could see the light changing in intensity. I could see it was me riding a bicycle.

I had a bicycle with a generator light, and the slower I peddled, the lower the light. The faster I peddled, the brighter the light.

That bicycle represents the Word of God. We each have access to that bicycle. By our devotion, we can delve deeper into God's Word and shine it out into the world. Some will desire to be drenched in the light, while others will shrink away. It is not up to us what others may do, but it is up to us to reach as deeply into God's Word and shine His light throughout our communities in whatever form the Lord is showing us. Sometimes the light will be brighter, and at other times, not so much, but as we allow more and more of His Word to sink in, the greater will be His Light reflected through us.

What I heard from the Lord:

"I have given you My promises. Some have been fulfilled, yet others have not. It is in these unfulfilled promises that you can and must place your hope. You know you can count on them. Look at My promises that have been fulfilled. I AM that I AM. I cannot lie. I will not lie. I give you My truth. What I have given you is not for you to keep for yourselves but to share freely with those I have placed in your path. Yes, hope will end when all things are realized. The end of hope is a new beginning where everything is made new. You will see not in a glass dimly but then face to Face. You will know and be fully known."

5 – Wait Patiently

"And thus Abraham, having patiently waited, obtained the promise."

Hebrews 6:15 ESV

My thoughts:

When I first read this, my thought was, "Well, that's not true; they weren't patient." I was thinking of the birth of Ishmael between Abraham and Sarah's slave, Hagar, because they got tired of waiting for God to honor His promise and so decided to speed things along. The result of that decision haunts Israel to this day. The time of Ishmael's birth was about twelve years after receiving God's promise. I have to look at myself and wonder if God had made such a personal promise to me and I was already up in years; wouldn't I be looking for ways to see God's promise fulfilled, and perhaps help Him along a little?

Now, let's look at the other side of the coin. I used to think it often seemed like a long time before I received answers to my prayers. In truth, He does answer. His answers are "Yes, no, or not yet." Probably more complex than that, but you get the idea.

Sometimes the fulfillment of those answers may take a while, but think about this: Are we waiting on God, or is He waiting more on us? Those things He sets in motion may require something of us, others, or events beyond our control.

What I heard from the Lord:

"You have patience, but in your world of instant fulfillment and gratification, you have lost much in the way of patience. Those who came before you were trained in patience, but you want everything now and from Me, that will not necessarily happen. You have seen My promises and My patience. You have also seen My actions. Those in the past support those fulfillments today and in the future. Have true patience, and you will be blessed."

6 – A New Spirit

"And I will give them one heart, and a new spirit I will put within them. I will remove the heart of stone from their flesh and give them a heart of flesh,"

Ezekiel 11:19 ESV

My thoughts:

All who serve Christ have received a heart that is one with all others who have received His Spirit as well. We all share the same Spirit. We no longer have hearts unfeeling but hearts longing to do God's will.

What I heard from the Lord:

"My people, those who call My Son Christ, the Risen One. Those who read My Word and receive understanding from My Spirit. My Spirit is fresh and new in your hearts of flesh, being renewed by the moment. Is there anything that I will withhold from you, you who call on My Son as Lord and Savior? Try Me and see. You have a new understanding. You have a new hope. You have a new destiny. I, I am your destiny. Come to Me, My children, and bask in My Glory. Commune with Me. I love you. I set no conditions except that you hold My Son first in your lives, then all will be well in your hearts. Trouble will come, but I will be there with you in the midst of it. I will never leave you. Stay in My Word. Breathe in My Spirit. Love your neighbors as yourselves and know that I am God."

7 – Worship Only the Lord

"Son of man, these men have taken their idols into their hearts and set the stumbling block of their iniquity before their faces. Should I indeed let myself be consulted by them?

Ezekiel 14:3 ESV

My thoughts:

It is the idols of the heart where it all begins. Those in the Old Testament had their idols fashioned by human hands that they would worship as gods. These gods were made of wood or metal with different designs. As they were fashioned by human hands, they were, in effect, subservient to those who prayed to them. Even those who did not worship these idols openly still worshipped them in their hearts.

We do not openly worship idols today, or do we? What in our hearts call out to us that we allow to be more important than God? Whatever they may be, are we not worshiping them as God? The big three; money, sex, power, and may I offer pride; if any of these are important enough to us that we honor them more than God, then they are our gods. They, in effect, grab our focus, and we cannot see the Lord. Whatever comes between us and God is our god. If that is where we are, then we are in great peril and need to re-focus on the Lord.

What I heard from the Lord:

"I am God, and there is no other. Open your hearts to My Spirit. Call on Me to search your hearts and cast out all iniquity. Be true to My Word, and you will be true to your own selves in all that you do. You are silly when you depend on your money, your strength, and your intelligence and think that it is by your power that has gained whatever riches you think you have. What of all that will you take beyond the grave? It is all folly. Trust only in Me, and you will have riches everlasting and so much more than what you have on this earth. Banish your idols and worship only Me."

8 – His Blood That We May Live

"He entered once for all into the holy places, not by means of the blood of goats and calves but by means of his own blood, thus securing an eternal redemption."

Hebrews 9:12 ESV

My thoughts:

Jesus gave His all so that we can have abundant and eternal life with God Himself.

Today, how many profess Christ yet live lives contrary to His teaching? How many give lip service to Christ yet keep their focus on the World? How many think they are going to Heaven but will never see it because if they do not want to be with God now, how could they want to spend eternity with Him? Wouldn't that actually be Hell for them? It's just a thought.

What I heard from the Lord:

"I gave My very best that you might have life eternal with Me. I hold nothing back. I am a jealous God. I am willing to go to the ends of the earth for you, pursuing you with My love so that you may not be lost. I don't want you to be lost for eternity but to enjoy the fullness of joy I have prepared for you. Be still and let My love penetrate your hearts and make you whole."

9 – No Pleasure in the Loss of the Wicked

"Have I any pleasure in the death of the wicked, declares the Lord God, and not rather that he should turn from his way and live?"

Ezekiel 18:23 ESV

My thoughts:

As I have been taught and shown, the Lord never takes pleasure in people going to Hell. We have witnessed Hamas murdering, raping, and pillaging Israel. We've seen the horrors of ISIS. I believe these are demon possessed and have no way back except for true repentance. Despite the terror they bring, eternity in Hell is far worse than anything they can do to us.

What I heard from the Lord:

"Never will I have pleasure in the death of those who refuse to acknowledge Me; to look upon Me as God. My pleasure would be for them to acknowledge their sin and repent, to come to Me. I would heap riches upon them as the World will never know; riches that will not rot, decay, or rust, but riches that last an eternity. Just turn to Me and repent. I will hear your prayer. If not, I will see you one last time, at the seat of judgement and then no more.

But of those who are steadfast in their love and obedience, oh, My loves, I welcome you into My eternity of blessings where every day is fresh and new, where love abounds in everything you see, say, and do. Come to Me, My dear children, and be blessed."

10 – Remember to Forgive Yourselves

"This is the covenant that I will make with them after those days, declares the Lord: I will put my laws on their hearts, and write them on their minds,"

Hebrews 10:16 ESV

My thoughts:

I know when I am doing right, and I know when I'm doing wrong. It is interesting that we don't have to teach our children how to do wrong, but what is right. That is just one indicator that we are all born with a sin nature. When Christ comes into our hearts, He puts His law right there. He makes us holy and sets us apart to do His bidding. Is that a hardship for us? I do not think so. When you love someone, you want to do things for them and show them your love. How are we loving Jesus today?

What I heard from the Lord:

"You have My new covenant written in your hearts from the time you were called by Me for your deliverance when you committed your lives to My Son. You know what is right and what is wrong. You know you have My forgiveness. You only need to be in the confession of your sins. My Spirit lives within you and knows all. As I have forgiven you, now you must forgive others, but begin with yourselves. Do not hang onto your sins but leave them behind. Do this and be blessed. You are blessed and forgiven by Me, the Lord of all."

11 – The Day Draws Near

"And let us consider how to stir up one another to love and good works, not neglecting to meet together, as is the habit of some, but encouraging one another, and all the more as you see the Day drawing near."

Hebrews 10:24-25 ESV

My thoughts:

Go to Church regularly. If not in Church, meet in other ways with those like-minded with yourselves. Encourage one another to love and do good work.

That's what I see, but let's dig a little deeper.

I've never thought of myself as a cheerleader. I do not have much pizzazz. I'm just me. I do not try to be what I'm not. I just try to do the next right thing as prompted by the Holy Spirit. I do love attending church and being with like-minded people. I want everyone to feel that way; after all, it is a command of Christ. (Hebrews 10:25)

I see the day drawing near for His return, and my prayer is that no one be lost who can be saved before it is too late. Perhaps I'm confused because of my age that Christ is coming soon, and instead, I'll be joining Him in the death of my body, but perhaps not. We all need to live as if this is our last day on Earth.

What I heard from the Lord:

"You are blind if you can't see the season. You will never know the day, but the season is clear when I will return. Look around. What do you see? Is it not what I said in My Word through My prophets and My apostles? Yes, the time is short. Do not hesitate but come to Me; stay in My love and be blessed. The darkness gathers and will soon be upon you. Stay by My side and rest in My light."

12 – Without Faith it is Impossible to Please God

"And without faith it is impossible to please him, for whoever would draw near to God must believe that he exists and that he rewards those who seek him."

Hebrews 11:6 ESV

My thoughts:

Hebrews chapter eleven is filled with "faith." What reason is there to live without God? Just to fill ourselves with sensual pleasure for a period and then be gone? How empty is that? Where is the gain in that? But to live our lives in the presence of the Creator; to be loved by Him; to be given the meaning of life by Him; and to spend eternity with Him, now that's living.

Without faith, we can't know that He exists, but when we have faith, we see Him everywhere. That's quite a reward in itself.

Augustine wrote, "God does not expect us to submit our faith to him without reason, but the very limits of our reason make faith a necessity."

Let's look at it slightly different:

God doesn't expect us to submit our faith to Him without reason.

But because our reason has limits, faith is required.

What I heard from the Lord:

"Seek Me, and you will find Me, sometimes in the most obscure places. Know that I am God, and I have plans for your lives. Just come to Me, trust Me, and know I love you more than anyone or anything else can, for I created you in My very image. You are no mistake, and you are not junk. I don't make junk, but I make you in My image. Know that from the depths of your spirits."

13 – Perfection Only Through Christ

"All these people earned a good reputation because of their faith, yet none of them received all that God had promised. For God had something better in mind for us, so that they would not reach perfection without us."

Hebrews 11:39-40 NLT

My thoughts:

All before Christ looked toward His coming in faith for their redemption. Christ came fulfilling their faith and providing for those of us who have come after Christ's redemption as well, that both those who came before Him and those who have come after Him receive redemption together, reaching perfection through Christ.

What I heard from the Lord:

"You have received perfection through My Son. I see you by your faith what you will be. As My Bride today is still in filthy rags, so you are. Today I cannot look upon My bride, but soon all will be fulfilled. You are blessed in My presence through your faith in My Son because of the work He did that you could never accomplish. After Adam, all were flawed, and none fit to be seen in My presence, but My Son, My Son, gave His very life that you should not only live but live in My presence and be perfect. Let My Spirit reign in your hearts."

As I read back what God had shown me, I saw that He called the Church His bride. I asked, "Shouldn't this be Christ's bride?" **His response was, "Are not My Son and I one?"** That should settle it for us. It does for me.

14 – Run with Endurance

"Therefore, since we are surrounded by so great a cloud of witnesses, let us also lay aside every weight, and sin which clings so closely, and let us run with endurance the race that is set before us,"

Hebrews 12:1 ESV

My thoughts:

Each of us who call on Christ as our Savior and Lord is in a race of endurance. That race is to do our very best in all circumstances, to keep our focus on the Prize, Jesus our Lord. We must set aside anything that holds us down or keeps us back, that draws us away from the finish line, especially depending on ourselves and our deeds. Anything that does that becomes our god, if even for a moment. We must depend on the Holy Spirit living in us and for His Word to sustain us in ever keeping us moving onward. If we do this, the outcome of our race is certain, and we can be secure.

What I heard from the Lord:

"You are on a path set before you. That path is unique and suited just for you. There is no other path like it. You suffer, and you are moved to exultation by what comes to you and affects your special likes, dislikes, things you love, and things you abhor. If I set you on such a unique course, you must know My great love for you. Because you are so special to Me, I move alongside you through My Spirit, and My Spirit knows all. Never shrink away but embrace both the good and bad that wait around every turn. Be blessed in the knowledge that you are not alone, and all things work for your good."

15 – Root of Bitterness

"See to it that no one fails to obtain the grace of God; that no "root of bitterness" springs up and causes trouble, and by it many become defiled;"

Hebrews 12:15 ESV

My thoughts:

A root of bitterness, if allowed to grow, turns joy into grief, happiness into sadness, and love into hate. It starts with anger, sorrow, or any number of negatives that come into our lives. We need to allow the Spirit to have His way and heal us through His tender mercies by getting out of the way and into His Word. In some cases that root can cause us to hold onto unforgiveness, which robs us of our joy.

What I heard from the Lord:

"Beware of the root of bitterness that feeds on itself and grows; that it turns you to wallow in your sorrow, never looking beyond your own perceived pain or the pain you cause others. Beware of the downward spiral as the root grows, crowding out all else until you are a shell of bitterness and enmity. That you curl up and begin to die inside, not wanting to be touched or to touch. Stay in My Word. Stay in My Presence. Confess and repent from your sins that you may be righteous in My courts and your joy may be complete."

16 – Love of Money

"Keep your life free from love of money, and be content with what you have, for he has said, "I will never leave you nor forsake you."

Hebrews 13:5 ESV

My thoughts:

In Timothy 6:10 it says, "For the love of money is the root of all evil."

I believe the love of money keeps people rooted in the World. In fact, there are those who bow to money rather than God, for money is their god. If we're rooted in the World, we can't be rooted in the Word. Money is a tool to get what is necessary to live in this world. If money is more than that to you, you need to get right with God, for he said, "I will never leave you nor forsake you." (Deuteronomy 31:8) Now that's a promise we can thank God for and be content with what He has provided.

What I heard from the Lord:

"Contentment; money; can you have both? Of course, as long as I remain your first and true Love. Money is a tool, like other necessary tools required for you to navigate the world you live in, but the love of money? That's something else again. Love of money separates you from Me. Like anything else that comes between you and Me, it becomes your god. Even if money is just another tool, it has a different significance, for with money you also can be trapped with more allure of the world. Your focus can drift from Me to the world. You decide. Live, and put your confidence in Me or place your trust in the world. You can't have both. Choose wisely."

17 – The Watchman

"But if the watchman sees the sword coming and does not blow the trumpet, so that the people are not warned, and the sword comes and takes any one of them, that person is taken away in his iniquity, but his blood I will require at the watchman's hand."

Ezekiel 33:6 ESV

My thoughts:

This sounds something like, "See something, say something." I see this world in mortal danger. Those who have been enlightened by Christ have an obligation to warn the world. The world cannot say it has not been warned, but people keep ignoring the message and the messenger. So, does that absolve the watchman from continuing with the warning? Perhaps the world has heard the warning so many times that it simply ignores the warning and the watchman. If that is true, do we just stop warning? Heavens no! We have been given a charge and must continue to the end. Not to do so leaves their blood on our hands.

What I heard from the Lord:

"To whom much is given, much is required. You have been given My Word. Take care of it. It is not only for you but for the whole world. You have been given a warning for the whole world. You have a message. Take it to those you love and those you don't. All deserve to hear it. As you have been given the message, so too have you been given the means to distribute it and the sense of timing in giving My message. When you know, don't hold back. Don't hesitate. I stand at the door knocking."

18 – Faith and Works

"But someone will say, "You have faith and I have works." Show me your faith apart from your works, and I will show you my faith by my works."

James 2:18 ESV

My Thoughts:

Though the church may be based on faith, it is wrong if it rests on faith alone, for the love of God will motivate those who love Him to do good work. The works are not for our salvation but because of our love for Christ. It is by His work on the cross that we have salvation, not by anything we could ever do. A man I thought to be a strong Christian told me he worked for Christ to get a better place in heaven. By saying that, he was saying he could be proud of his works. You cannot find that in the Bible. For me, I will do what He tells me and be glad just to have a foot in Heaven.

What I heard from the Lord:

"What are the spiritual gifts I give My own? Are they not works? Is the gift of teaching not for work? Is the gift of help not for work? Even the gifts of faith and healing, are they not for works? All are for works, not for your edification, but Mine. These demonstrate your love for Me. You truly show your faith by the works you do for Me by using those gifts for those in need. Your faith has saved you. Your works edify Me."

19 – Truth

"But the wisdom from above is first pure, then peaceable, gentle, open to reason, full of mercy and good fruits, impartial and sincere."

James 3:17 ESV

My thoughts:

These words from James are my truth. Before I accepted Christ, my heart was full of unclean thoughts and desires. My speech reflected what was in my heart. When Christ came into my heart, He swept all that away. At that time, I was an IT professional. I surrounded myself with machines that could not hurt me and things I could depend on. Christ came in and melted my heart of stone and gave me an instant love for people I had never known before. With that came a gentleness I had never known before. I was stirred to peace. My life was changed supernaturally. Oh, there was still lots of room for improvement and continues to this day, but my transformation was truly supernatural as is yours.

What I heard from the Lord:

"Let My peace rest upon you. I give it freely that your spirits may be gentle; that you bring peace; that you bring My peace to a generation that has forsaken My Word and My work on the cross. Stand as a testament to My saving grace even in the face of ridicule and so much more. You truly are My ambassadors. You have My wisdom. You have My love. You have My protection. Remember your armor. The battle is won, yet the enemy must linger for a moment more in all his fury until his final defeat at the hands of My Son. When you stand in My armor, you are a testament to Me and what I offer if they will only receive."

20 – Listen First to the Lord

"Instead you ought to say, "If the Lord wills, we will live and do this or that." As it is, you boast in your arrogance. All such boasting is evil. So whoever knows the right thing to do and fails to do it, for him it is sin."

James 4:15-17 ESV

My thoughts:

Don't boast about what you are going to do tomorrow, for only God knows what tomorrow will bring.

Let us be in total dependence on the Lord. When we say what we're going to do today, tomorrow, next week, or even next year, temper it with the Word of God. We can plan, but it is He who will deliver. James calls it boasting when we say that we're going to do anything without asking the Lord first. Keep Him first in our thoughts and be amazed by the results. Above all, we should be prepared to do the next right thing with the Lord leading our steps.

What I heard from the Lord:

"Why do you forget Me? Why, when you awake, am I not your first thought? Why do you make plans without asking for My Will? Take note and humble yourselves, for I am the Lord. You are My chosen. You are chosen for good works. You are chosen for My good pleasure. As you are Mine, though, so too am I yours. For it is you whom I've called to do My good works on the earth. Listen and obey. Plans are good, but do not be so arrogant as to leave Me from your planning. I have things to say that you must know. Wait upon Me as I wait upon you."

21 – Today, We are God's Temple

"And in the vestibule of the gate were two tables on either side, on which the burnt offering and the sin offering and the guilt offering were to be slaughtered."

Ezekiel 40:39 ESV

My thoughts:

Lord, I do not understand this temple description. I thought it would be the temple built after the Dispersion, the return of the people to Jerusalem, but it doesn't match it nor Herod's temple. It should not match the temple in the New Jerusalem because Christ has already paid the penalty for our sins, and no more sacrifice is required. What is it?

Note: Some think this could be the fourth temple yet to be built. Others think it is symbolic.

What I heard from the Lord:

"This is the template for what was to be built when my people returned. Their faith was insufficient for the task, so they built what they could in their own strength. Their hearts were willing, but their flesh was weak. So, I honored their work with My blessing.

Now, you have been given a template for living in My Presence. Your bodies are My temple regardless of whether your flesh is weak or strong. My Spirit lives in you. Let Me build you up. You, follow My Word, for it is life to you."

22 – Like the Grass Withering – On the Outside

"All flesh is like grass and all its glory like the flower of grass. The grass withers, and the flower falls, but the word of the Lord remains forever. And this word is the good news that was preached to you."

1 Peter 1:24-25 ESV

My thoughts:

Wow! Well, by this time in my life, I'm withered, and the flower has fallen. Even with that, there is still a roaring fire for the Lord inside. His Word remains forever, and that means forever in us. His Word is fresh and new morning by morning. This morning, I thought of the Holy Spirit. As I confess my sins regularly, I invite the Holy Spirit to come into the very throne room of my heart and to be firmly seated on that throne. From there, I pray that He directs me upon the path He has set before me through the day, that He protects me from evil, and that He keeps my focus on Him throughout the day. That does not mean that I can't notice things out of the corner of my spiritual eyes, but the focus needs to be on the Lord.

What I heard from the Lord:

"You received My Good News, and it sprouted within you and began to grow. To this day, it is still growing as it ever will. It grows within you both in the good and in the bad, for I make even the bad for your ultimate good. How could it be other than that? You keep trusting in Me. You keep My Spirit in your hearts, not in a dark corner, but exalted to the very throne of your hearts that you can know My presence now and forever more."

23 – Living Stones

"You yourselves like living stones are being built up as a spiritual house, to be a holy priesthood, to offer spiritual sacrifices acceptable to God through Jesus Christ."

1 Peter 2:5 ESV

My thoughts:

So, Jesus is the Cornerstone, and we are living stones making up His Church, His Bride. What a precious honor to be called in this way.

I love the term "living stone." This makes each of us part of the fabric of the living church of Christ. What an honor. Each of us, as a living stone, being called for specific tasks within the body of Christ. We are given spiritual gifts to accomplish those tasks. Our sacrifices are only acceptable to God through Christ if we do not see them as sacrifices. They are gifts freely given by us because we want to please Him, not as a hardship that we must give with an expectation of any return. It is such an honor to be allowed to give to our Lord and to be prepared for His good pleasure. Thank You, Lord, for calling us with the privilege of serving you. In Jesus' name, Amen.

What I heard from the Lord:

"Why do I ask for your sacrifices? Why do I want you to give Me things that are costly to you? Know this. I, too, give sacrificially. My chief sacrifice to you is My own Son. I give for a reason, and that is to bless and be a blessing to you. There, see, I have set the pattern for your sacrifice. As I feel good in My sacrifices to you, you too should feel good in your sacrifices to Me. You are living stones, each an important stone in My body, My bride. Give and be gracious. Give and be thankful. Give of your time, talents, and treasures as I give you Mine."

24 – The Righteous

"For the eyes of the Lord are on the righteous, and his ears are open to their prayer. But the face of the Lord is against those who do evil."

1 Peter 3:12 ESV

My thoughts:

Who are the righteous? Those who have heeded His call and bowed to Jesus Christ and invited Him into their hearts through the Holy Spirit to direct their paths daily. It is those who keep the focus of their hearts on Christ. They don't look for commands to follow; they just follow what the Spirit has placed in their hearts. Simply let go and let God be in charge.

Those who do evil are simply those without the Holy Spirit in their hearts. They may not appear evil in our eyes, but in the eyes of God, they are. You cannot make yourself holy. Only God can do that.

Some of these people are very kind yet have no thought of God in their lives. I admit that sometimes I am baffled by how some of the nicest people I know don't know Christ and are lost. Some of these we love very much. Pray for them and be an example.

What I heard from the Lord:

"If you are righteous in your own eyes, are you truly righteous? If you look for fault in others, do you have no faults? If you know right and do wrong, where are you? It is all about My Spirit. Remember the first Passover when the blood of the lamb was on the lintel and post? The angel of death passed over them. So, it is today. With My Spirit in you, I only see your righteousness in spite of your errors. Through My Son, I can only love you. I cannot do less."

25 – Perceptions

"If you are insulted for the name of Christ, you are blessed, because the Spirit of glory and of God rests upon you."

1 Peter 4:14 ESV

My thoughts:

Make certain you are being insulted for the name of Christ and not some offence you have committed to another, and it's a perceived insult. We all make mistakes. When someone says something negative about us because of our walk with Christ, we are truly blessed. If, however, you show off your Christianity expecting praise and get insults, you are being insulted for your failure to keep Christ first in your life. Do not come off as holier than thou.

What I heard from the Lord:

"My Spirit rests upon and within you. Insults may be hurled at you, but praise may also be heaped upon you for who you are. Many are those who do not want to understand and have misconceptions about Who I am. Many hate Me and will therefore hate you because of our special relationship. You are truly blessed if you follow in My footsteps and are insulted, but beware that it may be a wrong perception you have given to those who don't know Me. You must live according to My commandments that all may be well with you and that they see Me in you."

26 – Enlist Others in Prayer

"And told them to seek mercy from the God of heaven concerning this mystery, so that Daniel and his companions might not be destroyed with the rest of the wise men of Babylon."

Daniel 2:18 ESV

My thoughts:

The king of Babylon had just sent out a decree that all the wise men in the country be killed because they could not tell the king what his dream was. This included Daniel and his companions. Daniel had asked the king to give him until the next day to tell the king what his dream was and the interpretation.

Then Daniel asked his friends to pray to the Lord concerning the mystery that they may be spared. Daniel did not just pray by himself but enlisted all those he knew who had a heart for the Lord to pray that they would be saved. This shows that when we find ourselves in difficult situations, it is prudent to enlist those around us (our church) and others to join us in prayer. We are told in the New Testament that where two or more are together in prayer, He is in their midst. **(Matthew 18:20)**

An interesting point is that only Daniel and his three friends asked for a different menu that would not offend God. What about all the rest of the young men taken captive with these four? It was only Daniel and his friends who had a true relationship with the Lord.

What I heard from the Lord:

"Daniel, My friend. Be like him in your decisions. May your prayers and your thoughts be unselfish. When Daniel prayed that his friends and the others be saved, of course, he was included, yet he put others first. In this way, be like him. Always put others first in your lives and wait upon the riches that will be heaped upon you. And so, live your lives like Daniel. As he put others first before himself, he also put Me before all else."

27 – Sacrificed For the Truth

"For we did not follow cleverly devised myths when we made known to you the power and coming of our Lord Jesus Christ, but we were eyewitnesses of his majesty."

2 Peter 1:16 ESV

My thoughts:

Where is the scientific proof that there is a God, and that Jesus is His Son? There is none that I know of. However, if we look at what happens in a courtroom, witnesses are called to tell what they have seen and heard under oath. When we look at the apostles' lives, we see all but one of them were killed excluding Judas. They were martyred because of who they were. They were killed because they could not lie about what they had witnessed. They had been there and experienced His presence, His work, and His Word. To do anything else would have been a lie.

In this verse, Peter states they were eyewitnesses of His majesty because the apostles were there. When you are willing to give up your life for what you know you have seen and heard, that is very powerful. When Peter was crucified, he asked to be crucified upside down because he did not think he was worthy of being killed in the same manner as his Lord, and he could not deny his faith. I do not know about you, but that's more than good enough for me. I need no further proof.

What I heard from the Lord:

"Love, faith, and hope, all wrapped together, but the greatest of these is love. Those who followed My Son all gave their lives not because of their faith, for they were there and saw the miracles right before their eyes. They saw the wonder in the eyes of others and had great wonder of their own. Those who were there had to show the world that what happened was true and, therefore, could not say otherwise, for otherwise, it would be a lie. Only John was spared but for a very good purpose. All died in the true knowledge of the Truth before them that you can have a saving faith and live."

28 – Faith

"If this be so, our God whom we serve is able to deliver us from the burning fiery furnace, and he will deliver us out of your hand, O king. But if not, be it known to you, O king, that we will not serve your gods or worship the golden image that you have set up."

Daniel 3:17-18 ESV

My thoughts:

I love what Shadrach, Meshach, and Abednego told the king before they were thrown into the furnace. They believed God would spare them in the fire, but even if not, they wouldn't change their mind and worship the false god of the king. That's real faith. King Nebuchadnezzar is in heaven today because of the faith he saw in these three, the humility of Daniel, and the truths given for his dreams. This is the man who destroyed Jerusalem and many other kingdoms.

King Nebuchadnezzar wrote in Daniel 4:3, "How great are his signs, how mighty his wonders! His kingdom is an everlasting kingdom, and his dominion endures from generation to generation." For the great king to write this shows his belief in God. Oh, to have faith to even let myself be thrown into a furnace and know God will protect me from the flames.

What I heard from the Lord:

"They had no more faith than you. Exercise your faith and know Me. Do you think I will forsake you when the path you are on becomes rough or unknown demons' approach in the darkness? No, My children. For I am always with you. These happen to strengthen and grow your faith. I am always with you, protecting you, guiding you, and of course, loving you by turning the bad intended for evil and changing it for your good. Rest in My Word. Trust in My Son and live the rich lives you have been given. Pass it on."

29 – What Are Your Idols?

"The idols of the nations are silver and gold, the work of human hands. They have mouths, but do not speak; they have eyes, but do not see; they have ears, but do not hear, nor is there any breath in their mouths. Those who make them become like them, so do all who trust in them."

Psalm 135:15-18 ESV

My thoughts:

In the past, idols were fashioned by human hands. These idols were their gods made to serve their makers. They had mouths that didn't speak, eyes that didn't see, ears that didn't hear, and there was no breath in them. The Bible says that those who worshipped them became like them, and so it is today for those who do not serve the Lord. Their senses are tuned to the world and cannot praise God with their mouths, see His works, or hear His word, and there is no spiritual breath in them. As I wrote not long ago, these are lost. Most prefer it to be that way, but some can be turned to the light. These are our friends, relatives, and acquaintances. Many are lost, but some still may be chosen. Be ready.

What I heard from the Lord:

"As those who worship idols, they do indeed become like them. Their idols are dead, and so are they unless they turn to Me and renounce those things, those gods that draw them from Me. Behold, I give life. I give peace. I give joy, and most of all, I give true love, not the kind of love that's here today and gone tomorrow, but real, lasting love. You decide."

30 – Confession Lightens the Heart

"If we confess our sins, he is faithful and just to forgive us our sins and to cleanse us from all unrighteousness. If we say we have not sinned, we make him a liar, and his word is not in us."

1 John 1:9-10 ESV

My thoughts:

This is so clear and so concise. I learned the ACTS prayer model many years ago. **A**doration of God; **C**onfession of our sins; **T**hanksgiving, and **S**upplication. Now, I do not necessarily pray in that order, but I try to make certain all four aspects are in my prayers. First and foremost, I want to be sure my heart is right with God. I pray that He search my heart and ask Him to toss my sins as far as the East is from the West, then to keep His Holy Spirit on the throne of my heart, directing my paths and keeping my focus on the Lord.

I do not know how you might pray, and I am not trying to tell anyone how to pray, but I want His Word in my heart, and I want to be drenched in the Holy Spirit daily.

What I heard from the Lord:

"Your only righteousness is through My Son and His work on the cross. If you say you have any righteousness other than by Him, you are as Satan, a thief and a robber and there is no light in you. When you confess your sins, it is like Thomas who let his doubts out into the open where the Light could cleanse him of his doubts. So, it is and so it will be. Simply confess and My Spirit will take over the thrones of your hearts and lead you onward, onward on the path set before you. Confess and feel the lightness of heart."

Chapter 12: December

1 – Live in the World, But Love the Lord

"Do not love the world or the things in the world. If anyone loves the world, the love of the Father is not in him."

1 John 2:15 ESV

My thoughts, my prayer:

I find this a very serious warning. I have loved the world. I have loved its power, its excitement, and its riches. What have I gained from it? A hollowness. Nothing it offers has lasting satisfaction.

The Lord loves us and overwhelms us. The world uses us and casts us aside. The Lord lives in us through the Holy Spirit and pours His love on and through us. With all this in mind, I freely give all of myself to Him for eternity.

My prayer:

Help us, Lord, as we are in this world not to be of it in any way. **In Jesus' Name, Amen.**

What I heard from the Lord:

"Do not fret for I am with you. What the world offers does not last but is here for a moment. You may find gratification for an instant, but then it is gone, always leading you away from Me. Keep in My Word. Keep in communion with Me. Do not despair for I am with you always forevermore."

2 – Wash Me in Your Love

"See what kind of love the Father has given to us, that we should be called children of God; and so we are. The reason why the world does not know us is that it did not know Him. Beloved, we are God's children now, and what we will be has not yet appeared; but we know that when he appears we shall be like him, because we shall see him as he is."

1 John 3:1-2 ESV

My thoughts:

"See what manner of love the Father has given unto us – that we should be called the sons of God." That's how I memorized it, and how we sang it in church for many years. The word children here might be better translated "sons". The actual Greek word is teknon which can be a child, daughter, or son. Whether we are men or women, in the sight of God, we are all His first-born sons. As first-born sons we are joint heirs to His kingdom. Just think when He appears we will be like Him. I like to bask in these verses; to wash myself in these words and be clean all over. It is a great place to be.

What I heard from the Lord:

"You are My children. You are joint heirs of My kingdom. Oh, how I like to hold you and shower gifts upon you of such magnitude that you will be amazed. You will be amazed of the love I lavish upon you. Just hold to your course. It may seem hard at times now, but you shall see. It is all worth it. Now you have only a small portion of what is to come. I too anticipate the time when all will be yours, for you are My sons."

3 – Princes of the Kingdom

"The prince of the kingdom of Persia withstood me twenty-one days, but Michael, one of the chief princes, came to help me, for I was left there with the kings of Persia,"

Daniel 10:13 ESV

My thoughts:

Is the prince of Persia, Satan? Michael, an archangel was able to stand against him. Could this be why some of our prayers seem to take longer to be answered than others? It looks like a lot is happening in the spirit world.

What I heard from the Lord:

"There are princes in My kingdom, but also in the kingdom of darkness. Michael is one of my chief princes who has been given great power. You pray and expect Me to receive your prayers and I do. Your prayers are a wonderful aroma in My presence. My angels, My dear angels; My messengers and much more. They stand alongside you against the forces of evil. Some day you will understand that there are rules in the heavenly realms to be followed. Sometimes satanic forces are allowed to prevent my angels from their appointed tasks. Sometimes there are delays in answers to your prayers for such reasons, but that is not often the case. Do not be concerned but know that I hear your prayers. I always respond in time."

4 – It's a Two-Way Street

"So we have come to know and to believe the love that God has for us. God is love, and whoever abides in love abides in God, and God abides in them."

1 John 4:16 ESV

My thoughts:

It is a two-way street. We accept Christ into our hearts. The Holy Spirit comes to live in us. We live in God. Let us explore that further. We come and believe in the love God has for us through His actions.

What I heard from the Lord:

"John captured My essence in his writing. I am Love, but love is not Me. Only perfect love can be found in Me; perfect Love that casts out all fear; Love that inspires; Love that convicts; Love that is pure joy. That is who I am. Beloved, never fear. I am a gracious and loving Father. I know your steps. I know where you have been and where you are going. Walk side by side with My Spirit and you will never fear, but you will enter My rest."

5 – Where Shall I Go

"Where shall I go from your Spirit? Or where shall I flee from your presence? If I ascend to heaven, you are there! If I make my bed in Sheol, you are there! If I take the wings of the morning and dwell in the uttermost parts of the sea,"

Psalm 139:7-9 ESV

My thoughts:

Here we are in Psalm 139, my second most favorite psalm after Psalm 1. There is so much in this rich psalm. I memorized it a long time ago so I could meditate upon it sometimes just to feel closer to the Lord.

Where can I go from Your Spirit? Why would I want to ever be away from You except for sin in my life that I become shameful for until I confess it and receive Your precious forgiveness? You are everywhere through Your Spirit. Whether I'm in heaven or hell, You would still find me. You are relentless. You never give up on those You have chosen. Thank You, Lord, for choosing me. The only way I want to take the wings of the morning is to fly to You and never away.

What I heard from the Lord:

"Yes, I am here. I was here before you were born, waiting for that day. I am with you every moment of your life. It will be so throughout all eternity. Why would you flee from Me? Why would you doubt Me? Sin enters your hearts, but you need only stop, confess your sins, and see if I will not restore our fellowship. I am relentless. I would chase you to the ends of the earth, and yes even to the gates of Hell, for you are Mine. You are sealed by My Spirit. I will never let go."

6 – Pride Will Bring Us Low

"One's pride will bring him low, but he who is lowly in spirit will obtain honor."

Proverbs 29:23 ESV

I'm not sure I know anyone who doesn't struggle with pride. It has certainly been a problem for me, not so much today, but certainly in my younger days. Pride can bring us low. How can we get that understanding from our heads to our hearts? We know it in our minds, but it does not stick in our hearts. What can we do?

What I Heard from the Lord:

"Your pride must be based in Me. If it is based on your accomplishments, your strength, your intellect, your abilities, from where did these come? You did not do this yourself. I gave you everything you have. Your accomplishments are My accomplishments. Your strength comes from Me. Your intellect comes from Me as do your abilities. Your focus must shift from yourselves and back to Me. Otherwise, you will be puffed up and not even fit for your own company. Stop the seesaw of focusing on yourself and then back to Me. Keep your focus ever on Me and you will be humble in spirit and give Me joy."

7 – Mother's Womb

"For you formed my inward parts; you knitted me together in my mother's womb. I praise you, for I am fearfully and wonderfully made. Wonderful are your works; my soul knows it very well. My frame was not hidden from you, when I was being made in secret, intricately woven in the depths of the earth. Your eyes saw my unformed substance; in your book were written, every one of them, the days that were formed for me, when as yet there was none of them."

Psalm 139:13-16 ESV

My thoughts:

Read these verses carefully and slowly. What do you understand? I see that we are fearfully and wonderfully made by God in our mother's womb. Therefore, the way I read this is that to abort an unborn baby is murder. I see no other word for it. Even then all our days were written before we were born. How dare we take that from the defenseless unborn. I see no other way to look at this.

We are the ultimate creation of God. We share His DNA. We love and are loved. He gives us a love for others despite their actions, as He loves us. Let us reflect His love today.

What I heard from the Lord:

"Too many, too many follow their own desires regardless of the pain and suffering it causes others. When you take from others, is that not a sin? Think of the commandment where it says you shall not steal. Apply that command. When you take an object from another, that is theft. When you take another's life, that is theft. When you take the life of one helpless and show no mercy, the theft is compounded. To take the life of an infant or one not yet born is the ultimate in selfishness and though I forgive, there are consequences on this earth that will not pass easily. Listen to and obey My commands and you will be well."

8 – God's Thoughts of Us

"How precious to me are your thoughts, O God! How vast is the sum of them! If I would count them, they are more than the sand. I awake, and I am still with you."

Psalm 139:17-18 ESV

My thoughts, my prayer:

We pray, and we have thoughts of God. Sometimes we are ashamed of how little we might pray, or how few are our thoughts of God, yet night and day He's having thoughts of us. As it says in these two verses, His thoughts of us are vast, they are more than the sand on the shores. When we wake in the morning, our first thoughts should be of Him. I confess that often they are not, but that's my goal.

My prayer:

Lord, thank You that we are constantly in your thoughts. I pray that You prompt us to think of You when we wake in the morning. I pray You will prompt us throughout the day to think of you and pray. Help us, Lord, to share our day with You. In Jesus' name, Amen.

What I heard from the Lord:

"You have minutes, hours, and days. I have all eternity to be with each one of you. I yearn for your responses to My pleas for fellowship with you. I am God of creation. I have created all things, but of you I have a longing for fellowship. As I thought of you before your birth, I created you for fellowship with Me. I created a hollow place within your hearts that can be filled only by and with Me. There is also a place in My heart that only your presence can fill. Take joy in My fellowship as I do in yours. Be blessed now and for all eternity for you are covered in My Love."

9 – The Seven Stars

"As for the mystery of the seven stars that you saw in my right hand, and the seven golden lampstands, the seven stars are the angels of the seven churches, and the seven lampstands are the seven churches."

Revelation 1:20 ESV

My thoughts:

The apostle John founded seven churches. The number seven means completeness. So, as I read this it includes not only seven, but every church who calls Jesus Lord and Savior along with the infallible Word of God. Every church is a lamp stand. What is a lamp stand for except to hold light. Jesus is the Light of the world. It goes on to say that every church has an angel protecting it.

Let our churches shine the light of Christ into a dark world. Let us, as living stones, carry that Light into this dark world and bring His message through what we say and how we live.

What I heard from the Lord:

"You have My protection. As My church has angels, so do you. You are protected in many ways. You are protected from things you have never even imagined. I provide that protection. My angels are at your sides throughout your time on the earth. You know it because you have sensed their presence. You are My great love. Why wouldn't I go to any expense for your protection up to and including the sacrifice of My only Son? What greater love can I show you? Accept Me. Accept My Son that you may spend eternity in the joy of My presence."

10 – Your First Love

"But I have this against you, that you have left your first love. Therefore remember from where you have fallen, and repent and do the deeds you did at first; or else I am coming to you and will remove your lampstand out of its place—unless you repent."

Revelation 2:4-5 NASB1995

My thoughts:

The judgment of the seven churches begins with Ephesus. All is good except for one thing. They had lost that first love of Christ and were apparently doing works not for Christ, but for other purposes not named. If they would not come back to Christ and repent, they would be lost. Their lampstand would be removed for Christ was not there.

The night of my water baptism many years ago, I prayed for God's peace. I received it and a fire was lit inside me that has never gone out. When I look inside, I still see it burning brightly. I cannot imagine it going out and losing the Holy Spirit. That would be the darkest day of my life.

Lord Jesus, by your strength, renew Your Spirit in our hearts this day and forevermore.

What I heard from the Lord:

"Your first love. Remember when I was your first love. Do you remember your excitement? Where is that excitement today? Do you look in other places now for that excitement because you just cannot remember? Look in the mirror of your soul. What do you see? Yes, take a very good look. Do you see Me in any part of you or have you lost your first love? I have not forsaken you; I only want you to see the gifts awaiting when you again make Me first in your lives. Repent and be blessed."

11 – Do Not Dawdle

"And to the angel of the church in Sardis write: 'The words of him who has the seven spirits of God and the seven stars.'

"I know your works. You have the reputation of being alive, but you are dead."

Revelation 3:1 ESV

My thoughts:

Faith without works is dead. Works without faith leads to pride. As with the church of Sardis it is with some today. Always lead with faith but follow with works lest your faith be diminished. If we walk side by side with the Spirit, our works will come. If we walk ahead of the Spirit, our works lead to pride. Walk with the Spirit daily.

What I heard from the Lord:

"If you walk behind My Spirit, you are not with My Spirit any more than you are when you walk ahead of My Spirit. Do not try to lead Me. I lead you. Do not follow behind My Spirit for if you do, you are not in step and may dawdle and your works will never come. Just walk with Me and be blessed. You know when you walk with Me, we are united, and you are filled with My Spirit. We are in fellowship."

12 – Many Doors

"Behold, I stand at the door and knock. If anyone hears my voice and opens the door, I will come in to him and eat with him, and he with me."

Revelation 3:20 ESV

My thoughts – A vision:

I saw many doors. Some were open, but many were closed. Within the doors, I saw books inside of different colors. Those colors signified the degree of sin within the books. Those books are compartments within our hearts that we need to completely open to the Lord. Some books were open, many were closed. Jesus wants not only the door of your heart to be open, but the books within as well. Some want to open the door but have not. Others will never open their doors. Some who have opened their doors, haven't opened them all the way and need to give Jesus access to every chapter of every book that's written there. Nothing can be hidden. I was meditating on Revelation. 3:20.

The doors of our hearts can only be opened from the inside. Our Savior is patient and kind but let us not test His patience.

What I heard from the Lord:

"I knock. I knock on the door of every heart, but I do not knock forever. There is a time appointed when I must leave those who will not open the doors of their hearts to Me and move on. There are other hearts with doors that will open. I mourn for those who refuse to open the doors of their hearts but rejoice with those who do open the doors of their hearts. Be blessed in our fellowship."

13 – Who Not to Be Like

"So Haman came in, and the king said to him, "What should be done to the man whom the king delights to honor?" And Haman said to himself, "Whom would the king delight to honor more than me?"

Esther 6:6 ESV

My thoughts:

Who not to be like? Haman just had a 75-foot-high gallows built to hang Mordecai because Mordecai wouldn't bow down to him. Here we see the pride within Haman's heart. All this pride before he was hung on the very gallows he had built for Mordecai. Nobody liked him as is seen by the eunuchs, who when they saw the anger of the king toward Haman, pointed out the gallows just outside the window for Haman to be hung.

This is a lesson in humility. Mordecai who had been humble to God through the entire book of Esther was promoted to the highest position in the land. If we remain humble to our Lord, we too will be lifted up to be servants for the Master of the universe.

Help us, Lord to always be humble in Your presence. Let Your light ever grow in our hearts.

What I heard from the Lord:

"I honor you in all you do for My sake. I see your work and bless you. I see your heart and look for opportunities to fill it more and more by the day. I see your motives and know they are pure. I see you in My Son as you grow more and more like Him as time goes by. Keep your eyes ever on My Son and all will be well with you. Do not stray from the path before you for there is only dishonor there. Keep your focus and keep the faith."

14 – Golden Bowls

"And when he had taken the scroll, the four living creatures and the twenty-four elders fell down before the Lamb, each holding a harp, and golden bowls full of incense, which are the prayers of the saints."

Revelation 5:8 ESV

My thoughts:

Golden bowls filled with the prayers of the saints. All who have accepted Christ are saints. This is not as in the Catholic tradition but noted for those leading a life of virtue. I know some of us may have not in their own eyes led such a life, but that's not how God sees us. God the Father cannot look upon us because of our sins except through the mantle of Christ who prays for us constantly. He does see us for who we will be, and our prayers are heard.

It's so good to know that God, Master of all, does hear our prayers. He not only hears our prayers, He values them deeply. He values us so much that the Holy Spirit lives within us, directing our paths and certainly our prayers if we only let go and allow God to lead us.

What I heard from the Lord Jesus:

"I love it when you call on Me. Your thoughts, your requests, and yes, your praise are like fine gold with a breathtaking aroma. I wait for your prayers so I can act on your behalf. I wait to hear the love you have for Me. I wait that we can be in communion. I revel in sharing your prayers to the Father and I too wait patiently for His response. Dearly beloved, I am yours, and you are Mine."

15 – In You I Trust

"Let me hear in the morning of your steadfast love, for in you I trust. Make me know the way I should go, for to you I lift up my soul."

Psalm 143:8 ESV

My thoughts, my prayer:

So many misgivings this morning when I woke up in the dark. Fear crept in and I felt lost. I felt lost from the Lord. I know my time is short, and I thought of my body being set in a grave away from all light, sound, and care. But then, I'm no better than any who have gone before me. This body will be dead; lifeless, and I will be far from it.

My prayer:

Wherever You are, I want to be. You love us more than anything. We must trust You. Show us, Lord, the way we should go, for You lift up our souls for Your safekeeping. Our lives are Yours. We pray this in the name of Jesus, our Savior, Amen.

What I heard from the Lord:

"You need never fear. A spirit of fear is not from Me. Stay close and let Me speak to your very heart. Know that I am God. I am Love. You do well in bringing your fears to Me. My Spirit resides in you. You are Mine, and I will not let you go. You gave concern for the end of your life on this earth. Never fear. Your life on earth is not done until I say it is. You keep your focus on Me. Do not even let it linger elsewhere. I am your God. I am your Friend."

16 – Tithe?

"Bring the full tithe into the storehouse, that there may be food in my house. And thereby put me to the test, says the Lord of hosts, if I will not open the windows of heaven for you and pour down for you a blessing until there is no more need."

Malachi 3:10 ESV

My thoughts:

Malachi was the first book of the Bible I studied after accepting Christ. We did not have a lot of money then so we gave what we could. In the New Testament we are told to give what we can, and God will honor that. We are also told God loves a cheerful giver. That too was hard to accept.

It took a while to get to a point for giving an Old Testament tithe, but it felt good. Like it says in Malachi, blessings both spiritually and materially came upon us. We look forward to giving and know we are being rewarded. That is our experience.

You can give what you want, whether it is more or less than a tithe, but be a cheerful giver.

What I heard from the Lord:

"All you have and all you are is Mine. You have your life given by Me. Whatever possessions you have are from Me. If you say you worked for it yourself, who gave you the strength and intellect to acquire what you perceive as yours? In a breath I can take everything away and with the next I can restore it beyond all your expectations. Look to Me. Give what you can give to Me, but let it be of the first fruits, not what you may have left after you take care of your own perceived needs. See if I will not overflow what you have given, back to you."

17 – Be Available

"Then rose up the heads of the fathers' houses of Judah and Benjamin, and the priests and the Levites, everyone whose spirit God had stirred to go up to rebuild the house of the Lord that is in Jerusalem."

Ezra 1:5 ESV

My thoughts:

"everyone whose spirit God had stirred to go up to rebuild the house of the Lord...."

The Lord stirred their hearts. What about our hearts? Is He, or does He stir our hearts? Are we not stirred to do His bidding? Are we not stirred to provide for His church? Are we not stirred to pray and read His Word? There are two words that have always been very important to me when it comes to my relationship with Christ. Those words are "be available." To be available for His call for whatever it might be is to be ready to set all else aside.

That's what those in Ezra's time did. That is where I always want to be. My path to the Lord has been long and winding, but I have always tried to be available for His call. How about you on your path?

What I heard from the Lord:

"I stir up your hearts for many things. I stir your hearts to hear My Word, to set aside time for My presence. I stir you up to think beyond the trials of today and to look toward what's to come. I stir you up for greater things than you know and do today. I stir you up to give and provide for those less fortunate. I stir you up that you may know I am God, Lord of all, and know you have My love now and forevermore. Prepare yourselves for what is to come."

18 – Perception is Reality

"But many of the priests and Levites and heads of fathers' houses, old men who had seen the first house, wept with a loud voice when they saw the foundation of this house being laid, though many shouted aloud for joy,"

Ezra 3:12 ESV

My thoughts:

The old folks lamented, and the young folks shouted for joy. The old were at least in their 70s and were very young when they left Jerusalem. So, what if the temple didn't meet their expectations? At least they were building a temple where they had not had anything for 70 years. I am sure they were doing the best they could with what they had to work with.

Here we are more than 2000 years after the birth of Christ, and we are the temple. As it was at the time of Jesus, the Spirit of God inhabited the temple in Jerusalem; today He resides in our hearts. We are the Church, the Bride of Christ. Praise the Lord for making it so. Thank You, Lord Jesus, for living in us today and making our lives abundant and eternal.

What I heard from the Lord:

"I live in the least of you and the greatest of you. Wherever you are and whatever you have done, always look to Me. What are you looking for when you look for greatness? Is it the great works of mankind? Or is it perhaps the smallest and most insignificant life form? There is nothing insignificant in any life. The greatness of mankind is nothing in comparison to what I have created. Look to Me for greatness and I will show it to you in a mustard seed. Where My Spirit resides, there is My Church. There is My Temple."

19 – He is Greatly to Be Praised

"Great is the Lord, and greatly to be praised, and his greatness is unsearchable."

Psalm 145:3 ESV

My thoughts:

Our Lord deserves our praise, and He demands it. His greatness is beyond our comprehension. We read of His greatness, yet can we really comprehend it? I live in a beautiful place with unobstructed views of the desert and incredible mountains. I see magnificent animals walking and sometimes frolicking in our backyard. There are birds of every kind, and this hardly begins to describe the works of our Creator. When I look up at the night sky, I see just a glimpse of what He has made in the heavens.

Sometimes that makes me feel small in comparison to what He has made, but we are the capstone of His creation on this earth. Let us rejoice and praise Him in everything we think, say, and do. Let us pray for His swift return when we will see Him face to Face.

What I heard from the Lord:

"With only the nod of My head, I could command your praises, but that is not really praise. I want you to look at yourselves in a mirror. What do you see? Can you see at least even a glimmer of Me looking back? You are wonderfully and fearfully made, and you are made for worship. I who created the universe; all you can see and so much more that you cannot perceive. I will never demand your praise. I wait for it as you come to understand your places in My kingdom. All you have is vanity except for what I have placed in your hearts. Look and see if I am not worthy of worship."

20 – Gracious and Merciful

"The Lord is gracious and merciful, slow to anger and abounding in steadfast love."

Psalm 145:8 ESV

My thoughts:

Grace, mercy, slow to anger, and unending of love that is solid, gives us pause to think about these attributes of God. They also should give us pause to look at ourselves since we are supposed to be reflections of His love. Are we showing grace and mercy, and how will we do that today? Before we fly off the handle, might we want to hesitate for a moment and ask what Jesus might do? Might we use a bit more of the abounding and steadfast love that is given to us toward our neighbors? Maybe we should take more time to pause and reflect before reacting.

What I heard from the Lord:

"Have I not shown my graciousness to My people over the generations? Haven't you seen My mercy in the scriptures, how over and over again I forgave My people, and it continues to this day for those who have accepted My Son into their hearts and called Him Lord in the congregation of My saints? My love never stops. It never fails. Nothing can keep My love from you, no matter where you go or what you do. You are Mine, and I will not let you go. What is Mine is Mine. I am a jealous God. Do not stray. Let My Love abide in you as your love abides in Me and be filled by My Presence."

21 – The Lord Upholds

"The Lord upholds all who are falling and raises up all who are bowed down."

Psalm 145:14 ESV

My thoughts, my prayer:

Everyone who has ever lived has fallen except for Jesus. We, who are alive on this earth, have fallen and are falling. All fall short of the glory of God. He is ever ready to raise us up if we commit ourselves to Him. All of us who are bowed down in sin are lifted up when we call on Him and confess to Him.

Think of Jesus bowed down, carrying our sins on His cross. Think of His great work in taking our sins upon Himself so that we might live forever with Him. Not even the greatest among us were or are capable of His purity. Our very best works are as filthy rags compared to His righteousness.

My prayer:

Lord, uphold me, for I am falling. Lord, I am bowed down. Raise me up and let my eyes rest on You. You are my God. Let me ever remain in Your Presence. I ask for no more than that. In Jesus' Name, Amen.

What I heard from the Lord:

"I am always there for your rescue. My Spirit lives in you that you not fall. Never fear, for there is nowhere you can be that I am not with you. Whenever you feel overwhelmed, rest in My Spirit. It is He who upholds you and gives you righteousness. Know that I am God, and you should never fear. You are My children. Why would I ever send My children away without My provision? I am always with you."

22 – First and Foremost, Pray

"Open your mouth for the mute, for the rights of all who are destitute. Open your mouth, judge righteously, defend the rights of the poor and needy."

Proverbs 31:8-9 ESV

My thoughts:

We support our church which in turn supports those in difficult positions, but do we open our mouths? Not so much, but we support organizations that do it financially. Is that enough? We support a little boy and his family in Tonga so he can get a Christian education and meet some of his family's needs through Compassion International.

As I think about this, it is like the pastor who's always telling you you're not giving enough; not praying enough; not in the Bible enough; not loving enough. It never ends. I think we need to let the Holy Spirit be our guide. We cannot cure all the ills of the world, but we can make the presence of Christ felt as He leads us. He does not want us on a guilt trip. With Christ in our hearts, there should never be any guilt. We must keep our eyes on Him.

What I heard from the Lord:

"First and foremost, always pray. Pray before anything else. Even in helping those in need, pray first. Pray, lest you do good works on your own, and pride sets in. Pray that together the needs of the poor, the infirm, and the downtrodden can be lifted up. Then, and only then, should you proceed. See if your gifts are not multiplied through My strength. Give, but give with the guidance of My Spirit."

23 – Broken Faith

"And Shecaniah the son of Jehiel, of the sons of Elam, addressed Ezra: "We have broken faith with our God and have married foreign women from the peoples of the land, but even now there is hope for Israel in spite of this.""

Ezra 10:2 ESV

My thoughts:

There is a significant difference here than what Paul says in 1 Corinthians 7:12-15. Here we see men were forbidden to marry foreign women based on the idea that the men would be pulled away from their faith in God by their marriage partner and her religious faith. Though elsewhere, they could marry foreign women if she was willing to accept the Lord and His Law. Interestingly, it doesn't say anything about women marrying foreign men.

In 2 Corinthians 6:14 it says we should not be unequally yoked. I take that to mean in marriage or in any other partnership. Christians and those who are not should count the costs beforehand and be very certain before taking up marriage or any legal contract. If a person becomes a Christian who is married to an unbeliever, and that unbeliever wants out of the marriage, that person should be allowed to go, but the Christian partner is not allowed to go, but must remain in the marriage.

What I heard from the Lord:

"Should I not be first in your lives? Did I not make you from nothing? Do I not know you better than you know yourselves? I know your strengths, and I know your weaknesses. In many ways, you are the same. You all have weaknesses, and you also have strengths. Since I made you, have you ever wondered why I made you the way you are? Think about this. If you had only strength without weakness, would you not become full of yourselves and think of the fighting that would occur among you? You would not survive because pride would overcome you. If you only had weakness, how would you get anything done? How would you even take

care of yourselves? I made you just the way you are with a combination of strength and weakness so you can learn; you can understand the difference between pride and humility, hatred and love, but most of all, so you can learn dependence upon Me. Take satisfaction in who and what you are and stay in My presence."

24 – Arrow Prayers

"Then the king said to me, "What are you requesting?" So I prayed to the God of heaven."

Nehemiah 2:4 ESV

My thoughts:

Here Nehemiah does an arrow prayer. We all do it from time to time or should. There have been several arrow prayers in this writing. We find ourselves in positions where we need and want God's help, and there's no time to formalize our prayer, so we just shoot up a very brief prayer for help with what's at hand in that moment. That doesn't mean that your prayer life should be made up of arrow prayers. Our God covets the time we spend with Him in communion when we come alongside Him and give Him our hearts. At the same time, our hearts should be bent toward Him as well so that we have quality time with Him.

What I heard from the Lord:

"Prayers, your prayers, be they short or long, it's the time we spend together that counts, not just the time, but the quality of time. You are being looked out for constantly throughout your lives. Whether day or night, in the good times and the bad, I am with you. Though I covet your prayers, it is I who made you, and I know there are times you send Me brief messages for help. I'm right there with you, and I answer. I give you what you need when you need it, and I wait for when you make time for communion with Me. I always have time for you, and I wait, always."

25 – King of Kings

"They will make war on the Lamb, and the Lamb will conquer them, for he is Lord of lords and King of kings, and those with him are called and chosen and faithful."

Revelation 17:14 ESV

My thoughts:

On this Christmas day, we remember the birth of the Christ Child. We enjoy the Christmas carols and have renewed hope. All history before His birth looked forward to His coming, and all history since His birth looks not only back to His coming, but His second coming as well.

Jesus came into the world as an innocent babe. He never sinned, yet He died for our sins that we may have eternal life with Him. He was and is way more than an innocent babe. He will come next on this earth as a conqueror. All who fight against Him will fail and be conquered. All who fight against Him today will fail even though sometimes it looks like they are winning. We must keep our faith and stand our ground. He will not fail us. He loves us from before the beginning and after the end through eternity.

What I heard from the Lord:

"The battle against Me began eons ago and grows greater by each day's passing. They make war on the Lamb. In doing so, they make war on you. As it is written, "You who are with Me, you who are called, chosen, and are faithful." So, it shall be. The victory is Mine, but as you come with Me, you too are conquerors. Stay in your armor and keep the faith. Victory is at hand."

26 – Leadership

"I also persevered in the work on this wall, and we acquired no land, and all my servants were gathered there for the work."

Nehemiah 5:16 ESV

My thoughts:

The book of Nehemiah is, among other things, a book on leadership. As you read through the book, you can see the servant leadership style throughout. We are all leaders in one form or another, whether you are a CEO of a large corporation down to a child not yet an adult. If you are alive, you have influence on those with whom you have contact. Influence can be good or bad. Nehemiah displayed servant leadership with his willingness to get down, side by side with others, as Jesus did five hundred years later. Jesus asks the same of us.

What I heard from the Lord:

"You and all you know are leaders and followers at the same time. As iron sharpens iron, so you sharpen one another through your interactions, day by day. Beware that you not be influenced by anything ungodly, for it will not end well. Always look back to My Word and know the right path. Listen to My Spirit as He ministers to you, and all you do will succeed. Be blessed by My Word and by My Spirit."

27 – Angels, Fellow Servants

"Then I fell down at his feet to worship him, but he said to me, "You must not do that! I am a fellow servant with you and your brothers who hold to the testimony of Jesus. Worship God." For the testimony of Jesus is the spirit of prophecy.""

Revelation 19:10 ESV

My thoughts, my prayer:

John had an angel speak to him, thinking the angel was greater than himself in the eyes of Christ, but both angels and we are servants of Christ. As the angels are focused on their realm, so should we be in ours. As we look forward to the day when we and angels meet face to face, we need also to look forward to the marriage of Christ and His Bride (us). That's going to be spectacular beyond anything we can imagine. I look forward to both and so much more that Christ has in mind for us.

My prayer:

Thank You, Lord, that You give us the privilege to serve You on this earth as the angels serve You in heaven. As You have given them what's necessary to serve You in heaven, so have You given us what we need to serve You here on this earth. In the name of Jesus, Amen.

What I heard from the Lord:

"Angels, My beautiful, beautiful angels. They constantly minister to Me and also to you. They cover that which you can't see with your eyes but often point out dangers you can see with your spiritual eyes. Never fear My angels, neither bow down to them, for they, like you have a place in the now and in the hereafter."

28 – All People on the Earth

"Kings of the earth and all peoples, princes and all rulers of the earth! Young men and maidens together, old men and children!"

Psalm 148:11-12 ESV

My thoughts:

Let all praise Him. What a different world we would live in if we all praised the Lord and paid attention to His Word. What a difference if we allowed the Love of God to flow out to one another. What a magnificent place this would be if our selfish, prideful desires were no more and each of us looked out for the welfare of our brothers and sisters. It all started so well, but we know what happened, and this is what we live with. Come quickly, Lord Jesus. Come quickly.

What I heard from the Lord:

"I send my Son at the appointed time. It is good for you to pray for His return. It is good that you keep Him in the forefront of your thoughts and deeds. Look around. Can't you see the signs? They are all around you wherever you look. They all point to His return and all the terrors yet to come. As long as your focus remains on Him, you will not be caught unaware and will be blessed and not lost."

29 – Lake of Fire

"Then Death and Hades were thrown into the lake of fire. This is the second death, the lake of fire. And if anyone's name was not found written in the book of life, he was thrown into the lake of fire."

Revelation 20:14-15 ESV

My thoughts:

".... And if anyone/s name was not found written in the book of life, he was thrown into the lake of fire."

I don't have much of an imagination, but this verse sure fires up what I do have. I know my name is written in the Book of Life, but there are so many I know that this cannot be said of them. There are many that do not want to be bothered by Jesus. They just want to live their lives undisturbed by anything that challenges them. I view those in the lake of fire as set out of sight from those in the care of God, never to be heard of again, not to even be thought of again. If anyone living doesn't have time for Jesus now, wouldn't they be unhappy having to spend eternity with Him? For me, thank you, Lord, for writing my name in the Book of Life.

What I heard from the Lord:

"The Book of Life, yes. It contains so very many names, yet there are fewer names in the book than are not in the book. The terrors to come will drive many to the Book of Life, but so many more will still look away from Me and perish, never to be heard of again. My love shines on all, but too few reflect it back to me and to others. Your focus is so important at this time, more so than ever before. Focus or perish."

30 – All Things Made New

"And he who was seated on the throne said, "Behold, I am making all things new." Also he said, "Write this down, for these words are trustworthy and true.""

Revelation 21:5 ESV

My thoughts:

"Behold, I am making all things new." All things will be made new and from a vision I had several years ago, I saw all things will be made new all the time. I am not sure how time is measured in eternity, but it was ever changing with delightful beauty. It led all to praise Him all the time. Even today though, we should be praising Him all the time no matter where we are or what is happening.

What I heard from the Lord:

"It's not that I have made all things new, or I will make all things new. I am making all things new, and they will be shown at their appointed time. Once creation was fresh and new. It was unsoiled and perfect. When I am done, all, yes, all will know and understand why it is this way. It must be this way, for there is no other. Soon enough, you will see My new heaven and My new earth, for you are the reason for it all. Without you, it would never have been required. Know and accept My great Love for you from now in this present time before you have even seen my finished work until you see Me and the new creation face to Face. Until then, stand firmly for Me. I am always with you."

31 – Sanctuaries of Peoples' Hearts

"and came to Jerusalem, and I then discovered the evil that Eliashib had done for Tobiah, preparing for him a chamber in the courts of the house of God."

Nehemiah 13:7 ESV

My thoughts:

Nehemiah had just returned from some time away with the king to find a trusted friend had let the enemy in the temple. How do we feel when a trusted friend betrays us? For me, it has not happened often, but the pain, anger, and frustration must find an outlet. Our Christianity can be messy, and it certainly can be when this happens. I have not always acted graciously when this has happened, but we always need to take it to the Lord and place it in His hands, but not take it back.

What I heard from the Lord:

"As Nehemiah was enraged by Eliashib allowing Tobiah into the temple, so should you be when you see the enemy invading the sanctuaries of peoples' hearts. Nehemiah had the ability to cast Tobiah out. You have the ability to pray for the lost. How many friends and relatives do you know who have not accepted My Son into their hearts? Do you care enough about them to even pray for them? Do you know what happens after the second death? Take every opportunity to pray for them, to pray for their surrender to My Son. Do not leave this earth with their blood on your hands. Pray!"

A Deeper Look at the Beatitudes

Here are the eight beatitudes written to all the disciples of Christ found in Matthew 5:3 – 10.

My thoughts:

An introduction to the beatitudes:

Read the Beatitudes slowly and prayerfully. Take time to truly grasp their significance. I've read them hundreds of times, but it wasn't that long ago that I really saw them for the first time in all their glory. I would read them and identify myself in one or two of them. I just didn't get it.

Frankly, I didn't want to be meek, poor in spirit, or to be mournful. So, I just passed over them.

I see that we are to be all of them. All of them are to define us. Of the eight, I selected the verse above to start with. If we have pure hearts, shouldn't all the others apply?

Shouldn't we be poor in spirit when we see what's happening in the world? Shouldn't we mourn our failings before God? Shouldn't we put others before ourselves? Shouldn't righteousness be our goal in this life? Let us be merciful and forgiving. If our hearts are pure, shouldn't that be reflected by the way we live? Shouldn't we always seek peace with others? Shouldn't it be an honor to be persecuted for Christ? With all this, we should rejoice. Didn't Jesus pour His heart out to us in these verses?

The Holy Spirit resides in us as a down payment for what's to come. How great a comfort is that? Thank You, Lord, for opening our eyes just a bit further.

The Pure in Heart

"Blessed are the pure in heart, for they shall see God."

Matthew 5:8 ESV

According to popular definition, to be pure in heart means our hearts should be focused on the Lord and His Word. Our hearts should be fresh and pliable, not hard, and untouchable. They should not be contaminated in any way.

When we read His Word, we should not try to make it something other than what it is saying. That does not mean we should not study it to get a deeper understanding, but to be true to the Lord and His Word. We need to let His Word touch our hearts. We need to live with His Spirit in our hearts. Many years ago, the saying came out, "What would Jesus do?" If we are pure in heart that question will become automatic. It will become a part of us. If we are not there, that needs to be the goal.

What I heard from the Lord:

"It all starts in the heart. Whether your hearts are full of the fruit of My Spirit, or whether you give yourselves over to Satan, the root is the cause. Let your roots be deeply entrenched in My Word that your hearts are pure and nothing but the fruit of My Spirit grows in your lives. Again, the root of My fruit which gives freedom and life, or the fruit of evil which produces slavery and death? It's your choice."

The Poor in Spirit

"Blessed are the poor in spirit, for theirs is the kingdom of heaven."

Matthew 5:3 ESV

My thoughts:

For us to be poor in spirit is to look around and be truly thankful for where we are in Christ and his care. To see the injustice, hatred, arrogance, and perversion should hurt our hearts. It should make us want to look away and hide in Jesus, but we have been called to be in the world. As followers of Christ, through His strength, we must follow where He leads and do what we can with the gifts we have been given.

Jesus looked around and was poor in spirit. How can we do less? It is not an option as a disciple of Christ.

Thank You, Jesus, for the path You have set before us and the gifts You have given us for Your purpose. May you be blessed by this as I have been blessed. Amen

What I heard from the Lord:

"When you are poor in spirit, I can lift you up. It is here where we meet on hallowed ground. In your spirit, when it is poor, you truly know who you are and your place. You don't have to be told; you know. Cling to Me. Let Me lift you up."

The Mournful

"Blessed are those who mourn, for they shall be comforted."

Matthew 5:4 ESV

My thoughts:

For what are we supposed to mourn? Why should we mourn? To mourn is to feel regret or sorrow for our actions or those of others who will not listen to the Lord.

No matter where we are in our walk with God, no matter how close, we are still far away. Our righteousness is as filthy rags that we can mourn for throughout this life on earth.

We mourn the deplorable conditions so many people live in all over the world. We can do so little. We can say we do what we can, but it is never enough. We mourn slavery all over the world, from the lowest to the highest places in our society. We mourn for those we know and love that do not know Him or even want to. We mourn for the billions of people that do not know Christ or even want to know Him. We mourn for the carelessness people have toward this beautiful world God has provided for us. We mourn for a society that pushes the Lord away and has become its own god. We mourn over sinful past events and for a future on this earth without the Holy Spirit, for these things and more. As we mourn, let us ask for God's intercession. Come quickly, Lord Jesus, come.

What I heard from the Lord:

"You mourn, but the light is coming when there will be no more mourning. When you mourn, My heart mourns with you. I know things don't appear fair in this world but wait and look toward me. It is not finished. When it is finished, it will be right."

The Meek

"Blessed are the meek, for they shall inherit the earth."

Matthew 5:5 ESV

My thoughts:

Meek is an adjective that means quiet, gentle, and easily imposed on; submissive. It is also patient, long-suffering, and forbearing.

I have never thought of myself as meek. When I think of meek, I think of someone who will not stand up for themselves or their principles.

There's so much more to the word meek. We should want to be submissive to our Lord. We should want to be submissive to our wives or husbands as they are submissive to us. We should want to be submissive to the Word of God. We should want to be patient and long-suffering toward the Lord and to others. We need to understand that He has put us in this place, in this time, and in this way for His good pleasure, which is right and true. We simply would not fit anywhere else. So, we should be meek in accepting what God has done in our lives, what He's doing, and what He will do. That is good enough for me. I pray it is for you.

Moses was called the meekest person in the Bible toward God. Moses was no push-over when it came to leading the people or taking up their cause. We can be meek in that we are gentle.

What I heard from the Lord:

"To follow Me, you must let go of worldly views and look toward Mine. You are not foot mats. You have been called by the Creator of the universe. You have been called to be Mine. As such, you must follow the example left by My Son. Your power comes from Him. I will never give you more than you can handle. I am ever in your corner."

Those Who Hunger and Thirst for Righteousness

"Blessed are those who hunger and thirst for righteousness, for they shall be satisfied,"

Matthew 5:6 ESV

My thoughts:

Righteousness – morally right or justifiable – acting in accord with divine or moral law, free from guilt or sin – genuine. These are all meanings for righteousness, and aren't they all that we should have hunger for, or thirst for? Righteousness is in short supply these days. I see politicians act in the righteous indignation of a person or activity in the other party when they themselves may be far worse. This is a travesty. Do not try to remove a splinter in someone's eye when there is a board in your own eye.

We should want true righteousness. We read of His righteous acts, and we should hunger and thirst to be like Him as much as we can on this earth, but we have a sin nature that we constantly battle. We are to be dead to sin, yet seemingly out of nowhere, it appears and must be dealt with through confession and prayer. Those who hunger and thirst are hungry and thirsty for righteousness in themselves and in the world. To hunger and thirst for righteousness is to be in the Word and in prayer more and more.

What I heard from the Lord:

"True righteousness is only in Me. Your righteousness is as filthy rags, but We have a covenant. When you turn to me, when you call my Spirit to live in you, I will. I will be your Righteousness. But you must hunger and thirst for it. It is not just going to come to you without Me. I hide you under My mantel. That's the only way the Father can see you. And as He sees you, He sees you as you will be. You are sinful beyond repair except for My shed blood. You shall be satisfied, but only partially in the here and now, as My Spirit is only a down payment of what is to come in your life, but on the other side, and not now. Wait, watch, and listen with your whole being. You will be satisfied."

The Merciful

"Blessed are the merciful, for they shall receive mercy."

Matthew 5:7 ESV

My thoughts:

Christ's payment for our penalty is mercy. Mercy is benevolence and kindness within your power and control. When you have the power to make something right or something wrong for another and you choose doing right for them, that's mercy. I understand giving mercy to those we love and care for, but what about those who have hurt our loved ones? I can handle forgiveness and mercy for those who have wronged me, but when someone hurts my children or my spouse, that's a different matter. This is a hard thing. My desire is that if someone hurts a loved one, I want to put them in a place where it cannot happen again. I want to insert myself between my loved one and the perpetrator. I need Your help, Lord.

What I heard from the Lord:

"You must trust Me. You do not take up the offenses of others, even for your own children once they are grown. Your children are in your care for a while, but then you must release them. They will still be in My care. Remember all the times you were hurt by others? I was there. I saw. "All things work together for good, for those who love Me and are called according to My purpose." Romans 8:28 The good and bad work together to make each one whom I have called stronger and closer to Me. Now for children who don't know Me. I will place stumbling blocks in their paths to bring them to Me, but unless they give Me their hearts, I cannot do more. They have free will, which they must give over to Me, as have you. Your mercy must flow from Me."

The Peacemakers

"Blessed are the peacemakers, for they shall be called sons of God."

Matthew 5:9 ESV

My thoughts:

Being a peacemaker is being active and not passive in the cause of peace, but not peace at any price. Being a peacemaker is taking a role in squabbling among friends and relatives for conflict resolution. It means you cannot rest until the conflict is resolved.

We should always be peacemakers and never instigators of turmoil. We should long for peace and harmony not only with friends and relatives but in the church as well. There is no place in the church for conflict. I have seen it only rarely, and I hate it as does the Lord. It is ugly and reprehensible. We should always be ready to take the high road to peace. Peace in the church honors God.

Then there's peace in the world. That is a bit harder. The Bible tells us there will be wars and rumors of wars, but that does not mean we should just sit back. We need to be smart about our actions and act where and how we can do the most good. What kind of world would we have if there were more peacemakers and fewer troublemakers? And, too, don't you want to be called a son of God? All who know Christ are firstborn sons. It's the firstborn son who is the heir. No matter our gender, that is who we are in God.

What I heard from the Lord:

"Peace can appear illusive, but My peace, I bring to you. There is turmoil all around you, yet I give you My peace if you will only receive it. Yes, I give you peace in the midst of turmoil. Reach out and take it. It is a gift, but only if you receive it."

The Persecuted

"Blessed are those who are persecuted for righteousness' sake, for theirs is the kingdom of heaven."

Matthew 5:10 ESV

My thoughts:

To persecute is to treat another or others for being different by hostility or improper treatment. Personally, I have not been persecuted for being a Christian. I have seen it, though, right here in our own country. There are thousands if not millions of Christians being persecuted daily.

We have Christian missionaries who have been tortured and even put to death for their stand with Christ. It is happening now, and I expect it will get worse as we see our world changing. Even in this country, persecution will come and is at hand. I, for one, will not hide my belief in Christ. No, I will exalt His name wherever I can, not as a weapon, but to sincerely draw others to Him, even those who mock me. At the same time, I will not cast His pearls to the swine. If they do not listen, I will wait for another time as moved by the Spirit.

If the persecution is strong enough that we might be cast into jail, tortured, or even killed, we must take our stand for Christ. They can only kill us once, but they will die twice unless they come to Christ.

What I heard from the Lord:

"Take care when you are being persecuted. Ask the question, "Am I being persecuted for Christ or myself?" If it is for Christ, count it as a blessing. If you are being persecuted for something you said or did outside My Word, that is on you. You have been given everything you need to stand persecution for My Name. It may hurt, but only for a while. I am coming soon."

www.ingramcontent.com/pod-product-compliance
Lightning Source LLC
Chambersburg PA
CBHW041134110526
44590CB00027B/4013